LIMITS AND LOOPHOLES

LIMITS AND LOOPHOLES

The Quest for Money, Free Speech, and Fair Elections

Victoria A. Farrar-Myers
University of Texas at Arlington

Diana Dwyre
California State University, Chico

CQ PRESS

A Division of Congressional Quarterly Inc.
Washington, D.C.

CQ Press
1255 22nd Street, NW, Suite 400
Washington, DC 20037

Phone: 202-729-1900; toll-free, 1-866-4CQ-PRESS (1-866-427-7737)

Web: www.cqpress.com

Cover design: Designfarm
Composition: Auburn Associates, Inc.

∞ The paper used in this publication exceeds the requirements of the American National Standard for Information Sciences—Permanence of Paper for Printed Library Materials, ANSI Z39.48-1992.

Printed and bound in the United States of America

11   10   09   08   07   1   2   3   4   5

Library of Congress Cataloging-in-Publication Data to come
Farrar-Myers, Victoria A.
  Limits and loopholes : the quest for money, free speech, and fair elections / Victoria A. Farrar-Myers, Diana Dwyre.
      p. cm.
  Includes bibliographical references and index.
  ISBN 978-0-87289-329-0 (alk. paper)
  1. Campaign funds—United States. 2. Elections—United States. 3. United States—Politics and government—1989- I. Dwyre, Diana. II. Title.

  JK1991.D993 2007
  324.7'80973--dc22

  2007038669

This book is dedicated to

Jason

and

Joe, Quinn, and Pauline

CONTENTS

Figures and Boxes   ix

Preface   xi

1 Competing Values and the High Stakes of Campaign Finance Reform 1
   The "Mischiefs of Faction" and Campaign Finance   3
   Campaign Finance Regulation in Historical Context   8
   The Multiple Layers of Campaign Finance Reform   19
   Plan of the Book   22

2 Campaign Finance Reform in the 105th Congress:
  A Tale of Unorthodox Policymaking   27
   The Battle Begins in the Senate: Bargaining, then Defeat   28
   The Fight Continues in the House:
     An Issue Whose Time Had Come?   35
   Promises, Promises: The Republican Leadership Stalls   40
   Scramble for Control: Reform Proponents Fight Back   44
   The Republican Leadership's *Death by Amendment* Strategy   47
   Getting around Poison Pills: Developing Issue Networks   50
   In Spite of It All, the Bill Passes the House   53
   Conclusion: Negotiating the Labyrinth   57

3 Clearing a Pathway through the Labyrinth:
  Passing Campaign Finance Legislation   65
   History Repeats Itself in the 106th Congress   66
   The 2000 Elections   73
   Clearing the Path for Final Passage   75
   Lessons from BCRA's Passage through the Legislative Labyrinth   90

4 From the Halls of Congress to the Supreme Court:
   The Impact of Judicial Interpretation on Public Policy   99
   The Founders' View of the Judiciary   100
   The Judiciary and Campaign Finance   102
       Buckley and Its Progeny   102
       McConnell and Its Progeny   108
   Extending the Labyrinth: Implications of Judicial Interpretation   116

5 Through the Regulatory Wringer:
   The Federal Election Commission Takes on BCRA   123
   As Clear as Mud   124
   The Politics of Regulation   126
       Lost in Translation or Purposely Undermined?   126
       Take 'em to Court!   127
       The Legislative Approach   129
       It Matters Who Writes the Rules   130
   The Politics of Little or No Action: 527s and the FEC   132
   An Ongoing Process   137

6 Elections in the Post–BCRA World   141
   Political Parties   142
       National Party Committees   142
       State and Local Parties   148
   A New Frontier: The Rise of 527s and Other Nonprofit
       Groups   149
       Section 527 Organizations after BCRA   151
       Moving on to Other Nonprofits   154
   The Next Frontier: Taxable Corporations   156
   More or Less Free Speech?   157
   So, Where Are We and Where Are We Going?   159

7 Values, Choices, and Consequences   165
   The Policy Labyrinth   165
   The State of Campaign Finance Policy   169
   Campaign Finance, Popular Sovereignty, and the Dynamics of
       the American Political System   172

Index   177

FIGURES AND BOXES

Figures

1-1   James Madison's Analytical Framework in *Federalist* No. 10   5
1-2   Average Expenditure of House Candidates, 1980–2006   14
1-3   Average Campaign Expenditures by Senate Candidates,
      1980–2006   15
1-4   Total PAC Contributions to House and Senate Candidates,
      1980–2006   16
1-5   Party Committee Soft Money Receipts, 1992–2002   18
6-1   National Party Committee Receipts, 2000–2006   144
6-2   National Party Committee Receipts by Committee, 2000–2006   144
6-3   Federal Candidate Contributions to Congressional Campaign
      Committees, 2000–2006   146

Boxes

3-1   Summary of Major Provisions of the Bipartisan Campaign
      Reform Act of 2002   86
5-1   Spending by Top Federal 527 Organizations Active in
      the 2004 Election   134
6-1   Spending by Top Federal 527 Organizations Active in
      the 2006 Election   154

PREFACE

Approximately ten years ago, we were about to begin our appointments as American Political Science Association Congressional Fellows. Our time on Capitol Hill from late 1997 through the summer of 1998 immersed us in the world of campaign finance. From late-night sessions on the floor of the House of Representatives to being part of meetings in which key strategic decisions were made, we lived firsthand the debate over if and how to reform our nation's campaign finance laws.

In the subsequent years of reflection from our time as Congressional Fellows, we have come to appreciate that amidst the cacophony of voices in campaign finance, people often lose sight of the common thread that binds these voices to one another. Where others see intractable positions, we see connections. Where others see ideology and politics, we see core beliefs and values. Where others experience frustration and defeat in the perpetual state of reform, we see the beauty of the original constitutional design.

Campaign finance is more than a tale of how a bill becomes a law or how the legislative process functions. It is a window into how core values that are at the bedrock of our political system both motivate and constrain all actors in the American representative democracy. Campaign finance, therefore, is more than just a reform issue; it is the very embodiment of the ongoing founding debate over equality and freedom of speech and the manner in which our system of government and political actors work through the policy process and various institutional structures to achieve a delicate balance. The aim, therefore, of this book is to explore the richness of the melody that underlies campaign finance and to reveal the song and not just the noise.

This book is the product of many perspectives. Most fundamentally, our time on Capitol Hill serving as legislative assistants to Reps. Christopher Shays, R-Conn., and Sander Levin, D-Mich., provided us with an appreciation for the inner workings of Congress and for the relevant interest groups and participants in the campaign finance debate. Our countless hours working with Hill staff and key participants allowed us to see the detailed, complicated, and often seemingly irreconcilable positions that can develop around a single issue. We gained an appreciation for context, leadership, and how individuals can make significant contributions at critical junctures as an issue evolves. Living this experience motivated us to write our first book, *Legislative Labyrinth: Congress and Campaign Finance Reform* (CQ Press, 2001). We wanted not only to tell the story of campaign finance, but also to share the lessons it can teach about the legislative and policymaking processes.

In the years that have followed, we have often been asked to revise *Legislative Labyrinth* with a second edition, but we resisted because the insider perspective that informed the first book could not be replicated. The more the issue of campaign finance evolved, the more clear it became to us that the issue provided the basis for more than just telling a story of the legislative process. Campaign finance is a policy area that serves as a case for understanding a deeper narrative that drives American politics—that of competing, and sometimes conflicting, core values. It was recognizing this that motivated us to write this new and different book.

In the context of this theoretical framework, we examine not only the intense and complex legislative process that led to congressional passage and presidential approval of the Bipartisan Campaign Reform Act (BCRA) of 2002, but also the journey that this most recent round of campaign finance reform has traveled through the *entire* policy process. This book also analyzes BCRA's path through the judicial branch, with more than one appearance before the Supreme Court, in which the law continues to be interpreted according to each new challenge to the constitutionality of its various provisions. We then explore how laws are implemented by the executive branch with the often controversial actions, and inactions, of the Federal Election Commission in its efforts to execute and enforce the new law. Not surprisingly, both judicial interpretation and agency implementation of BCRA featured the same partisan and ideological battles that played out in Congress during the law's passage as the debate over fair elections versus freedom of speech continued.

Then, we explore how various affected actors reacted to the new law. We ask how candidates, parties, interest groups, corporations, unions, and wealthy individuals responded to the new regulatory regime during the 2004 and 2006 elections, the first two elections after BCRA's enactment. Finally, we note the cyclical nature of the policy process with a look at the various proposals being advanced in Congress to address the issues that BCRA did not cover as well as in response to the (sometimes unintended) consequences of the new law. Given this broad treatment of the entire policy process and the current interest in campaign finance as a fundamental policy issue, we expect that students and scholars of American government in general, of Congress and the legislative process, and of public policy and policy making will find *Limits and Loopholes* of interest.

Acknowledgments

As with all work, our theory, thoughts, and ideas have benefited from contributions and insights developed over the years. Our own scholarship in various books, articles, and chapters has honed our thoughts and arguments and served as the foundation for the analysis presented herein. We are grateful to those discussants, editors, reviewers, and colleagues—and even critics—of *Legislative Labyrinth* who helped us refine our work along the way.

This book might never have seen the light of day if it were not for a number of scholars who have encouraged us, as well as for the encouragement we received from the four thoughtful reviewers who CQ Press commissioned: Anthony J. Corrado (Colby College), Lori Cox Han (Chapman University), Douglas B. Harris (Loyola College in Maryland), and Craig W. Thomas (University of Washington). We owe a huge debt of gratitude to Charisse Kino and Brenda Carter, who saw our vision for a new book that would move beyond a simple revision of *Legislative Labyrinth*. Charisse in particular was our confidant, counselor, cheerleader and champion. She stuck with us through medical issues, administrative follies, and a myriad of commitments that incessantly distracted us from completion of this work. She never stopped believing in the project or providing a nudge when necessary. For all these efforts we owe our deepest appreciation. We also thank our copy editors, Michael Coffino and Anna Socrates. And finally, we want to thank the staff at CQ Press, especially Steve Pazdan and Allyson Rudolph, for their wonderful work to ensure that the subtle nuances of our arguments were not lost in the editing and production process.

Additionally, we wish to thank our respective universities and colleagues for their support as we worked on this project. To our students, we deeply appreciate your questions, which often prompted us to reconsider how best to convey the complicated world of campaign finance and reminded us to avoid jargon and keep the text accessible.

Last but not least, we wish to thank our respective spouses, Jason Myers and Joe Picard. Their unflappable support, guidance, and countless hours of hearing about and reading the various iterations of this work have made this process even more a labor of love.

Victoria A. Farrar-Myers and Diana Dwyre
September 2007

LIMITS AND LOOPHOLES

1

COMPETING VALUES AND THE HIGH STAKES OF CAMPAIGN FINANCE REFORM

The concept that government may restrict the speech of some elements of our society in order to enhance the relative voice of others is wholly foreign to the First Amendment, which is designed to secure the widest possible dissemination of information from diverse and antagonistic sources and to assure unfettered interchange of ideas for the bringing about of political and social change desired by the people.

U.S. Supreme Court, *Buckley v. Valeo* (1976)

When the Supreme Court said, in the Buckley case, that fairness to candidates and their convictions is "foreign" to the First Amendment, it denied that such fairness was required by democracy. That is a mistake because the most fundamental characterization of democracy—that it provides self-government by the people as a whole—supposes that citizens are equals not only as judges but as participants as well.

Ronald Dworkin, "The Curse of American Politics,"
New York Review of Books, October 17, 1996

In *Federalist* No. 10 James Madison reminded us that in trying to find political solutions to conflicts involving core values and underlying beliefs, we

1

must be careful to ensure that the remedy is not worse than the disease. Over two hundred years later, Madison's warning still echoes loudly in the contemporary debates surrounding campaign finance reform. Similarly, much of the Founding debate played out in Madison's *Federalist* writings provides a framework for understanding campaign finance reform as more than just a policy debate over the rules and regulations governing the use of money in elections. It is an issue that reflects the value choices and compromises that are woven into the fabric of our governmental structure. Viewed in this light, campaign finance reform can be seen as a battle for power between competing factions as well as being an arena in which competing core values (such as those highlighted in the quotations above) must somehow be balanced with one another.

To fully understand campaign finance reform, one cannot examine the issue from a single perspective, but must look at it from various approaches. The issue itself is one that invokes and affects many vital interests in American politics. Campaign finance touches upon issues ranging from the conduct of elections in our system of representative democracy to fundamental individual rights protected by the Constitution. As a result, campaign finance regulations also impact the process of determining the composition of our governing institutions, which in turn affects the nature and types of policies our government produces. Thus, the rules governing the financing of elections can have a direct or indirect impact on almost every aspect of the American political system.

Unfortunately, however, one problem in crafting legislation to address campaign finance issues is that, due to short-term interests, time limitations, political expediency, and previous policy and judicial decisions, legislators are not often able to approach the matter in ways that examine the questions at hand from multiple perspectives. Lawmakers have difficulty developing campaign finance legislation that addresses the issues in a comprehensive way. As a result, legislative efforts to address campaign finance have been characterized by arduous—and sometimes unorthodox—approaches to policymaking. The study of campaign finance reform from a multilayered perspective, however, provides greater insights into the legislative process in general, and at the same time illuminates related issues in judicial interpretation of campaign finance laws, regulatory implementation, and the problems of governing from different sides of the political spectrum. Further, this multifaceted approach offers greater understanding of this policy area and demonstrates one of the basic lessons of democracy—namely, that political participation is vital in determining which values guide the debate.

The "Mischiefs of Faction" and Campaign Finance

During the founding period in the late 1700s, as the Federalists drafted and sought to obtain passage of the Constitution, Federalists and Anti-Federalists alike offered their thoughts on such fundamental questions as the proper structure of the institutions within government, human nature, and the most appropriate path for the emerging nation to follow. James Madison used the *Federalist Papers*—a collection of essays by Madison, Alexander Hamilton, and John Jay published in New York state newspapers in 1787 and 1788 to urge New Yorkers to ratify the proposed Constitution—as an opportunity to explore the connections among these issues. In doing so, he provided not only a justification for ratifying the new Constitution, but enduring historical evidence of the values that were important to the Federalists and of the choices they made to promote and protect those values, even when the values themselves were at times in conflict.

In perhaps his most famous exposition on human nature and the need to craft governmental structures that took that nature into account, Madison wrote in *Federalist* No. 10 about the Federalists' concern with factions, which he defined as "a number of citizens, whether amounting to a majority or minority of the whole, who are united and actuated by some common impulse of passion, or of interest, adversed to the rights of other citizens, or to the permanent and aggregate interests of the community." Implicit in this definition was Madison's concern about groups in society being organized around and acting on their collective self-interest without regard for either the general public good or the interests of any other group in society.

Madison then set out an analytical framework for assessing the most appropriate way to cure what he described as "the mischiefs of faction" (see Figure 1-1). One approach would be to remove the causes of faction, with two possible ways to do so. The first would be to destroy the liberty that nourishes the growth of factions. It was here, though, that Madison cautioned us that the remedy must not be worse than the disease. Liberty, Madison wrote, is essential to political life in a free society. Destroying it would undermine one of the fundamental tenets of the political system he and others were trying to construct. The second way to remove the causes of faction was to give every citizen the same set of opinions, passions, and interests. This approach, however, was also flawed. It "is as impracticable as the first would be unwise," Madison wrote, because as long as the reason of man is fallible and he has the liberty to exercise such reason, different people will inevitably differ in their opinions, interests, and concerns.

James Madison, the author of *Federalist* No. 10 and fourth president of the United States (1809–1817).

Since "the causes of faction cannot be removed," Madison concluded, "relief is only to be sought in the means of controlling its effects." When the faction consists of a minority of the populace, a majority-rule system will protect against tyranny by that minority. The more difficult problem, however, is posed by the threat of tyranny of the majority: "To secure the public good and private rights against the danger of such a faction, and at the same time to preserve the spirit and the form of popular government, is then the great object to which our inquiries are directed." The two ways to accomplish this objective are either to ensure that the development of a majority's

Figure 1-1   James Madison's Analytical Framework in *Federalist* No. 10.

FACTION: "A number of citizens, whether amounting to a majority or minority of the whole, who are united and actuated by some common impulse of passion, or of interest, adverse to the rights of other citizens, or to the permanent and aggregate interests of the community."

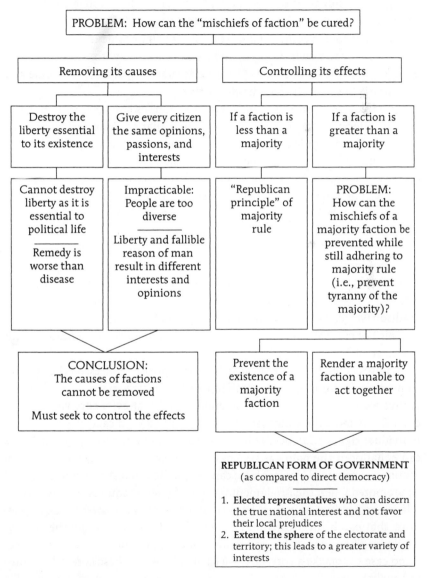

PROBLEM: How can the "mischiefs of faction" be cured?

Removing its causes

Controlling its effects

Destroy the liberty essential to its existence

Give every citizen the same opinions, passions, and interests

If a faction is less than a majority

If a faction is greater than a majority

Cannot destroy liberty as it is essential to political life
———
Remedy is worse than disease

Impracticable: People are too diverse
———
Liberty and fallible reason of man result in different interests and opinions

"Republican principle" of majority rule

PROBLEM: How can the mischiefs of a majority faction be prevented while still adhering to majority rule (i.e., prevent tyranny of the majority)?

CONCLUSION: The causes of factions cannot be removed
———
Must seek to control the effects

Prevent the existence of a majority faction

Render a majority faction unable to act together

REPUBLICAN FORM OF GOVERNMENT (as compared to direct democracy)
———
1. **Elected representatives** who can discern the true national interest and not favor their local prejudices
2. **Extend the sphere** of the electorate and territory; this leads to a greater variety of interests

Source: Developed by Victoria A. Farrar-Myers.

passion or interest in the first instance is prevented, or if such majority-based interest does arise, to render the majority unable to be so organized as to utilize their majority position to pursue their self-interest. Madison focuses on the second of these by extolling the virtues of a republican form of representative government. By utilizing representatives to serve in government, thus enlarging the sphere of the electorate, "you make it less probable that a majority of the whole will have a common motive to invade the rights of other citizens; or if such a common motive exists, it will be difficult for all who feel it to discover their own strength, and to act in unison with each other." Indeed, the separation of powers and an electorate dispersed over a wide area are barriers to quick and coordinated action.

One final point from *Federalist* No. 10 deserves consideration, particularly in reference to the issue of campaign finance. Madison noted that the "latent causes of faction are thus sown in the nature of man," where diverse opinions, preferences, and passions lead people to band together with others of a common viewpoint against the interests of others. Even in a political system where citizens had "perfect equality in their political rights," they would not be (and it would be erroneous to assume they would be) "perfectly equalized and assimilated in their possessions, their opinions, and their passions." Madison also observed that "the most common and durable source of factions has been the various and unequal distribution of property," leading to the development of a variety of economic and social interests and classes. "The regulation of the various and interfering interests," Madison wrote, "forms the principal task of modern legislation, and involves the spirit of party and faction in the necessary and ordinary operations of the government."

Madison's analysis in *Federalist* No. 10 expressly addressed the issue of competing factions—groups similar to the political parties and interest groups we know today. But it also emphasized that even core values of an open and democratic polity can come into conflict with each other. How can individual rights and liberties be protected in a majority-rule system? How can equality in the political system be achieved in a society with different economic and social classes? How can the public interest and common good be promoted when the fundamental value of liberty requires that exercise of self-interested human nature be permitted? The basic answer to these questions that can be derived from *Federalist* No. 10 is to promote the positive attributes of any core value and to limit or check the negative attributes, but in no case to forsake a core value—a *balance* between these core values must be sought.

Perhaps there is no more significant venue in a representative democracy where these issues of competing factions and competing values play out than in elections. Fair and open elections constitute one of the basic mechanisms that sustain our representative democracy. They are a means by which a sense of the public will is regularly expressed and through which the people who will be handed the reins of government are chosen. Much is at stake in any given election. The winning side (or faction, to use Madison's term) comes away from the election with more power to wield within the governmental system and more influence over the outcome of any political or policy matter. They are better able to promote their interests, passions, and views of what constitutes the public good.

As a practical matter, money is a necessary part of elections because it is needed to produce campaign literature, pay for campaign rallies, and generally enable a candidate to communicate his or her message. This was as true in the founding period as it is today. The primary concern about money in elections, though, is not about the mechanics of waging a campaign, but about the potentially corrupting force that the presence of money can have. Clearly, money can have a corrupting effect when an elected official is bribed or otherwise improperly influenced by receiving money. As Madison eloquently put it in *Federalist* No. 10, "men of. . .sinister designs, may, by intrigue, by corruption, or other means, first [be elected to office], and then betray the interests of the people." Money, however, can also be a corrupting force by distorting the representational relationship between the electorate and elected officials—by, for example, providing a larger voice to a minority faction with greater financial resources than a majority with fewer such resources.

The potentially corrupting force of money in elections would appear to present a threat to such fundamental values as equality of representation and the principle of majority rule. The protection of these values, therefore, would seem to justify campaign finance regulations designed to limit the potential corruptive effect of money in the electoral process. But, just as Madison wrote of the need to balance competing values in order to control factions, so too must other values be taken into account in addressing the issue of money in politics.

As Madison asserted, equality of political rights does not equate to equality of property, and the differences of interests must be allowed to exist in our system based on liberty and freedom. The importance of individual rights in the world of campaign finance was heightened by the Supreme Court's 1976 decision in *Buckley v. Valeo,* where the Court held that the need to protect individuals' First Amendment rights to freedom of speech significantly restricted the federal government's ability to regulate money in elections.

In doing so, the Supreme Court expressly set out the competing core values that largely define the debate about campaign finance regulation: equality versus freedom of speech. [1] Ultimately, the *Buckley* decision helped shape the debate that ensued in Congress and elsewhere about the appropriate regulations, if any, that should be placed on money in elections. This debate has played out often in the years since *Buckley,* from failed attempts to pass additional regulations in the wake of the Court's decision through the mid-1990s; through the momentum that reform legislation gained in the late 1990s culminating in the passage of the Bipartisan Campaign Reform Act (BCRA) in 2002; and, in the years since, as Congress, the Federal Election Commission (FEC), and the judiciary have sought ways to interpret and implement BCRA's regulations. To have a proper understanding of BCRA and other recent campaign-finance regulation issues, though, one should first understand the issue of campaign finance regulation in its historical policy context.

Campaign Finance Regulation in Historical Context

Prior to the 1970s, the financing of federal elections in the United States was virtually unregulated and very little campaign finance activity was disclosed to the public. Only a few rules applied to the fundraising and spending connected with federal elections. For example, in 1905 President Theodore Roosevelt called attention to the participation of corporations in campaigns (ironically, several had financed his own 1904 campaign) in his annual message to Congress. Following a similar call by Roosevelt in his 1907 annual message, Congress passed the Tillman Act, which banned corporations and national banks from making contributions to candidates for federal office. In 1910, Congress passed the Publicity Act, which required House campaign committees that operated in two or more states to disclose contributors over $100 within 30 days after an election. Later, in 1911, Congress extended filing requirements from the 1910 law to Senate candidates. This law also limited the amount candidates could spend to $10,000 for Senate campaigns and $5,000 for House campaigns.

Following the Teapot Dome scandal, in which Secretary of the Interior Edward Fall accepted money in connection with granting leases for the Teapot Dome oil field in Wyoming, Congress passed the Federal Corrupt Practices Act in 1925. This Act was the basic campaign finance law until the reforms of the early 1970s. It closed a loophole in the law that allowed candidates and contributors to avoid disclosing monetary contributions in non-election years. It revised the amount candidates could spend and made it illegal to offer money to anyone in exchange for a vote. Its scope was limited to general elections and did not apply to campaign committees operating within a single state. The Act also did not include any enforcement provisions. In 1939 Congress enacted the Hatch Act. This Act barred federal employees from active participation in national politics. In 1940 the Hatch Act was revised to limit to $3 million the fundraising and expenditures of party committees operating in two or more states, and to limit individual contributions to $5,000 a year. The Act also sought to regulate primary elections. Finally, in 1947, the Taft-Hartley Act was passed. It aimed to ban political contributions by labor unions. [2]

The campaign finance regulations passed in the first half of the twentieth century primarily addressed concerns over undue influence and corruption. The Tillman and Taft-Hartley Acts sought, respectively, to limit the influence that corporations and labor unions could exert. The Federal Corrupt Practices Act sought to limit certain undisclosed financial activities, such as those that gave rise to the Teapot Dome scandal in the first place. The Hatch Act placed a firewall between political activities and government employees charged with implementing the nation's laws and policies.

Each of these acts targeted potentially corruptive or corrosive forces that could have a deleterious effect on our nation's democratic processes by improperly privileging certain individuals or groups over others. Together, they demonstrated recognition that some individuals or groups had the potential to create a fundamental inequality in the exercise of political rights. Corporations, labor unions, and those working in government are in a powerful position to influence the electoral and/or political process, an advantage not enjoyed by the average voting citizen. Therefore, the federal government's role was to step in and ensure that our representational system would not be undermined by those who had the means and access to influence the system in a way that ordinary voters could not.

Interestingly, legislative efforts to limit the influence of privileged individuals and groups during the early part of the twentieth century also often included restrictions on contributions and candidate spending. Although these issues would be at the core of the debate over campaign finance regulation starting in the 1970s, this approach was not challenged at the time. Although campaign funds were necessary, they were not as critical to waging a viable campaign that they are today. Elections into the 1960s were *party-oriented* in nature; that is, candidates were selected primarily by party leaders and, particularly on the congressional level, candidates relied on the party organization for support in financing and waging a winning campaign. Starting in the 1960s and continuing into the 1970s, efforts were undertaken to make government more open and accessible, and this included efforts related to how elections were conducted. For example, at the presidential level, the McGovern-Fraser Commission in 1968 changed the methods by which the Democratic Party selected candidates for its national conventions in presidential years. These changes led to more states holding presidential primaries in order to select convention delegates and the party's nominee for president, thus resulting in a loss of power for party leaders.

At the congressional level, elections became more *candidate-centered,* meaning that the emphasis of the campaign focused on the candidate and not the party. The movement toward candidate-centered campaigns allowed political outsiders—that is, people who were not specifically tied to a political party's leadership—to run and be elected to office. One impact, though, of the various efforts at the presidential and congressional levels to open up the political and electoral processes was to increase the need for candidates to raise money independently. Previously, candidates could rely on their parties for much of their financial support. But in the more open system that started to emerge in the 1960s and 1970s, candidates needed to raise their own funds separate from any party funding and, in the case of the presidential nomination, wage campaigns in a greater number of primaries throughout the nation. In other words, trying to make the electoral process more open helped foster an environment that facilitated the rise of candidate-centered campaigns; this environment, in turn, resulted in the unintended consequence of putting a greater emphasis on money in campaigns.

The 1971 Federal Election Campaign Act (FECA) represented Congress's effort to open up the electoral process by reducing the influence of *fat cats*— that is, wealthy individuals who were willing to contribute extraordinary amounts of money to get a candidate elected. FECA (and its amendments of 1974, 1976, and 1979) and the Revenue Act of 1971 (and its 1974 amendments) dramatically changed the landscape for the financing of congressional and presidential campaigns. The Revenue Act of 1971 provided public funding for presidential elections through a check-off on income tax forms by which taxpayers could divert one dollar of their tax liability to the public fund (this later was raised to $3). Presidential candidates were eligible for the public funds if they agreed to limit their overall spending. FECA strengthened the existing prohibition against contributions from corporations and labor unions; it also provided the legal basis for business, labor, and other organizations to form political action committees (PACs—the campaign financing arms of interest groups), the entities through which they legally could spend money in federal elections. FECA limited personal contributions by candidates and their immediate families, and it tightened campaign finance reporting and disclosure requirements and extended these requirements to primary elections. Finally, the 1971 law placed strict limits on the amount of money candidates could spend on media advertising.

The break-in at the Democratic Party headquarters at the Watergate complex in Washington, D.C. on June 17, 1972, began one of the most highly publicized scandals in American political history. The Watergate hearings documented numerous transgressions by the Nixon administration, including the burglary, millions of dollars in illegal campaign contributions, arm-twisting for contributions, money laundering, lists of enemies, and a cover-up conspiracy. The scandal brought down President Richard Nixon, and Congress responded to the public's demand for change with a number of amendments to FECA that represent the most comprehensive campaign finance laws ever adopted.

New campaign finance legislation is not contingent on the occurrence of political scandals like Watergate or the Teapot Dome. Such scandals do, however, provide windows of opportunity for pursuing reform. Often, scandals serve to highlight the existence of a problem and result in the public demanding changes to prevent a similar scandal from occurring in the future. Legislators seeking to promote change to the status quo are given a warrant for action, while those opposed to change risk being perceived by the public as defending a flawed system or, worse, defending the corrupt actions exposed in the scandal. Thus, these opportunities lend themselves to revisiting the very values that motivate political actors and underlie their actions.

Following the Watergate scandal, the 1974 amendments to FECA included these major provisions:

(1) **limits on contributions** from individuals, PACs, and party committees were established, as was a monetary limit for total contributions by individuals;

(2) **limits were established on the amount of money political party organizations could spend on behalf of federal candidates** (these expenditures are called coordinated expenditures);

(3) **limits on expenditures** by House, Senate, and presidential candidates replaced the media expenditure ceilings in the 1971 FECA;

(4) **limits were set on independent expenditures,** that is, expenditures made independently of a candidate's campaign by individuals or in-

terest groups to advocate the election or defeat of a federal candidate,[3] and cash donations over $100 were prohibited;

(5) **the Federal Election Commission** (FEC) was established to implement and enforce the federal campaign finance laws;

(6) **new disclosure and reporting rules** were passed that required candidates to file quarterly reports on their contributions and expenditures
with the FEC, and that made these records available to the public;
and

(7) **the presidential election public funding system** was amended to
allow presidential nominees for the major parties to receive public
funds equal to the aggregate spending limit if a nominee agreed not
to raise additional private money (minor party and independent candidates were eligible for a proportional share of this subsidy), and a
voluntary system of public matching funds was established for presidential primary campaigns.[4]

These provisions created a new landscape for the financing of federal elections, but they were almost immediately challenged in the courts by such
plaintiffs as a conservative senator still in office (James Buckley of New York)
and a liberal former senator and presidential candidate (Eugene McCarthy
of Minnesota). However, in 1976, the Supreme Court in *Buckley v. Valeo*[5] upheld FECA's limitations on contributions to candidates as appropriate
legislative tools to guard against improper influence, or at least the appearance of improper influence, stemming from candidates' dependence on large
campaign contributions. In doing so, the Court gave credence to concerns
about the potentially corrupting effect that large amounts of money in elections could have:

> Of almost equal concern as the danger of actual quid pro quo arrangements
> is the impact of the appearance of corruption stemming from public aware-
> ness of the opportunities for abuse inherent in a regime of large individual
> financial contributions. . . . Congress could legitimately conclude that the
> avoidance of the appearance of improper influence is also critical if confi-
> dence in the system of representative Government is not to be eroded to a
> disastrous extent.[6]

At the same time, however, the Court invalidated FECA's limitations on
independent expenditures (expenditures for communications made by individuals, interest groups, or parties without any coordination or consultation

with any candidate), candidate expenditures from personal funds, and over-all candidate campaign expenditures. By striking down these limitations, the Court emphasized the rights of individuals, framing the issue in the context of the individual's First Amendment right to free speech:

> A restriction on the amount of money a person or group can spend on polit-ical communication during a campaign necessarily reduces the quantity of expression by restricting the number of issues discussed, the depth of their exploration, and the size of the audience reached. This is because virtually every means of communicating ideas in today's mass society requires the ex-penditure of money. [7] . . . It is clear that a primary effect of these expendi-tures limitations is to restrict the quantity of campaign speech by individu-als, groups, and candidates. The restrictions, while neutral as to the ideas expressed, limit political expression at the core of our electoral process and of the First Amendment freedoms. [8]

Buckley v. Valeo set into motion two conflicting principles: one that al-lows limits on campaign *contributions* as a means to reduce corruption or the appearance of corruption in the political system, and another that views limits on campaign *expenditures* as unconstitutional limitations on free speech and, therefore, allows candidates to spend as much as they choose. [9] The Court's ruling is often criticized by regulation proponents for the latter principle's suggestion that "money equals speech," which, given the magnitude of some contributions, could imply a very unequal right to free speech. According to this approach, critics say, wealthy individuals and groups are entitled to *more* speech than an individual $100 contributor. But critics of campaign finance regulation also found fault with the *Buck-ley* decision. These critics contend that restricting the amount of money permitted in political campaigns, regardless of whether it is a contribution or an expenditure, impermissibly restricts both the quantity and quality of political discourse and ideas.

Beginning in the 1980s and continuing through much of the 1990s, those concerned with the perceived inadequacies of the campaign finance regula-tory system focused on two main issues: (1) the rising cost of campaigns (see Figures 1-2 and 1-3, showing the average expenditures of House and Senate candidates from 1980 to 2006); and (2) the substantial reliance on PACs as a source of major funding for campaigns and the resulting influence of wealthy and powerful interest groups (see Figure 1-4, showing the growth of PAC contributions to congressional candidates from 1980 to 2006).

Figure 1-2   Average Expenditure of House Candidates, 1980–2006

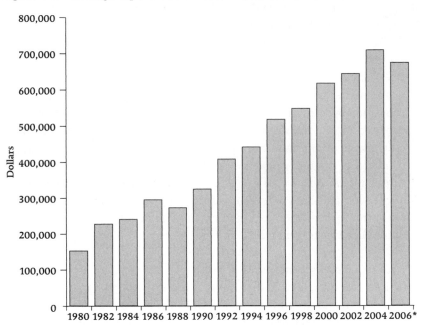

Source: For 1980–1998, compiled from data in Norman J. Ornstein, Thomas E. Mann, and Michael J. Malbin, *Vital Statistics on Congress, 1999–2000* (Washington, D.C.: AEI Press, 2000), 80. For 2000–2004, compiled from CQ's Vital Statistics on American Politics Online Edition, Table 2-6 Congressional Campaign Costs, by Party and Incumbency Status, 1993–2004, available at http://library.cqpress.com/vsap. For 2006, compiled from Federal Election Commission, "Congressional Campaigns Spend $966 Million through Mid-October," press release, November 2, 2006, available at http://www.fec.gov.
Note: Data for 2006 election reflects expenditures up through 20 days prior to the 2006 election.

Additionally, many political scientists, journalists, public interest groups, and regulation-oriented legislators argued that the incumbency advantage and the lack of electoral competitiveness in congressional elections were detrimental to our system of representative democracy. Challengers were (and still are) generally far outspent by the incumbents they take on, and House incumbents were reelected at rates often well over 80%, and sometimes at rates over 90% during the 1980s and 1990s, a pattern that continues today.

These issues, together with the stage set by the Supreme Court with its *Buckley* decision, characterized attempted campaign finance reform legislation throughout the 1980s and early 1990s. For example, in 1987 the leading reform bill, S.2, included public financing for congressional campaigns in ex-

Figure 1-3   Average Campaign Expenditures by Senate Candidates, 1980–2006

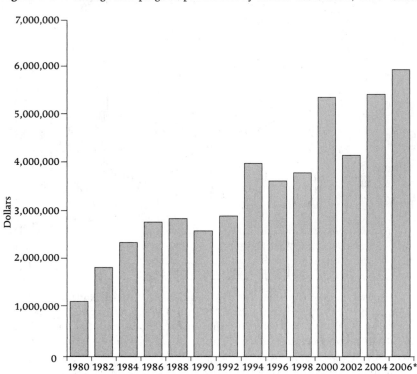

Source: For 1980–1998, compiled from data in Norman J. Ornstein, Thomas E. Mann, and Michael J. Malbin, *Vital Statistics on Congress, 1999-2000* (Washington, D.C.: AEI Press, 2000), 80. For 2000–2004, compiled from CQ's Vital Statistics on American Politics Online Edition, Table 2-6 Congressional Campaign Costs, by Party and Incumbency Status, 1993–2004, available at http://library.cqpress.com/vsap. For 2006, compiled from Federal Election Commission, "Congressional Campaigns Spend $966 Million through Mid-October," press release, November 2, 2006, available at http://www.fec.gov.
*Note: Data for 2006 election reflects expenditures up through 20 days prior to the 2006 election.

change for voluntary spending limits by congressional candidates, aggregate PAC limits, limits on PAC "bundling," [10] and limits on independent expenditures. The 102nd Congress (1991–1992) actually passed similar campaign finance reform legislation, but it was vetoed by President George H.W. Bush. The 103rd Congress, with Democratic majorities in both chambers and a new pro-reform Democratic president, Bill Clinton, came close to passing campaign finance reform, but the sponsors of the reform legislation could not overcome Republican delaying tactics and filibusters in the Senate.

Figure 1-4   Total PAC Contributions to House and Senate Candidates, 1980–2006

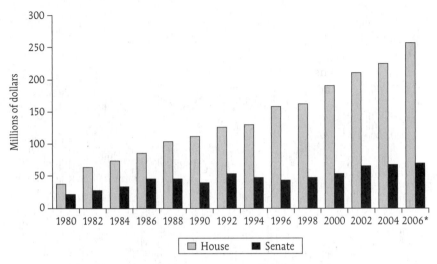

Source: Federal Election Commission, Compiled from: (a) "FEC Releases Information on PAC Activity for 1997–1998," news release, June 8, 1999; (b) "PAC Activity Increases for 2004 Elections," news release, April 13, 2005; (c) "Congressional Candidates Spend $1.6 Billion During 2003–2004," news release, June 9, 2005; and (d) "Congressional Campaigns Spend $966 Million through Mid-October," news release, November 2, 2006.
*Note: Data for 2006 election reflects expenditures up through 20 days prior to the 2006 election.

Critics of the *Buckley* decision also complained that by limiting contributions the Supreme Court had restricted the supply of money for campaigns but not the demand for it, thus encouraging both campaign-fund raisers (e.g., candidates and parties) and spenders (e.g., individuals, PACs, and parties) to look for loopholes in the law that would allow them to raise and spend more money. One way this occurred was through the growth of *soft money,* which originally stemmed from efforts to strengthen political parties to help counterbalance the growing impact of outside or special interests in the electoral process. The FEC promulgated regulations to assist parties with activities to revitalize themselves, namely get-out-the-vote drives, generic party advertising (such as advertisements that say "Vote Republican, For a Change"), and the like. Yet these activities themselves quickly became avenues for the proliferation of unregulated party money (i.e., soft money) from the wealthy interests they were intended to curb. Ironically, by limiting contributions, the *Buckley* decision helped open the door to soft money.

Additionally, in the *Buckley* decision, the Supreme Court defined narrowly what is considered a campaign communication to include only those communications that *expressly advocate* the election or defeat of a clearly identified candidate. Communications that fell inside this definition of express advocacy were subject to federal contribution limits and reporting requirements, while those that fell outside of this narrow definition were *not* subject to those restrictions even if they conveyed a similar substantive message as express advocacy ads. The proliferation of so-called issue ads (ones that fell outside the express advocacy test) funded by outside interests resulted in candidates beginning to notice that their own campaign messages were being drowned out by competing advertising. Yet these issue advocacy ads, especially when run in the final weeks of the election, came very close to advocating the election or defeat of a particular candidate. These new developments kept the push for reform alive and shifted the focus of reform endeavors in Congress, particularly after the 1996 elections.

After over a decade of reform efforts that attempted to limit campaign spending, restrict contributions, and provide for public financing of congressional elections, the focus of reform shifted to various perceived *loopholes* in the campaign finance system. While many of these loopholes in the law were evident toward the end of the 1980s, concern escalated as the loopholes began to engulf the whole system, which was especially evident after the 1996 elections. According to Representative Christopher Shays, R-Conn., a key reformer in the House, the system began to "collapse on itself." In 1996 record amounts of soft money were raised and spent, the president and his party were accused of violating numerous campaign finance laws, [11] and more and more issue advocacy ads filled the airwaves and our mailboxes while their sponsors escaped any regulation of these activities. Reformers—led by John McCain, R-Ariz., and Russell Feingold, D-Wis., in the Senate, and Shays and Marty Meehan, D-Mass., in the House—thus turned their attention to the various loopholes that allowed such campaign finance practices, including:

- *Bundling:* The collection by an intermediate agent of checks made payable to a specific candidate. This allows PACs and interest groups to raise money in excess of what they can legally contribute directly to a candidate and to receive recognition from the candidate for their endeavors.
- *Soft money:* Money that may "indirectly influence federal elections but is raised and spent outside the purview of federal laws and would be illegal if spent directly on a federal election." [12] Soft money raised by the national Democratic and Republican national party organizations rose

Figure 1-5   Party Committee Soft Money Receipts, 1992–2002

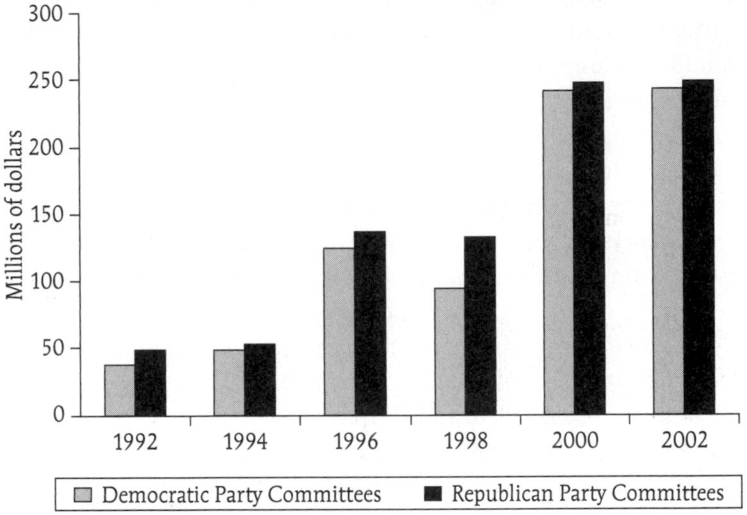

□ Democratic Party Committees   ■ Republican Party Committees

Source: FEC, "Party Committees Raise More than $1 Billion in 2001–2002," press release, March 20, 2003.

from $86 million in 1992 to $262 million in 1996 to over $496 million in 2002 (the last year that the national parties were permitted to receive soft money contributions—see Figure 1-5). [13]

- *Independent expenditures:* Money spent by individuals or groups on communications with voters to support or oppose clearly identified candidates, as long as there is no coordination or consultation with any candidate.
- *Issue advocacy:* Advertisements that do not *expressly advocate* the election or defeat of a candidate by using the so-called *magic words,* such as "vote for" or "vote against." Such a communication could be paid for with unregulated and undisclosed funds (i.e., soft money), for it was not technically considered campaigning.

The terms of the campaign finance reform debate began to shift with the growing acknowledgment that these loopholes posed a more severe threat to the campaign finance system than past concerns about PAC influence and high campaign costs. Political action committees, which were once perceived as a source of corruption that threatened to undo the system, were now seen as one of the more legitimate avenues for raising and spending campaign money. After all, at least PACs are regulated and their activities disclosed. Moreover, while concerns over fundamental issues like competition and the incumbency advantage were still in the background, the Republicans helped knock the wind out of these arguments with their decisive victory in the 1994 congressional elections by taking control of the House for the first time in forty years and winning the Senate for the first time since 1986.

The explosion of soft money, though, also raised questions about increases in the amount of money that outside groups were spending on issue advocacy ads. Many of these ads may not have used the *magic words* to expressly advocate for the election or defeat of a candidate, but the intended message was usually very clear. The controversy over issue advocacy ads began when the Democratic National Committee (DNC) used a combination of soft money and hard (or regulated) money to run issue ads in 24 states in 1995 and 1996. Since the ads did not use the magic words, the DNC could use soft money to pay for part of them. Moreover, by transferring the soft money to state party committees so that they could buy the ad time locally, the DNC was able to conserve its hard money, which is more difficult to raise since it must be raised in small increments and is the only party money that may be given to or spent directly on behalf of candidates. [14]

Together, soft money and issue advocacy seemed to be the most egregious campaign finance practices in the 1996 elections, and reformers turned their attention to proposing remedies for these *twin evils*. Campaign finance reform efforts starting in the 105th Congress were, therefore, a dramatic shift away from the traditional reform proposals to restrict contributions, limit campaign spending, and provide public financing of congressional elections. Senator John McCain and Senator Russell Feingold had introduced in 1995 a comprehensive reform bill that attempted to take a multi-layered approach to campaign finance legislation. But by scaling back their proposal and attacking these *twin evils*, the reformers sought to take advantage of the media attention focused on these legal loopholes during the 1996 election and to bring together a larger coalition in support of their reform bill, the Bipartisan Campaign Reform Act. [15]

The Multiple Layers of Campaign Finance Reform

As noted at the outset of this chapter, properly analyzing the issue of campaign finance reform requires that it be looked at from multiple perspectives. Further, within each perspective, many other questions and issues arise. For example, examining campaign finance reform from a policy per-

Source: David Nather with Jill Barshay, *CQ Weekly*

(left to right) Sen. John McCain, R-Ariz.; Rep. Martin T. Meehan, D-Mass.; Rep. Christopher Shays, R-Conn.; and Sen. Russell D. Feingold, D-Wis.

spective, one must ask "what is the primary problem or set of problems that one would want to remedy within the system?" As the above historical summary shows, in the years following the *Buckley* decision, the primary focus of regulation proponents shifted from spending by PACs to the *twin evils* of soft money and issue ads, with a number of other issues taken into consideration along the way. But regulation opponents, too, if given their choice, likely would want to remove the limitations on contributions permitted under *Buckley*.

From a legislative process perspective, the question is not so much what bill each side would want passed, but what bill can they get passed through the two chambers of Congress and approved by the President. Just as Madison counseled in *Federalist* No. 10 that the interests around which factions could be organized needed to be dispersed across an enlarged electorate to protect against the tyranny of the majority, so too the powers of the government needed to be separated among the political branches, so as to require that each branch would check the others' wielding of their respective powers. Madison wrote in *Federalist* No. 51 that "ambition must be made to counteract ambition. . . . It may be a reflection of human nature, that such devices should be necessary to control the abuses of government." [16] Although the system of separation of powers and checks and balances is necessary to control the government, it sometimes also results in making compromises in the legislative process in order to achieve a legislative outcome. For example, in discussing the decision to scale back a legislative proposal to focus on soft money and issue ads, Representative Marty Meehan, D-Mass., one of the primary sponsors of reform legislation in the House of Representatives, acknowledged that the proposal "represent[ed] a compromise struck between what Chris [Shays, R-Conn.] and I wanted to pass and what we believed could pass in the current political climate. It's not the perfect bill. But perfection is too often the enemy of the good."

From a policy implementation perspective, one can focus on what happens after campaign finance reform legislation is passed by Congress and put into action within the political system. The FEC is responsible for developing regulations to flesh out the details of the legislation and to oversee enforcement of the rules and regulations governing the conduct of campaign financing. Yet, the FEC's decisions can have a dramatic impact on the campaign finance landscape, as was the case with the FEC regulation that gave rise to soft money. Similarly, the judiciary has played a significant role not only in deciding whether any given limitation is lawful, but also in shaping discourse on the issue by expressly placing protection against corruption and the appearance of corruption as one core value competing with the First Amendment right to freedom of speech as the other. Further, how candidates, parties, interest groups, and others conduct themselves in the course of an election cycle not only gives meaning to prior legislation, but also identifies loopholes that are being exploited and that may need to be addressed in the future.

Overlaying each of these perspectives, though, is the issue of competing core values inherent in campaign finance legislation. In this regard, the analytical framework offered by James Madison in *Federalist* No. 10 also helps frame the issue of campaign finance. Just as Madison could not conceive of a way in which to cure the cause of problems associated with factions, one cannot cure any the problems associated with the campaign finance system simply by removing one of the competing values. Permitting corrupt elections or severely restricting the expression of political thought and speech as a solution would surely be a remedy worse than the disease.

Indeed, we must accept the tension between the desire to eliminate corruption and the need to allow free expression of political speech, but do so in a way that addresses the effects of this tension. Guarding against a modern-day tyranny of the majority in the context of campaign finance requires preserving the individual right to political expression. But such protection of the individual should not give rise to tyranny of the minority—in other words, it should not distort either the majoritarian principle or equality of political rights, both of which are bedrocks of our nation's political system.

Taking each of these perspectives into account, though, one can distill many of the policy issues to one guiding question: *what is the appropriate mechanism to balance competing values in our political system?* Put another way, are we going to rely upon a system of extensive governmental regulation to achieve balance between the competing values, or, are we going to remove what some see as artificial and improper limitations, and instead let the political marketplace of ideas determine what is acceptable campaign finance behavior, and what unacceptable? Each side of this debate—each faction, if you will—has (or at least has had) its share of proponents in the halls of Congress, the Oval Office, judicial chambers, and bureaucratic offices. The outcome of the continuing battle between these factions will have dramatic consequences for the future of our nation's representative democracy. For this reason, we are compelled to delve into the labyrinth that defines the making of campaign finance policy.

Plan of the Book

In Chapter 2, we pick up where the historical overview left off and begin to tell the story of the most recent attempt to reform the campaign finance laws of the United States. We examine the events and circumstances leading up to and during the 105th Congress (1997–1999) and discuss this important round in the battle for and against changes to the campaign finance system. This tumultuous legislative story illustrates some of the unorthodox lawmaking methods that often characterize modern policymaking and compares such methods against what is often called the *textbook* description of how a bill becomes a law. Further, we explore the nature of inter-chamber politics, the role of important policy entrepreneurs and issue leaders, and the impact of external actors like the president, interest groups, and the media.

In Chapter 3, we discuss not only what happened during each round of the debate over campaign finance reform in the House and Senate during the 106th and 107th Congresses, but also what changed (and did not change) from one round to the next. We find that lawmakers and others involved in the debate went through a process of political learning and that the issue itself evolved over time. For example, key leaders changed (House Speaker

Newt Gingrich, R-Ga., was replaced by Dennis Hastert, R-Ill.), different scandals arose (Enron), interest groups and other outsiders helped broker new compromises, and John McCain's 2000 presidential bid helped place campaign finance reform higher on the nation's political agenda. We explore the high-stakes battle over the issue, a battle in which both sides feel equally passionate about what values deserve greater weight and what mechanisms should be used to promote them.

In Chapter 4, we explore the role of the judiciary in determining, interpreting, and implementing campaign finance policy. One of the most interesting and unusual aspects of the Bipartisan Campaign Reform Act was its mandated process for judicial appeal. Knowing that the law would be challenged before the ink was dry on the president's signature, lawmakers provided for what they hoped would be a fast-track process of judicial review. In 2003, the Supreme Court decided to uphold the main provisions of BCRA, but the Court's decision did not provide the clear direction for which BCRA's proponents and opponents alike had hoped. Instead, the court's decision was just one in a line of cases that helped shape and continuously affect how the issue of campaign finance reform is addressed. This chapter will explore the dynamics of attempting to utilize the courts to resolve the underlying clash of values associated with campaign finance, as well as the effect that judicial decisions have had on the policymaking process.

In Chapter 5, we take a look at how the opposing sides tried to get the FEC to write rules and regulations that favored their perspective. Of course, the pro-regulation side had won many of the battles thus far, but BCRA's sponsors (John McCain and Russell Feingold in the Senate, and Chris Shays and Marty Meehan in the House) criticized the FEC for what they saw as misinterpreting and gutting BCRA, the law they had so carefully crafted. The pro-regulation interest groups and some of the media (most notably the *New York Times* and *Los Angeles Times*) also pressured the FEC in congressional hearings and in editorials, respectively. The FEC itself became even more of a focus of reform than it had been in the past, as pro-reform legislators began proposing legislation to completely overhaul the agency. The FEC's decisions prompted new rounds of proposals to try to close what pro-reform legislators saw as new loopholes created by the FEC's regulations.

The 2002 election was the last election in which political parties could raise and spend soft money, and all of the national party committees raised and spent record amounts of it. They rushed to construct new buildings, purchase computer equipment, and pay off debts. And, of course, they spent it on the few competitive House and Senate races around the country. In Chapter 6, we look at how the 2004 and 2006 elections begin to tell a fascinating story about party development and adaptation, and about political learning by various political actors. Many predictions abounded at the time about what life would be like once BCRA took effect, with some observers predicting that the parties would be seriously weakened without the ability to raise and spend soft money. This was not the case at all. The parties and their allied groups found new ways to raise huge amounts of money. The parties raised more hard money than they had ever raised before. In addition, new organizations that acted much like shadow parties were created as 527 organizations (nonprofit political groups named after the section of the tax code that regulates their activities), and lawmakers and their party leaders found new ways to help each other win.

Additionally, neither presidential candidate was lacking in funds. The experiences of the 2004 election, particularly the rise of 527 organizations, offered fertile ground for additional calls for new remedies to the ills of the campaign finance system, yet little appeared to change in the 2006 election cycle. Rather, 2006 saw ever-increasing pressure on the system with the advent of widespread use of blogs, the Internet, and other alternative forms of political communication. Future elections will reveal more fully how these political actors changed and adapted to the new campaign regime, but the 2004 and 2006 elections give us a very good look at the implications of the choices previously made and an indication of those that may lie ahead. Therefore, in this chapter, we explore the immediate impact of BCRA on political behavior within campaigns and elections and address the ramifications associated with its implementation.

Finally, in Chapter 7, we examine how the clash of core values that characterizes the issue of campaign finance leads the opposing camps to identify different problems and different remedies to those problems. As a result, the compromise legislation that emerges addresses symptoms rather than root causes. As we saw with the Madisonian analysis of the issue, however, the best that can be hoped for is to address the effects of the choices made between competing values. The story that unfolds is one of learning and adaptation, unorthodox policymaking processes, piecemeal legislation, and unintended consequences. The lessons learned from this story of campaign finance reform help us clarify how policies are really forged in our system of representative democracy in which at times certain core values compete with one another.

NOTES

1. For a discussion on balancing issues of representation with First Amendment rights in the context of campaign finance reform, see Victoria A. Farrar-Myers, "Campaign Finance: Reform, Representation, and the First Amendment," in *Law and Election Politics: The Rules of the Game,* ed. Matthew J. Streb (Boulder, CO: Lynne Rienner Publishers, 2005).
2. See Karen Foerstel, "From Teddy Roosevelt On: A Century of Changes," *CQ Weekly,* May 13, 2000.
3. When making independent expenditures, there can be no coordination or consultation with the candidate, and these expenditures must be paid for with funds raised in accordance with FECA and reported to the FEC.
4. For a thorough history of federal campaign finance laws, see Anthony Corrado, "Money and Politics: A History of Campaign Finance Law," in *Campaign Finance Reform: A Sourcebook,* eds. Anthony Corrado, Thomas E. Mann, Daniel R. Ortiz, and Trevor Potter (Washington, D.C.: Brookings Institution Press, 2005).
5. *Buckley v. Valeo,* 424 U.S. 1 (1976).
6. *Buckley v. Valeo,* 424 U.S. 1 at 27 (1976). The other two interests proffered by regulation supporters that were deemed "ancillary" by the Court were to "equalize the relative ability of all citizens to affect the outcome of elections" and "to open the political system more widely" (*Buckley v. Valeo,* 424 U.S. 1 at 26). Of these, the Court considered the purpose of stemming corruption or the appearance of corruption to be the only reason sufficient to potentially justify an infringement on free speech rights.
7. Ibid, 424 U.S. at 19.
8. Ibid, 424 U.S. at 39 (internal quotations, citations, and punctuation omitted).
9. In *Buckley* the Supreme Court ruled that spending limits would be permitted if they were linked to public funding of campaigns, so that candidates who accept public funds would, in turn, agree to limit their overall spending. The key point here is that such limits on campaign expenditures are voluntary (in exchange for public funding) and therefore do not violate the Court's ruling that campaign expenditures are protected political speech and therefore cannot be involuntarily limited.
10. Bundling involves an intermediate agent, usually a PAC or interest group, collecting checks that are made payable to a specific candidate, and delivering those checks to the candidate bundled together.
11. For example, Democrats were accused of accepting illegal foreign campaign contributions. President Clinton was charged with trading overnight stays in the White House's Lincoln Bedroom for campaign contributions, and Vice

President Al Gore was accused of holding a fundraising event at a Buddhist Temple. Democrats countered with their own accounts of Republican campaign finance irregularities. For a comprehensive look at these investigations, see the final report of the Committee on Governmental Affairs of the United States Senate, "Investigation of Illegal or Improper Activities in Connection with 1996 Federal Election Campaigns," Volumes 1–6 (Washington, D.C.: U.S. Government Printing Office, 1998).

12. See Joseph Cantor, *CRS Issue Brief—Campaign Financing, Report # IB87020,* updated October 16, 1998, page 4.

13. Federal Election Commission, "Party Committees Raise More than $1 Billion in 2001–2002," News Release, March 20, 2003.

14. Anthony Corrado, "Financing the 1996 Elections," in *The Election of 1996: Reports and Interpretations,* ed. Gerald Pomper (Chatham, NJ: Chatham House Publishers, Inc., 1996), 147.

15. While many argued that the original version of the bill, which included free television time in exchange for voluntary spending limits and provisions to deal with bundling, was preferred, supporters of BCRA in both chambers contended that the updated version still had enough teeth to accomplish meaningful reform of the campaign finance system. The revised version also dealt with foreign money, coordinated independent expenditures, and, to some extent, the advantages enjoyed by wealthy candidates. Perhaps more importantly, supporters of the revised version of the bill believed that it actually had a chance of passing.

16. Madison famously continued: "But what is government itself, but the greatest of all reflection on human nature? If men were angels, no government would be necessary. If angels were to govern men, neither external nor internal controls on government would be necessary. In framing a government which is to be administered by men over men, the great difficulty lies in this: you must first enable the government to control the governed, and in the next place oblige it to control itself."

2

CAMPAIGN FINANCE REFORM IN THE 105TH CONGRESS: A TALE OF UNORTHODOX POLICYMAKING

Students of Congress are accustomed to discussing the flowchart model of "how a bill becomes a law," complete with a predictable journey charting the bill's introduction, committee and subcommittee action, floor action, conference committee review, final floor consideration, and, finally, presidential approval. But this textbook model does not accurately describe the way that many bills make their way through Congress. In both chambers, legislation often proceeds along a much less predictable path. The modern legislative process features a variety of unorthodox or nontraditional strategies to both assist and hinder passage of particular bills. As a result, some measures travel unpredictable and often unique pathways through the legislative process. [1]

When the stakes are high and powerful players like party leaders, bipartisan groups of legislators, or congressional-presidential coalitions strongly desire a particular outcome, the inclination toward innovation is also high. Beginning in the 1970s, the use of innovative and unorthodox strategies in the legislative process became more common. Now, these special procedures and practices have become the norm rather than the exception. Barbara Sinclair's survey of the procedures used for major legislation in the House and Senate in the late 1980s and early 1990s reveals that four out of five measures in the House and two out of three measures in the Senate were considered under some unorthodox or unusual process. She found that employing unorthodox procedures tends to make legislating easier in the House but more difficult in the Senate. [2] The textbook model, then, is clearly not the primary one used in the modern Congress. Similarly, the journey of campaign finance reform legislation through the Senate and the House during the 105th Congress (1997–1998) was characterized by many of these unorthodox procedures, and reveals much about how and why they were used as well as the different outcomes that can result in the two chambers. [3]

The Battle Begins in the Senate: Bargaining, then Defeat

The self-proclaimed "Darth Vader" of campaign finance reform stood on one side of the debate, while a former prisoner-of-war turned crusader and maverick stood on the other. [4] Although both men were from the same party, they were definitely not on the same side of this issue. It seemed like a match-up destined for headlines. But this legislative battle played out under very little media scrutiny.

Senator Mitch McConnell, R-Ky., chair of the National Republican Senatorial Committee (NRSC) for the 1998 election, was well aware that the GOP enjoyed a significant financial advantage over the Democrats under the campaign finance regulations in place at the time. As a result, Senator McConnell was hardly motivated to change the laws, for the current system allowed him to raise record amounts of money, much of it soft money, for Republican Senate candidates. For example, in the 1998 election cycle, McConnell's NRSC raised over $123 million in hard and soft money for GOP candidates.

He also articulated the well-formed view shared by most of his Republican colleagues that they were generally opposed to further government regulation and intervention in this area. Moreover, most GOP lawmakers like McConnell believed that many of the campaign finance reform proposals would impinge on fundamental First Amendment free speech rights. Throughout his years in the Senate, McConnell has been consistent with respect to his passionate belief regarding the need to protect First Amendment rights, even if it has meant that at times he must defy his party's position. For example, McConnell voted against a constitutional amendment that would have prohibited flag burning, a measure that most of his Republican Senate colleagues supported. McConnell has become a relentless crusader against attempts to reform the campaign finance laws and has led more than one filibuster to kill the measures in the Senate. The various descriptions of McConnell as the "black night" or the "Darth Vader" of campaign finance reform capture his determination to defeat reform that he considers to be an "evil" that threatens the First Amendment to the Constitution. [5]

Among McConnell's arguments against campaign finance legislation during floor debate on the issue, he mocked the reform proponents' definition of issue ads as campaign ads. "Sham issue advocacy is the reformer's favorite pejorative term of art for First Amendment protected speech," he said. "They say it is sham speech because—brace yourself—it might actually affect an election." Contending that interested voters and organizations should be able to freely express their viewpoints on issues, McConnell continued, "there could be some citizen group with all their 'sham' issue advocacy spoiling the election, messing the election up, fussing the election up with issues, for goodness sake—with issues." [6] McConnell proclaimed that the "proponents of this proposal seem to me to be dismayed at all of this speech out there polluting our democracy and our campaigns. The presumption underlying that, of course, is that we as candidates somehow ought to be able to control elections, as if only our voice should be heard." [7]

On the other side, leading the reform legislation efforts in the Senate was Senator John McCain, R-Ariz. Although the McCain-Feingold Bipartisan Campaign Reform Act (BCRA) was the product of a bipartisan effort by two senators, Senator McCain clearly was the more identifiable of the two. Perhaps it was because of his status as a war hero. McCain spent over five years as a prisoner of war in Vietnam, where he endured torture and solitary confinement after his Navy fighter plane was shot down. Like other public figures who have fought for their country, McCain enjoys a special kind of respect, especially because of his POW experience. Or maybe McCain received more attention because he was willing to take such a prominent position on an issue his party did not support. He has a reputation for being independent or a maverick, and he has defied his party leaders on other issues as well, such as the tobacco settlement legislation he sponsored in 1998. [8]

McCain, like Senator McConnell, was quite sincere in his position regarding campaign finance reform. Indeed, his reform efforts have not been confined to campaign finance. In this regard, McCain was the perfect GOP advocate for campaign finance reform. He is a conservative, and being out front on this contentious issue sent a signal to other legislators that it was legitimate for a conservative to support campaign finance reform. His tell-it-like-it-is, no-nonsense style also helped keep reporters interested.

Russell Feingold, for his part, seemed to complement and balance McCain quite well. Feingold—seen as one of the most liberal members in the Senate—provided evidence that campaign finance reform legislation was something that both sides of the ideological spectrum could support. Similarly, where McCain was seen as fiery and sometimes combative, Feingold had been

Source: Congressional Quarterly

Sen. Mitch McConnell, R-Ky., the leading opponent of campaign finance reform in the Senate.

known to take unorthodox (and somewhat humorous) approaches to matters. For example, during his first campaign for the Senate in 1992, Feingold painted his contract with the voters of Wisconsin on his garage door [9] and even accepted the endorsement of an Elvis Presley impersonator. Feingold, however, shared McCain's commitment to campaign finance reform, to the point of conducting his 1998 re-election campaign with a set of self-imposed restrictions that he sought to impose on others as part of the McCain-Feingold legislation.

Because of the generally more flexible rules in the Senate than in the House, and with the support of a majority of senators, reform proponents hoped that it was only a matter of time before the legislation would receive Senate approval. Senators McCain and Feingold introduced the Bipartisan Campaign Reform Act of 1997 (S. 25) on January 21, 1997. [10] The bill started out as a comprehensive reform measure with provisions that included free television and radio time for candidates in exchange for campaign spending limits, reduced political action committee (PAC) contribu-

Lead sponsors of the Bipartisan Campaign Reform Act in the Senate, Sens. Russell D. Feingold, D-Wis. (left), and John McCain, R-Ariz.

tion limits, and prohibitions on bundling. Some of the provisions, such as those providing candidates with free television and radio airtime, were controversial. [11] Additionally, Republican leaders argued that proposed limits on PAC contributions violated the First Amendment by infringing the right of free speech. Senators McCain and Feingold realized that they had to build a larger and more bipartisan coalition in order to overcome an inevitable GOP filibuster.

Herein lies one of the major problems lawmakers face when they try to craft a bill that will lead to a winning coalition. One group of legislators might insist that a certain provision be included in the bill if they are to support it. If the sponsors of a bill include that provision, however, they risk losing the support of other legislators who might otherwise support the bill if it were not for that provision. Negotiating with groups on different sides of the partisan aisle magnifies the problem. As a result, debate surrounding a bill often focuses on ancillary provisions rather than the core issues that the bill addresses. Political realities often dictate that lawmakers significantly alter their proposals to accommodate the need for a larger and broader coalition of supporters.

So, McCain and Feingold modified their bill to improve its prospects in the Senate. The revised bill was pared down to focus on efforts to regulate

Source: Congressional Quarterly

sources of funding that were outside the control of candidates themselves. The bill aimed to limit the raising and spending of soft money by political parties and to bring spending on issue advocacy communications by interest groups, parties, corporations, labor unions, and wealthy individuals in the last sixty days of an election under the already-existing regulations of the Federal Election Campaign Act (FECA).

The revised McCain-Feingold bill began making its way through the Senate in the charged atmosphere of ongoing House and Senate investigations into campaign finance abuses that took place during the 1996 election. Reformers hoped this environment would enhance the prospects of a bill that sought to change the nation's campaign finance laws. However, they did not count on the heightened partisanship that would steer the process. Senate GOP leaders narrowed the scope of the committee's deliberations to only investigation of illegal activities. This move put the investigative committee's activities and findings on a separate track from reform efforts. The committee's narrowed scope demonstrates how legislative leaders can use unorthodox procedures to inhibit (or advance) the progress of legislation.

Reform proponents had much working against them from the beginning. As the end of the first session of the 105th Congress grew near, Senate majority leader Trent Lott, R-Miss., still had not moved to bring campaign finance reform up for a vote before the chamber adjourned for the year. Not until President Clinton threatened to use his authority to reconvene Congress if it adjourned without considering campaign finance reform did Senate leaders agree to bring the revised McCain-Feingold bill up for a vote. [12] Whether or not President Clinton's intervention to keep campaign finance legislation alive was merely a political show, as some contended, presidents rarely use this power or even threaten to do so.

Although GOP Senate leaders may have agreed to consider campaign finance legislation, they did all they could to kill the McCain-Feingold bill. For example, Majority Leader Lott used a parliamentary tactic known in legislative parlance as *filling the amendment tree* with his own amendment, thus preventing anyone else from offering another amendment. [13] Although filling the amendment tree is a fairly common tactic among rank-and-file senators, Senate leaders rarely use this maneuver. When they do use it, however, their goal is to defeat a piece of legislation. [14] Lott's amendment was called the Paycheck Equity Act (also known as the paycheck protection measure). The amendment required that labor unions undertake the costly administrative burden of receiving authorization from both union and non-union members before using any dues, fees, or payments for political purposes. Since the political activities of unions usually and overwhelmingly favor Democratic candidates, this measure, which Democrats referred to as the "worker gag rule," was "vehemently opposed by Democrats as a 'poison pill' " designed to split the fragile coalition of reform supporters. [15] Senator Lott hoped that bringing this amendment forward would force the Democrats to filibuster the proposal, making it appear that they—and not the Republicans—were responsible for killing campaign finance reform.

Sen. Olympia Snowe, R-Maine (after working with Senate minority leader Tom Daschle, D-S.Dak.) and Sen. James Jeffords, R-Vt., offered the Snowe-Jeffords amendment to the McCain-Feingold bill. [16] In an attempt to soften the McCain-Feingold bill's restrictions on issue advocacy ads in order to gain more support for the measure, the Snowe-Jeffords amendment sought to narrow the kinds of communications that would be considered express advocacy and therefore be subject to new, more restrictive regulation. The amendment replaced the broad definition of express advocacy in the McCain-Feingold bill with the term *electioneering communications* and narrowly defined such communications as those that referred to a candidate for federal office and were broadcast in the last sixty days of a general election or the last thirty days of a primary election. The Snowe-Jeffords amendment further required that once a group spent $10,000 in a year on such electioneering messages, it had to disclose these activities to the Federal Election Commission (FEC). More controversially, Senators Snowe and Jeffords's amendment sought a compromise between the Republican leadership's desired paycheck protection language and the reformers' position. To this end, the Snowe-Jeffords amendment would require all membership organizations, including labor unions, corporations, and interest groups, to get the consent of their members or stockholders before spending dues or profits on political activities. [17] Such a measure would affect important fundraising constituencies for both Republicans and Democrats.

This high-stakes bargaining over campaign finance reform illustrates how much each side stood to gain or lose depending on whether and how the rules of the game changed. As one might expect, no compromise on union and corporate political activity was reached. The Senate debate on the pared-down McCain-Feingold bill led to three failed attempts, on October 7, 8, and 9, 1997, to get the sixty votes necessary to invoke cloture and stop the GOP filibuster. For the moment, passage of the McCain-Feingold bill had been stopped.

Despite this defeat, Senate reformers had hope for the future. Even though the reformers failed to end the filibuster, they had garnered support on each of the three votes from a majority of senators. This implied that if campaign finance reform were ever voted on directly in the Senate (where it would only need majority support, rather than the supermajority necessary to overcome a filibuster), the bill would likely pass. Additionally, even though the three votes had generally split along partisan lines, seven Republicans had crossed the aisle to vote with the Democrats for cloture. So, reform supporters in the Senate continued to press for a vote on the McCain-Feingold bill itself.

As a result, Majority Leader Lott and Minority Leader Daschle agreed to a unanimous consent agreement (UCA), a procedural method used in the Senate to move business along by setting the terms for consideration of a bill. Although any one senator can potentially block a UCA, such agreements serve as the primary means by which the Senate organizes proceedings on certain bills. The UCA provides the Senate leadership with "a tool for scripting proceedings" by, for example, setting time limits on each component of debate, deciding which senators will control debate time, and establishing certain voting procedures. [18] The Lott-Daschle UCA called for a vote on the McCain-Feingold bill sometime before March 6, 1998. According to the UCA, after the vote on the McCain-Feingold bill, Senator Lott "would be permitted to hold a vote on an alternative bill to his liking," [19] expected to be the controversial Paycheck Equity Act.

Shortly after the start of the second session of the 105th Congress in January 1998, the Snowe-Jeffords language was added to the McCain-Feingold bill by voice vote. But the very next day, reformers failed to end a GOP filibuster of the amended bill, securing only fifty-one of the sixty votes needed for the cloture vote that would cut off debate. Immediately after, the Senate considered Senator Lott's Paycheck Equity Act, and it too was defeated when only forty-five senators voted for cloture to end a Democratic-led filibuster. These votes left the Senate in a stalemate. So Senator Lott pulled the bills from the floor and moved on to consideration of other legislation.

As noted above, during the course of the Senate floor debate in the 105th Congress, Republican leaders framed the debate over campaign finance reform as a discussion about the First Amendment and freedom of speech. Senator McConnell conceded that candidates (himself included) do not like independent issue advocacy ads, particularly those run against them, but, he argued, campaigns are not for candidates to control. McConnell noted, "the Supreme Court has given no indication that the political candidates are entitled to control all of the discourse in the course of a campaign." [20] This line of argument put reform proponents on the defensive, for they had to show that the McCain-Feingold bill would not exclude healthy dialogue from electoral debates. Although campaign finance reform proponents used well-known outside groups to contend that McCain-Feingold was constitutional, McConnell responded that the "American Civil Liberties Union [ACLU], America's experts on the First Amendment, say that the bill falls short of the free speech requirements of the U.S. Supreme Court in the First Amendment." Having the leaders of this traditionally liberal free speech advocacy organization on his side was a bit of a coup for Senator McConnell and one in which he took great pride.

The reform legislation opponents' constitutional arguments had caught some of McCain-Feingold's supporters off guard. In the end, however, the reform legislation was stymied by a filibuster, not necessarily by the force of convincing constitutional arguments. The McCain-Feingold bill did have the support of a majority of senators, but not the supermajority of sixty votes needed to invoke cloture to end the filibuster. Additionally, opponents of the McCain-Feingold bill had the majority party leadership on their side, allowing them to use procedural rules for considering campaign finance legislation to their advantage.

The Fight Continues in the House: An Issue Whose Time Had Come?

By early 1998 the climate for campaign finance reform in the House was more favorable than it had been in the recent past. House reformers had been working on campaign finance reform for some time, but had originally agreed that the Senate should take the lead. In early 1997, most reformers were convinced that little or no action would take place in the House because House Republican leadership would never allow discussion, let alone a vote, on campaign finance reform. By the time the McCain-Feingold bill was filibustered for the second time in the Senate in late February 1998, though, many campaign finance reform bills had already been introduced in the House, including the Bipartisan Campaign Reform Act (BCRA) sponsored by Christopher Shays, R-Conn., and Martin T. Meehan, D-Mass. The Shays-Meehan measure was similar to the original McCain-Feingold bill, and would eventually emerge as the leading campaign finance reform bill in the House. As expected, though, House Speaker Newt Gingrich, R-Ga., and the Republican House leaders would not schedule debate or votes on campaign finance reform legislation.

For Christopher Shays, reforming government and making it accountable were issues that he had pursued since his days in the Connecticut state legislature, and he continued these reform efforts after being elected to Congress in 1987. For example, he was the lead sponsor of the Congressional Accountability Act, the first bill passed out of the Republican Party's *Contract with America*—the party's manifesto that served as its platform in gaining majority control of the House of Representatives in 1994 for the first time since the 1950s. Shays strongly believed in the principles underlying the *Contract* and the role of the Republican Party to achieve those principles, to the point of providing crucial support for Newt Gingrich, the primary author of the *Contract*, when party conservatives sought to replace Gingrich as Speaker of the House in a coup attempt in 1997.

Publicly, Shays tried to emphasize the campaign finance reform effort more than himself. In fact, he usually referred to the Shays-Meehan bill as the "Meehan-Shays" bill or the "House version of McCain-Feingold." This humility no doubt contributed to his diplomatic effectiveness. Still, those outside of Congress identified Shays with the House reform effort. Similar to John McCain, the *David versus Goliath* character of Shays's challenge of his own party's leaders was irresistible fare for the media.

Source: Congressional Quarterly

Reps. Martin T. Meehan, D-Mass. (center), and Christopher Shays, R-Conn. (right), sponsors of the Bipartisan Campaign Reform Act in the House of Representatives.

Shays, for example, highlighted the differences between what the GOP party leaders said they would do in 1994 as part of the *Contract with America* and what they actually did in the course of the campaign finance reform debate. As Shays noted at one press conference, "when the Republicans took over, we said things were going to be different, but I have not seen that to be the case." [21] Thus, despite his increasingly favorable reputation outside of Congress and the fact that he had been seen as a dedicated party member, Shays had to fight his own party leaders and fend off often hostile attacks from his own party caucus. [22] Even Shays's relationship with Gingrich became strained, thus leading Shays to ask his friend in a very public moment "do you and I have a problem?" [23]

Like Shays, Marty Meehan also had a background of pursuing reform efforts prior to entering Congress. As the Massachusetts Deputy Secretary of State for Securities and Corporations, for example, Meehan was credited with taking the Securities Division "from a frequent embarrassment to gaining a national reputation as hard-hitting and activist." [24] Upon entering Congress in 1993, Meehan took on efforts, for example, related to tobacco regulation. His 111-page prosecution memorandum written in 1994 served as the basis for the Justice Department's investigation and litigation against major tobacco companies. Meehan's reform credentials both inside and outside of Congress enabled him to step into a prominent role in campaign finance reform legislation very easily.

Reform proponents in the House had to find ways to push the issue if they expected any reform legislation to see the light of day in the 105th Congress. For example, on October 7, 1997, thirty House Republicans sent a letter to Speaker Gingrich requesting an "opportunity for a full and fair debate on all aspects of campaign finance reform," urging the Republican leaders not to act as the Democrats had when they were in the majority in 1993 and refused to allow a vote on a bipartisan proposal. Later that month, the Blue Dog Coalition, a group of moderate and conservative House Democrats, primarily from the South, circulated a discharge petition to force campaign finance reform legislation out of committee and to the floor for consideration by the full House.

Discharge petitions are rarely used in the House. Indeed, since 1910, when the rule allowing discharge petitions was adopted, only two discharged bills have become law. [25] Yet, in recent years, discharge petitions have been used more frequently, not so much actually to dislodge a bill from a committee, but as leverage to get a committee or the majority party leadership to move on a bill. [26] If 218 or more House members (one-half of the membership of the House) sign a discharge petition, the measure immediately proceeds to the floor under the rule specified in the petition, and the majority party leadership loses control of the process. The petition's rule would, in effect, bypass the Rules Committee, which under normal circumstances writes the rules governing the procedural matters for each bill brought before the House.

The campaign finance reform discharge petition, which became House Resolution (H.R.) 259, was introduced by a leader of the Blue Dog Coalition, Rep. Scotty Baesler, D-Ky. The petition created a special rule under which campaign finance reform would be considered. [27] Interestingly, the Blue Dog discharge petition did not call for consideration of the Shays-Meehan bill. Yet many in the press and the Republican leadership mistook the petition as one designed to bring that specific bill to the floor. This misperception became reality and drove many reform interest groups and newspaper editorial boards to push for the petition. Moreover, it encouraged more members to sign the petition. It may seem odd that some House members were not aware of the true contents of the petition. But with so many issues and projects on members' agendas, and limited time to focus on each item, legislators often rely on secondhand sources for information. Those in the know, therefore, control a powerful commodity on Capitol Hill.

During the week of October 24, 1997, 172 House members signed the discharge petition, including five Republicans. Reformers were getting closer to the 218 signatures needed to force consideration of campaign finance reform. This swift gain in support for the petition clearly worried Republican leaders. Speaker Gingrich held a press conference on November 13, 1997, announcing that campaign finance reform would be brought to the floor for a "fair, bipartisan process of voting" sometime in February or March of 1998.[28] After the Speaker's promise to take up campaign finance reform, active efforts to get the 218 signatures on the discharge petition were dropped.

While support for the Shays-Meehan bill was solidifying, others were offering their own campaign finance bills. In all, more than 134 such bills were introduced in the House of Representatives during the 105th Congress. [29] One in particular attracted a good deal of attention: the so-called Freshman bill introduced by a diverse group of Republican and Democratic House freshmen headed by Republican Asa Hutchinson of Arkansas and Democrat Tom Allen of Maine. This group of legislators enjoyed a degree of legitimacy among their colleagues because they were first-term House members who perhaps could offer an untainted perspective on the campaign finance system. Although freshmen members were generally not expected to jump right into crafting legislation, this quick action by the new legislators earned them respect from their more senior colleagues. The process by which their bill emerged was, like many aspects of modern legislating, unconventional. The bipartisan group formed outside of party or committee structures and without the support of party leaders. The freshmen established their own bipartisan task force, bypassing the normal committee process. They studied the issue and held their own hearings to craft a reform measure that could gain support from both parties. When it was introduced, the freshmen's proposal had more Republican support than the Shays-Meehan bill.

Like the Shays-Meehan bill, the Freshman bill focused on the *twin evils* of soft money and issue advocacy. However, it was seen as a less palatable option by some reformers, primarily because the bill still allowed political party organizations on the state level to raise and spend soft money in ways that could potentially benefit federal candidates. The Freshman bill did not include a ban on state party soft money because the bill's sponsors believed that such a ban might violate the Tenth Amendment to the Constitution, which provides that all powers not delegated to the federal government or prohibited to the states are reserved to the states or the people. Critics of the Freshman bill pointed out that because soft money would still be directed to and spent in the states on federal elections, the bill did not close the soft money loophole in federal law. Ironically, a similar state soft money provision was included in the BCRA that became law in 2002, added during final negotiations to garner needed support. [30] In addition, the Freshman bill had a weaker issue advocacy provision than the Shays-Meehan bill, calling only for disclosure of expenditures for issue ads, while not requiring disclosure of the sources of these funds.

Although supporters of the Shays-Meehan bill and supporters of the Freshman bill shared the general objective of reforming the campaign finance system, the two camps competed for support from their fellow members. On February 26, 1998, Shays and Meehan met with the Freshman bill sponsors in an attempt to merge the Shays-Meehan and Freshman bills. Negotiations broke down over the state party soft money language.

The intricacies of policymaking do not always lend themselves to singular solutions to major policy problems. In this case, the problem was complicated by the bipartisan nature of each of the coalitions, making it difficult to keep Democrats and Republicans together on one bill. Moreover, it was unlikely that a compromise bill could obtain the same level of support. Many observers criticized the reformers for not presenting a united front against GOP leaders and others opposed to their legislative efforts, and they warned that

infighting among reform proponents could dash all hope of enacting comprehensive campaign finance reform legislation. Indeed, the Republican leadership would later use this split among reformers to try to kill the reform effort
altogether.

Promises, Promises: The Republican Leadership Stalls

House Speaker Gingrich's pledge to conduct a "fair, bipartisan process of voting" on campaign finance reform was the first in a series of promises broken
by GOP leadership during the 105th Congress. Even though rescheduling of
debates and votes on legislation is commonplace in Congress, the Republican leaders had established a record of not honoring their promises regarding campaign finance reform during the previous Congress (1995–1997).
Thus, when Speaker Gingrich promised in November 1997 to bring up campaign finance reform in February or March of 1998, most reform proponents
were skeptical. Some thought, however, that the bad press and increased public attention that would result from yet another broken promise on campaign
finance legislation might motivate GOP leaders to make good on their
promise this time. Moreover, pressure to consider meaningful reform proposals was coming from some key members of the Republican Conference,
not just from the Democrats.

Source: Congressional Quarterly

Rep. Newt Gingrich, 58th Speaker of the House, January 1995 to January 1999.

On February 4, 1998, thirty-four Republicans, including Chris Shays, Asa Hutchinson, Zach Wamp of Tennessee, William Goodling of Pennsylvania, Mark Sanford of South Carolina, and Porter Goss of Florida, sent a letter to Speaker Gingrich urging that he not only keep his promise of a vote in February or March, but that "during the floor debate, there be an opportunity for a vote on one or more bipartisan alternatives that include a ban on soft money." One hundred ten Democrats, under the direction of House Oversight Committee ranking minority member Sam Gejdenson of Connecticut, sent a similar letter on February 12, 1998. In this letter the Democrats promised to "renew and redouble our efforts to secure the final 31 signatures needed to complete the discharge petition" if the Speaker would not allow a vote on bipartisan campaign finance reform. February, however, passed without any such vote.

By mid-March there was still no sign from the Republican leadership that the issue would be scheduled for a vote. Shays and Meehan used this time to solidify further support for their bill. On March 17, Meehan met with Minority Leader Richard Gephardt, D-Mo., and Minority Whip David Bonior, D-Mich., to secure the House Democrats' endorsement of the Shays-Meehan bill. The Democratic leaders were sensitive to the fact that many Democrats had introduced campaign finance reform bills, and they were particularly cautious not to slight supporters of the Freshman bill. They agreed to recommend endorsing the Shays-Meehan bill to the full Democratic Caucus, but would not rule out support of the Freshman bill. [31]

Good-government interest groups, such as Common Cause, the Public Interest Research Group, the League of Women Voters, and Public Citizen, were also pressuring the Democratic leaders to support the Shays-Meehan bill, because they believed it was the more comprehensive bill and the one most likely to pass. Lobbyists from these groups, especially Common Cause, had been involved in crafting and advocating for campaign finance reform legislation for many years. Interest groups opposed to reform legislation, by contrast, did not mobilize until later, when passage of the Shays-Meehan bill started to look like a real possibility.

The Democratic leadership first sent the campaign finance issue to the Democrats' Task Force on Campaign Finance Reform, yet another use of an unorthodox legislative method (similar to the task force used in connection with the Freshman bill). Although the Task Force, chaired by caucus chairman Vic Fazio, D-Calif., did not completely rule out supporting the Freshman bill, it ended up backing the Shays-Meehan bill. In the case of campaign finance reform, the Democrats had little to lose. It was an issue that set them apart from the increasingly unpopular Republican leadership. Moreover, the Democratic Party was worried about its financial situation as compared to the Republicans. Clearly, the party was motivated in part by pragmatic self-interest by closing the soft money and issue advocacy loopholes.

The Democratic Party endorsement was an important turning point for campaign finance reform in the House. The Democratic Caucus and its leaders had made the issue a priority, which meant the party would devote resources to the effort. One of the most important resources that a party can offer is *whipping*, that is, lining up votes of support from party members. The party's designated whip and his or her deputies encourage discipline and mobilize the party's members on behalf of the party leadership's legislative priorities. Votes are counted and recounted as the whips work to persuade their colleagues to vote with the party. Whipping is a vital function of party strategy, since it is helpful to know if there are enough votes to achieve the desired legislative outcome before moving on a measure. Whipping also involves more of the party's members in the party leadership. This builds party loyalty and gives members a stake in the party's success.

With the Democrats set to push for reform, the Republican leaders canceled their plans to bring campaign finance reform to the floor during the week of March 23. Many speculated that the GOP leaders canceled floor consideration after discovering they were likely to lose a key procedural vote on the issue to the Democrats, and losing control of the House floor was not a desirable option. [32] Reform interest groups, the media, and congressional reform proponents publicly scolded the GOP leaders and accused them of breaking yet another promise. The *New York Times* ran an editorial on March 27, 1998, chastising the Republican leadership for "desperation tactics [that] are an abuse of power reminiscent of conduct Mr. Gingrich himself deplored for years." [33]

Perhaps in reaction to this kind of portrayal by a large number of news outlets, GOP leaders announced on March 27 that they were scheduling votes on campaign finance for the following Monday, March 30, the day of Republican Representative Steven H. Schiff's funeral in New Mexico. Usually, votes are canceled on the day of a fellow member's funeral to allow members to attend the services. Many speculated that the schedule was designed to keep pro-reform members from returning from the funeral in time to vote on the measures. Four bills of the GOP leaders' choosing, some of which had not even been introduced yet, were to be considered under suspension of the rules, a procedure usually reserved for non-controversial measures. Bills on the suspension calendar are limited to forty minutes of debate, no amendments are allowed, and a two-thirds vote is required for their passage. Although the suspension-of-the-rules procedure is used much more frequently today than in past years, it is still meant for non-controversial measures and not for rushing through major bills. [34] Campaign finance reform clearly was not a non-controversial issue, and reform supporters and the media were quick to note the disingenuousness of the leadership's plan.

When debate on the Republican bills began, the main bill, the Campaign Reform and Election Integrity Act of 1998 (H.R. 3485), sponsored by Representative Bill Thomas, R-Calif., was soundly defeated in a 74–337 vote. [35] The Paycheck Protection Act (H.R. 2608) also was defeated with a mostly party-line vote of 166–246. The two other bills, the Campaign Reporting and Disclosure Act (H.R. 3582) and the Illegal Foreign Contributions Act (H.R. 34), were not objectionable to reform proponents but did not really address what reformers viewed as the main issues of campaign finance reform. As a result, these measures passed by large margins as members from both parties saw no reason to vote against them, particularly since a "no" vote might be perceived as a vote against reform regardless of how inadequate the bills really were. In the end, it was clear that what reform proponents viewed as meaningful

"I KEPT MY PROMISE TO TAKE IT UP"

from Herblock: A Cartoonist's Life (Times Books, 1998) ©1998 HERBLOCK

Source: "I Kept My Promise to Take It Up" A 1998 Herblock Cartoon, copyright by The Herb Block Foundation

campaign finance reform had not been considered in the four bills brought up under suspension of the rules.

GOP leaders had hoped to put the issue to rest by arguing that campaign finance reform had been duly considered under the suspension-of-the-rules process. Again, we see lawmakers using unorthodox methods to achieve legislative goals in campaign finance reform, but this time it did not have the desired effect. Instead, the *Washington Post* and others accused Republican leaders of hypocrisy: "Republicans have spent a year and a half claiming to be indignant about the fund-raising abuses in the last campaign. . . . But given the chance to change the law to ban the principal abuse, having to do with the raising and spending of so-called soft money, they flinch." [36] The editorial was accompanied by the cartoon shown here of Gingrich hanging campaign finance reform. Clearly, GOP leaders had not avoided public criticism and bad press in their effort to put campaign finance reform to rest.

Scramble for Control: Reform Proponents Fight Back

In the wake of this failed attempt by GOP leaders to preempt the reform effort, the House Blue Dog Coalition revived the discharge petition effort. By March 31, 1998, the petition had 191 of the 218 signatures needed to force a vote on their preferred campaign finance reform bills. The pro-reform interest groups, especially Common Cause, also worked to raise the profile of the campaign finance reform issue in members' home districts. The groups put many legislators on the spot in community meetings back home, and they spoke with editorial boards of local newspapers to urge editors to cover the issue. Many lawmakers paid attention when accused by their own constituents of not supporting reform. One House member, Tom Davis, R-Va., noted that his decision to sign the discharge petition had been influenced by a Common Cause volunteer at a district meeting. [37] A 1993 House rules change requiring that the names of those who had signed a discharge petition be made public also helped reform supporters put pressure on uncommitted members. [38] On April 18, 1998, in an unusually forceful editorial, the *New York Times* published a list of who was and was not on the discharge petition. Other newspapers across the country also urged their local House members to sign the petition and support reform.

By late April, a critical mass of twelve Republicans had signed onto the discharge petition, including such previously unlikely signers as Zach Wamp of Tennessee and Frank Wolf of Virginia. [39] This alarmed the Republican leaders, who did not want to lose control of the floor to the Democrats. The Speaker and key GOP leaders offered Shays and other Republican reformers yet another promise to bring campaign finance reform to the floor by mid-May in exchange for Republican members removing their names from the discharge petition. [40] The Republican reformers and GOP leaders agreed that several bills would be considered in an "open" process (as compared to the suspension-of-the-rules process of the last round) and that the base bill would be the Freshman bill, with consideration of other bills, including the Shays-Meehan bill. On April 22, nine of the twelve Republicans, including Shays, removed their names from the petition. The next day, two more Republicans removed their names, leaving Connie Morella, of Maryland, as the only Republican on the petition.

Shays himself suggested the Freshman bill as the base bill for consideration, knowing it would be more palatable to the Republican leadership, who saw it as a means to defeat the Shays-Meehan bill. The agreement, however, would at least give Shays the opportunity to bring his bill to the House floor. The Republican leaders, for their part, were willing to accept this agreement, since the Freshman bill was untested in the Senate and unlikely to be acceptable to key reformers there. Despite these strategic decisions, Republican leaders held out hope that if the laborious process in the House did not kill reform, the Senate would. Many would suggest that because of the *promise* of another Senate filibuster, the House process and subsequent votes became *free votes*. In other words, House members would be able to vote and claim credit for passing campaign finance legislation knowing it would eventually be defeated in the other chamber.

The deal angered many Democrats, for they felt the reform coalition was close to getting what it wanted—an up or down vote on the Shays-Meehan bill with no amendments to water it down or alter it in ways that would cause the reform coalition to fall apart. Moreover, making the Freshman bill the base bill reinvigorated the freshman reform supporters to push for their bill over the Shays-Meehan bill. This, of course, reinforced the split between the two camps. This divide-and-conquer strategy kept reform proponents busy trying to persuade one another to support each others' bills. Representative Meehan met with the Freshman Democratic Task Force on April 28 to try to persuade the first-term legislators to back the Shays-Meehan bill. He offered to give the freshmen the lion's share of the credit for passing campaign finance reform. The freshmen, however, were not persuaded and they continued to try to gain more support for their own bill. Opponents of reform legislation used this time and the prospect of a "more open debate" to craft amendments that would have the potential of dividing the reform coalition. [41] All sides were preparing for the big showdown.

Securing support from the White House was another important goal for both camps of reform proponents. President Clinton had helped keep the campaign finance reform issue on the political agenda by, for example, mentioning it as one of his legislative priorities in the State of the Union address in January 1998. The president had also publicly supported the McCain-Feingold bill in the Senate, which was almost identical to the Shays-Meehan bill. At a meeting with White House staff on April 29 to discuss strategy for a tobacco settlement bill, Meehan used the opportunity to express his concern about the president's plan to meet with the primary sponsors of the Freshman bill. High-level White House staffers, including Clinton's chief of staff, John Podesta, agreed with Meehan that the president should endorse only one bill, and that his meetings with members should reflect that decision. With lobbying help from Common Cause, the president decided to meet only with Shays and Meehan. On May 12 they met with both President Clinton and Vice President Al Gore, and the president offered to help pass the bill. This was another important step for the Shays-Meehan bill in solidifying support for the measure and raising the public profile of the issue; it was clearly a blow to the freshman reformers, who had hoped to get a hearing at the White House. Yet President Clinton's efforts on this and other issues

Source: The White House

President Bill Clinton in the Oval Office with Reps. Martin T. Meehan, D-Mass. (*left*), and Christopher Shays, R-Conn. (*right*), on May 12, 1998.

were becoming increasingly overshadowed by charges that he had had an affair with a White House intern. [42]

By the time the Shays-Meehan bill received the White House's endorsement, Representatives Shays and Meehan had introduced another measure, less sweeping than their original bill. The new bill (H.R. 3526) closely mirrored the pared-down final version of the McCain-Feingold bill that had been blocked in the Senate in February. As with the Senate bill, controversial provisions were removed to build bipartisan support. There was growing consensus among reformers from both parties, the interest group community, and many newspaper editorial boards that this revised Shays-Meehan bill could gain more support and was the best vehicle for meaningful campaign finance reform. Moreover, since the McCain-Feingold bill had garnered majority support in the Senate, there was increasing optimism that House passage might force the Senate to consider the bill again.

The Republican Leadership's *Death by Amendment* Strategy

After GOP leaders struck the deal with the Republican reformers for an "open" process, the matter was handed over to the House Rules Committee to come up with a procedure to consider campaign finance reform legislation. Thirty-eight members testified at the Rules Committee meeting on May 20, 1998, and thirteen substitute bills (substitutes to the Freshman bill) and more than three hundred amendments were submitted to the committee for consideration. In the end, the Rules Committee made, in order, the Freshman bill as the base bill, eleven substitute bills, including the Shays-Meehan bill, hundreds of germane amendments (a germane amendment is one that is relevant to the section of the bill that it seeks to modify), and an unprecedented 258 nongermane amendments (amendments that are not related to what they seek to modify—nongermane amendments are generally allowed in the Senate but not in the House). [43] Allowing this extraordinary number of amendments meant that debate over campaign finance reform legislation could drag on for a very long time. Representative Rick White, R-Wash., sponsor of one of the other substitute bills, said he expected the process to be as "open as you can possibly imagine. . .maybe too open. It might just go on forever." [44]

The openness of the process itself invited several possible lines of attack on reform bills. Indeed, reform proponents considered many of the amendments to be poison pills. Democratic leaders, reform House members, many of the pro-reform interest groups, and some editorial boards accused GOP leaders of devising a process of "death by amendment" in order to kill the Shays-Meehan bill, the Freshman bill, and other comprehensive reform measures.

The process the GOP leadership established was a *queen-of-the-hill* rule. Under this scenario, the base bill (the Freshman bill) and each of the substitute bills were entitled to a vote and whichever bill received the most votes, as long as it received a majority, would prevail. Special rules like this are powerful tools in the hands of the majority party, for they allow the majority party to structure the options from which legislators must choose. Such special rules are among the parliamentary devices and other unorthodox procedures used more frequently in recent years by the House majority party to improve the chances of achieving their desired legislative outcome. The Republican leaders no doubt hoped that this process would bring about the defeat of comprehensive campaign finance reform, since both the Shays-Meehan and the Freshman bills were to be subject to many poison pill amendments and were up against other reform bills that might trump them.

In particular, a bill known as the Commission bill had a good chance of gaining more votes than the Shays-Meehan bill. The Commission bill was a bipartisan measure to establish an independent campaign finance reform commission that would study the issue and propose reform legislation to Congress. The Commission bill was sponsored by, among others, John Dingell, D-Mich., known as the Dean of the House and who actively sought support for the bill among his fellow Democrats. Commission bill supporters from both parties argued that the partisan and contentious process of campaign finance legislation was not likely to result in any new laws on the matter. They believed that a commission operating outside of the political arena, much like the independent commission on military base closings, stood a better chance of suggesting reforms that could garner significant bipartisan support in both chambers. Moreover, the Commission bill offered a way for Republicans in particular to cast a vote for campaign finance legislation without supporting the Shays-Meehan bill. By doing so they could claim to support reform and, for these reasons, avoid criticism back home, as well as escape the wrath of their party leaders. Thus, the Commission bill was a serious threat to the Shays-Meehan and Freshman bills.

The substitute bills were only part of the puzzle. The hundreds of amendments presented a tremendous challenge as well. The purpose of the GOP's death-by-amendment strategy was to weigh down the reform bills with poison pill amendments, preventing a clean vote and inducing defections among supporters. For example, many amendments proposed to attach some

version of the so-called paycheck protection measure to the Shays-Meehan bill. Others were attempts to weaken the "motor-voter" law by, for example, requiring extraordinary procedures for verifying the citizenship of prospective voters. [45] Other amendments would have weakened the issue advocacy provision in the Shays-Meehan bill, softened the restrictions on soft money, and created what reformers saw as loopholes in the name of protecting the First Amendment right to free speech.

In early May, GOP lawmakers, led by Majority Whip Tom DeLay, R-Tex., formed what they called the Free Speech Coalition to raise First Amendment–based arguments similar to those made during the Senate's consideration of the McCain-Feingold bill. The Capitol Hill newspaper *Roll Call* reported that DeLay's Free Speech Coalition was created "to bury the various reform proposals with a pile of partisan amendments designed to shift the debate to the First Amendment and the fundraising allegations swirling around President Clinton." [46] The Free Speech Coalition assailed the reform proposals with floor speeches, talk-radio appearances, op-ed pieces, and a series of "Dear Colleague" letters distributed to House members. [47] These letters had titles such as "Oppose the 'Bipartisan' Gag Order, Protect Your Constituents' Right to Speak," "Protect Free Speech, Oppose Unconstitutional Campaign 'Reform,' " "The Shays-Meehan Bill's Year-Round Restrictions on

First Amendment Rights," and "Unconstitutional 'Campaign Reform' Means 'Government Control.' " One Dear Colleague letter from DeLay featured the cartoon shown above with this message from DeLay:

> Dear Colleague: Don't be seduced by so-called campaign finance 'reforms.' Stand true to the principles which have guided our country for more than two hundred years—free speech. Oppose Shays/Meehan (H.R. 3526) and the Freshman Bill (H.R. 2183) which betray our constitutional rights.

Getting around Poison Pills: Developing Issue Networks

The Shays-Meehan supporters had originally said that they would accept no amendments at all. But the sheer number of cleverly crafted amendments made it politically impossible to insist on that. [48] Staffers quickly mobilized to evaluate all the amendments to determine which ones were poison pills that endangered passage of the Shays-Meehan bill, and which would not weaken the bipartisan reform coalition and thus would not be opposed. In a flurry of activity, supporters attempted to shore up support for the Shays-Meehan bill and ensure that killer amendments would not hit their mark.

To do so, Shays and Meehan relied upon the *issue network* they had developed while pursuing campaign finance legislation. More than just a coalition of supporters, an issue network is a group of individuals who are committed to the policy goal at hand and who will assist in fending off complex (and perhaps unfair) rules or dilatory tactics by their opposition. The most successful issue networks are comprised not only of key legislators on the issue and their staffs, but of outside interest groups, the media, and governmental actors such as the president and others in the executive branch. An expansive issue network confers an informational advantage on its members and disadvantages those who are excluded from or oppose it. This sort of network is also able to move beyond the mere pursuit of votes to play an educational role that assists in widening the support network and, therefore, increases the likelihood of legislative success.

As an example of the efforts undertaken by the Shays-Meehan issue network, the Republican working group focused on countering the more powerful arguments lodged against the Shays-Meehan bill, like charges that the measure violated the First Amendment. They also had face-to-face meetings with other GOP members to explain the bill and answer any concerns. Several GOP members, such as Tom Campbell, R-Calif., and Zach Wamp, R-Tenn., were vital in fending off conservative groups, such as the Conservative Action Team (CAT) whose members opposed, in the words of Tom Delay, " 'liberal' proposals that created a 'bureaucracy' that tramples our electoral systems and certainly tramples on the First Amendment to the Constitution." [49] Republican supporters of Shays-Meehan also had to counter lobbying efforts by the GOP leadership and CAT members. Gaining more Republican votes was the priority for the Shays-Meehan network, for virtually all Democrats already supported the bill, whereas fewer than 40 of the 227 Republicans were on board at that point.

The Democrats had the support of their leadership, which greatly enhanced their ability to shore up and maintain Democratic support for the bill. Minority Leader Dick Gephardt, R-Mo., committed staff resources and vocal public support to the effort. He included campaign finance reform on the agenda of many leadership meetings held during this period. Minority Whip David Bonior, D-Mich., conducted whips on many of the amendments and substitute bills. The Democratic Caucus chairman, Vic Fazio, D-Calif., worked closely with important Democratic reformers such as Marty Meehan of Massachusetts, Sander Levin of Michigan, and Sam Gejdenson of Connecticut, and he called regular meetings of the Democratic Caucus Campaign Finance Reform Task Force to build and maintain support for reform.

Only a few Democrats opposed the Shays-Meehan bill, among them some members of the Congressional Black Caucus who were pressured by religious organizations and pro-life groups to oppose the Shays-Meehan bill. These groups guarded their membership lists closely and had avoided disclosing them thus far by conducting only activities that technically would not be considered campaigning, such as running issue advocacy advertisements and distributing ostensibly nonpartisan voter guides. Under the Shays-Meehan bill some of these activities would be considered campaigning if they were conducted in the last sixty days before an election. The chairman of the Democratic Congressional Campaign Committee (DCCC), Martin Frost of Texas, also expressed opposition to the Shays-Meehan bill, because it contained a severability clause that would allow sections of the law to remain intact even if the courts struck down other sections. [50] Frost argued that such selective enforcement of the bill could put the Democratic Party at an even greater financial disadvantage in relation to the Republican Party.

Shays and Meehan ensured that members were armed with far more information and strategic material than is usual for legislative battles. For example, extensive briefing books were put together for Shays-Meehan core supporters, which included a proposed response to each argument against the reform legislation and a detailed explanation of the reformers' position on it. [51] The briefing books also included arguments against the other substitute bills as well as the Freshman bill. Additional materials were prepared by Democratic staff to counter the expected attacks on President Clinton and the Democratic Party regarding the fundraising scandals of the 1996 election. Each anticipated attack was paired with an example of a past Republican campaign financial irregularity.

At this crucial stage of the process, public interest groups—a key external component of the Shays-Meehan issue network—were once again extremely active in securing positive news coverage. This positive coverage emboldened some members to defy interest groups opposed to reform. The reform groups also worked with congressional staff to help lobby other members and other groups for support. Many of the public interest group lobbyists were veterans of other campaign finance reform battles. These efforts affirmed Shays's comment that "people outside of Washington do care about campaign finance."

The use and growing effectiveness of their issue network was one of the most visible signs of the transformation of Shays and Meehan from issue leaders on the subject of campaign finance legislation into policy entrepreneurs. For a bill to succeed, it generally has to be championed by an issue leader advocating some policy change—a member of Congress who devotes his or her time and resources to an issue and introduces legislation to address some perceived policy problem. Issue leaders are a focus point for the public, the media, and fellow lawmakers, someone to look to for expertise and voting cues. In the 105th Congress, campaign finance legislation had many issue leaders in addition to Shays and Meehan. People like the leaders of the Freshman bill or Senators McCain and Feingold were issue leaders in favor of campaign finance legislation; those who opposed such legislation could look to Senator McConnell or Representative DeLay to provide cues on the matter.

Shays and Meehan, though, distinguished themselves from other issue leaders by "identifying problems, networking in policy circles, shaping the terms of the policy debates, and building coalitions"—in other words, they were policy entrepreneurs. [52] The qualities that characterize a policy entrepreneur include: electoral security or a chance of gaining it by establishing oneself as a leading policymaker; the respect of one's colleagues in Congress and of important actors outside of Congress, such as the relevant interest groups; a deep commitment to an issue; a willingness to expend extraordinary amounts of time, energy, and resources on that issue; and a superb sense of timing. Throughout the process in the 105th Congress, Shays and Meehan adapted to and took advantage of changing circumstances, identified and successfully pursued legislative strategies, and found ways to bring potential competitors for votes into the fold of their coalition.

Being a policy entrepreneur is yet another unorthodox way in which a legislator can bring about policy changes. Neither Shays nor Meehan had any formal institutional position (such as a key committee chairmanship) that would provide them with a forum to promote their legislation. Yet, even lacking such a formal position, they became recognized both in and outside of Congress as leaders of *the* reform coalition on campaign finance, and from this informal position of power and authority promoted their legislation.

In Spite of It All, the Bill Passes the House

Consideration of campaign finance reform was delayed again until after the June 2 primary election in California, where a paycheck-protection style proposition that would limit union political activity was on the statewide ballot. The California ballot initiative was ultimately defeated. By early June, though, as campaign finance legislation approached consideration on the House floor under the unorthodox and complex process set out for it, the Commission bill continued to worry the Shays-Meehan reformers. In the final days before floor consideration, however, Democratic Shays-Meehan supporters struck a deal with primary sponsors John Dingell and Carolyn Maloney, D-N.Y. They agreed to vote "present" on their Commission bill and to merge it into the Shays-Meehan bill as a friendly amendment. [53] This move was backed by many supporters of the Commission bill, but it enraged several Republican backers, such as Commission bill cosponsor Rick White of Texas, who had wanted the Commission bill to replace the Shays-Meehan bill. Nevertheless, adding the reform commission to the Shays-Meehan bill actually improved the proposal, for it allowed a commission to consider issues that were not covered by the bill. More important, the deal ensured that the Commission bill would not trump the Shays-Meehan bill. Without the support of its original Democratic sponsors, the Commission bill failed on June 17 with 156 yeas, 201 nays, and 68 (including Dingell and Maloney) voting present.

With the Commission bill out of the way and support mounting for the Shays-Meehan bill, the challenge that remained for the bill's supporters was the barrage of potentially coalition-destroying amendments to the Shays-Meehan bill. General debate on the Shays-Meehan substitute bill began on June 18, 1998. One of the first challenges faced was an amendment offered by Republican Bill Thomas that would have made the Shays-Meehan bill "non-severable," meaning that if part of the act were struck down by the courts, then the entire law would fall with it. Martin Frost, the DCCC chairman, spoke in favor of the amendment, but other Democrats and GOP reformers saw it as a poison pill amendment. It failed on June 19 by a 155–224 vote. This challenge had been met, but the death-by-amendment process ensured that many more amendments were waiting in the wings.

Reform staffers met regularly to develop strategies to respond to upcoming amendments. They developed responses to critiques and strategized about how to use the rules of debate, such as the five-minute rule, to their advantage. The House limits debate on an amendment offered in the Committee of the Whole to five minutes for its sponsor and five minutes for an opponent. [54] With unanimous consent, more time can be granted. The staff and members also were versed in using a pro forma amendment entitled *strike the last word*. A member gains recognition to speak from the chair by asking to "strike the last word" spoken by the last speaker and, therefore, to pick up where he or she left off. When a member uses this amendment, he or she does not intend to offer any changes to the measure under discussion but, rather, seeks to have five minutes of further debate. However, a member may use *strike the last word* only once. Strategic use of these parliamentary procedures allowed both sides to exercise more control over the debate.

The battle over campaign finance legislation was waged on other fronts as well. For example, fourteen Republican reform members met on June 24 with the Campaign Reform Project's Business Advisory Committee, which included such prominent business executives such as Jerry Kohlberg of Kohlberg & Company and Warren Buffett, chairman of Berkshire Hathaway.[55] These corporate executives favored reform, in part because they were tired of being asked by both parties for huge soft money contributions and of fearing that they would be shut out of the legislative process if they did not contribute. This meeting sent a message to the Republicans that at least some leaders in the business community, perhaps the most important GOP constituency, strongly supported campaign finance legislation. President Clinton once again assisted the reform proponents, when the Department of Justice sent a letter to Speaker Gingrich indicating that several of the amendments to be offered to the Shays-Meehan substitute were legally unacceptable. [56] Additionally, the reformers were emboldened by a statement from nine leaders of the ACLU, who "rejected the group's long-standing basic argument that campaign spending is a form of free speech." [57] One of the reform legislation opponents' best ace-in-the-hole had been the ACLU. But this statement by some high-profile ACLU members that limits on campaign spending are not a violation of free speech rights weakened one of the reform opponents' most powerful arguments.

Many Dear Colleague letters that attacked various provisions of the Shays-Meehan bill were also beginning to surface. One in particular drew a good deal of attention—a July 13, 1998, letter entitled, "Vote NO on the Shays-Meehan 'Campaign Finance Reform' Bill," signed by fifty-three non-profit, issue-oriented citizen advocacy groups. These groups claimed that they could end up violating several provisions in the Shays-Meehan bill if they publicly commented on the views held by members of Congress or candidates, even if they did so outside of an election season. This was an argument that just might have defeated the Shays-Meehan bill, so Shays-Meehan supporters knew they needed to work hard to address it. It became clear that educating people about the bill's contents was going to be vital in this game. In the battle for control of the debate, both sides made considerable use of Dear Colleague letters. A war of paper ensued, as a stream of these letters clogged House members' fax machines and mailboxes.

The number of amendments to be offered to the Shays-Meehan substitute alone suggested that this process might never end, an outcome neither side desired. Thus, Republican Bill Thomas of California helped broker a deal between Shays-Meehan supporters and the Republican leadership in early July for a unanimous consent agreement that would whittle down to fifty-five the number of amendments offered to the Shays-Meehan substitute. [58] Even though unanimous consent agreements are common in the Senate, they rarely are used in the House. This agreement was an important part of the bill's unorthodox legislative journey. Although the Shays-Meehan bill still faced many potential pitfalls, this agreement not only decreased the number of amendments that would be considered but clearly listed what the amendments would be and in what order they would be considered. This made preparation for both sides much easier. The unanimous consent agreement also made clear that if a particular amendment was not offered when it came up for consideration on the floor it could not be brought up again. This was an option that would prove helpful to reform proponents as the debate waged on. However, while the unanimous consent agreement improved the process, it did not shield the Shays-Meehan bill from poison pill amendments intended to kill it.

Chief among the potentially fatal amendments was one offered by the Republicans Tom DeLay and John Doolittle. Their amendment aimed to gut the issue advocacy provisions of the Shays-Meehan bill in the name of protecting free speech rights under the First Amendment. DeLay and Doolittle, who were criticized by some for "delaying" and "doing little," argued that the Shays-Meehan bill would ban the use of voter guides, a favored tool of the Christian Coalition and other conservative groups. A voter guide specifies candidates' positions on various issues important to the guide's sponsor. The Christian Coalition distributed its voter guides in churches across the nation up to the Sunday before election day. Reformers pointed out that the Shays-Meehan bill already contained a provision to allow for printed voter guides, and that the DeLay-Doolittle amendment would continue to allow outside groups to spend unlimited and unreported amounts of money anonymously to broadcast campaign ads (masquerading as issue advocacy ads) in federal elections. This was indeed a poison pill amendment. For many members, reining in the uncontrolled use of issue advocacy ads was the primary purpose of the reform effort, and they would not support the Shays-Meehan bill if it did not do that.

The reformers were well prepared to fight this and other amendments. The Senate battles had familiarized them with the possible constitutional attacks. Many times the debate dragged on toward midnight and, as one might expect, these late-night debates made it difficult to keep members focused on the issue and motivated to debate it on the floor. Part of the GOP leadership's strategy, it seemed, was to wear down the reformers. Thus, a great effort was made to ensure that there would always be reform members available to speak on the floor, especially for the late-night sessions. Members were asked to sign up to be available for certain time slots prepared to speak about campaign finance reform. Such extensive planning was rarely seen for floor debates. The opposition appeared to be less organized, offering the same speakers and arguments over and over again.

The DeLay-Doolittle amendment was defeated, effectively neutralizing the First Amendment issue. After each defeat of a poison pill amendment, outside public interest groups, as well as Shays and Meehan themselves, made positive statements to the press about key members' support. Additionally, Shays and Meehan sent personal thank-you notes to everyone who helped defeat these key amendments.

During the course of June and July, the Shays-Meehan bill encountered a series of amendments, with most of the debate coming on July 20 and July 30, 1998. Shays and Meehan provided vote cards describing each amendment and their position on it to all representatives who wanted them. Of the forty-one amendments voted upon, twenty-three passed, including eight by voice vote. One important amendment was a compromise crafted out of the six individual amendments offered by Representative Linda Smith, R-Wash., regarding voter guides. This compromise was achieved through long negotiations between Shays, Smith, and their respective staffs. With the support of the reformers, this amendment passed 343–84. Passage of the Smith amendment essentially slammed the door on other amendments about voter guides. The reform proponents defended their bill from what they regarded as fourteen poison pill amendments. The sponsors of five other poison pill amendments chose not to offer their amendments for the House's consideration. [59]

Moreover, Reps. David Obey, D-Wis.; John Tierney, D-Mass.; Sam Farr, D-Calif.; and Tom Campbell, R-Calif., withdrew their substitute bills. On August 3, the Shays-Meehan substitute bill passed the House by a margin of 237 to 186. The remaining substitutes, the Doolittle and Freshman bills, were defeated on August 6 by votes of 131–299 and 147–222, respectively. [60] In a symbolic gesture of appreciation for the efforts of the freshmen, Shays and Meehan allowed their bill to amend in whole (and replace) the Freshman bill, thus passing the Shays-Meehan bill as H.R. 2183, under the original Freshman bill number. The final vote for the Shays-Meehan bill was on August 6, 1998, with 252 members voting for its passage and 179 voting against it, far more than the 218 votes needed for passage.

In all, sixty-one Republicans voted for final passage, a blow to Republican leaders who were seen as the "big losers" of the day. [61] Ironically, the GOP leadership may have contributed to the final passage of the bill they sought to kill. Republican Marge Roukema, who previously had signed the discharge petition, noted, "the odd thing is that the House Republican leadership improved the bill's chances by trying so hard to kill it. This prolonged the debate, made the issue more prominent and put more members on the spot." [62]

After the long, hard fight, supporters of reform legislation were hopeful that the measure might pass the Senate this time around. However, GOP Senate leaders were reluctant to consider the issue at all, having already done so twice before in the 105th Congress. The reform effort failed to attract enough votes to thwart a filibuster for a third time in the Senate, and despite all the legislative maneuvers in the House, Congress's consideration of the issue in the 105th Congress came to an end.

Conclusion: Negotiating the Labyrinth

The journey through Congress of the Shays-Meehan campaign finance reform bill was unusual, and it illustrates many important characteristics of contemporary congressional policymaking. The unique character of the issue itself forces lawmakers to consider their personal ambitions and motivations as well as the issue's impact on important constituencies, their districts, and the country. The structure of campaign finance regulations affects each legislator's professional life, and the political parties potentially have much to gain or lose if changes are made to that system. The experience of the McCain-Feingold and Shays-Meehan bills also illustrates many of the unorthodox procedures used in contemporary policymaking. It is unusual for one bill to be subjected to so many unconventional procedures by both sides to try to either promote or kill the issue. As the political scientist Barbara Sinclair points out, a hostile political climate often forces innovation in the legislative process, and the story of campaign finance reform in the 105th Congress supports her theory. [63]

The extensive use of so many unconventional procedures reflects the high stakes involved in the outcome of legislative efforts to change the nation's campaign finance laws. Those high stakes, in turn, reflect the tension between the competing values of fair and open elections versus individual freedom that underlies the issue. Members of Congress highlighted these values during floor debate on campaign finance, most notably Senator McConnell in his argument based on the First Amendment. Reform supporters were equally committed to achieving fair and open elections. Nevertheless, the legislative process often forces members to move off of their principled positions in order to achieve legislative results. The need to compromise may require issue leaders and policy entrepreneurs to evaluate and prioritize their objectives, and perhaps subordinate lower priority items, no matter how steeped in principle they may be, in order to build a broad enough coalition to obtain their higher priority goals. But even when doing so, our system of separation of powers and checks and balances, and the rules that govern the consideration of legislation in Congress, do not guarantee that a bill—even one that may be supported by a majority of congressional members—will become law.

Campaign finance reform had been on the policy agenda for years and even passed Congress in 1992, only to be vetoed. [64] What the political scientist John Kingdon has called the "policy window" had been open before, and once again the circumstances and attitudes that seemed ripe for success were present. [65] Why had the issue made it onto the agenda so many times without actually being enacted into law? The nature of the issue itself is undoubtedly part of the explanation. The high stakes involved and strong possibility of unintended consequences (for example, the rise of thousands of political action committees in the wake of passage of the Federal Election Campaign Act and its amendments in the 1970s) make resistance to change understandable. Moreover, despite a new crop of campaign finance scandals from the 1996 election, the public was not focused on campaign finance reform as a top policy priority. Although the policy window may have been partially open, perhaps the idea's time had not fully come.

NOTES

1. Barbara Sinclair, *Unorthodox Lawmaking: New Legislative Processes in the U.S. Congress* (Washington, D.C.: CQ Press, 1997).
2. Ibid., 72.
3. This chapter draws significantly from our book, Diana Dwyre and Victoria Farrar-Myers, *Legislative Labyrinth: Congress and Campaign Finance Reform* (Washington, D.C.: CQ Press, 2001).
4. Amy Keller and Ed Henry, "Will the Campaign Finance Reformers Finally Prevail in '98?" *Roll Call*, January 26, 1998, A36.
5. Ibid.
6. 144 *Congressional Record*, 981 (1998).
7. Ibid.
8. McCain's notoriety as a reformer also may have stemmed from the fact that he himself was caught in the Keating Five scandal a decade earlier, where McCain's own ethics were called into question and which resulted in a rebuke from his Senate colleagues. More than one commentator has speculated that McCain's drive for campaign finance reform might be to reform his own image.
9. Feingold painted the following contract terms on his garage door: (1) I will rely on Wisconsin citizens for most of my contributions; (2) I will live in Middleton, Wisconsin. My children will go to school here and I will spend most of my time here in Wisconsin; (3) I will accept no pay raise during my six-year term in office; (4) I will hold a "Listening Session" in each of Wisconsin's 72 counties each year of my six-year term in office; and (5) I will hire the majority of my Senate staff from individuals who are from Wisconsin or have Wisconsin backgrounds.
10. An earlier version of the McCain-Feingold bill was introduced in 1995 and was defeated with a filibuster in 1996.
11. Paul Farhi, "GOP Hill Leaders Oppose FCC on Free Air Time," *Washington Post*, March 7, 1998, A8. For examples of the positive press, see "The Cleansing Power of Free TV," *New York Times*, editorial, March 11, 1998, A30, and David Broder, "The Broadcasters and Their Friends on the Hill," *Washington Post*, March 10, 1998, A17.
12. Amy Keller, "Without House, Senate Reform Deal Doesn't Matter," *Roll Call*, September 25, 1997, 14.

13. Amy Keller and Ed Henry, "Senate Goes Another Reform Round Today," *Roll Call*, October 9, 1997, 1. An amendment tree is the name given to the structure of a pending bill and its attached amendments. The base bill represents the tree's trunk, and the proposed amendments are the branches stemming off from the trunk. The Senate's rules allow only two degrees of amendments (or to continue the tree analogy, two types of branches): first-degree amendments that would modify the base bill and second-degree amendments that would change a first-degree amendment. When all the positions on the amendment tree (the pending bill, the first-degree amendments, and the second-degree amendments) are occupied, the amendment tree is filled. The number of first- and second-degree amendments for any given bill is dictated by the rules established for consideration. Charles Tiefer, a scholar on congressional procedure, noted senators make tactical use of the amendment tree in three ways: (1) so that their amendment is voted upon first; (2) to preclude their amendment from itself being amended; or (3) perhaps the "most common maneuver is to attempt to prevent any further amending at all." Charles Tiefer, *Congressional Practice and Procedure: A Reference, Research and Legislative Guide* (New York: Greenwood Press, 1989), 679.

14. Keller, "Parliamentary Moves Thwart Reform, Burton 'Filling the Tree' Blocks McCain Bill," *Roll Call*, February 26, 1998, 1. According to Senator Byron Dorgan, D-N.D., "this is a rarely used approach. It is true that this approach has been used by the Majority Leader a couple of times last year, but in history, it has been rarely used in the Senate. And the reason is, it is almost exclusively used to block legislation."

15. "Nickles Vows to Fight Limits on Corporate Political Action," *National Journal's Congress Daily*, January 5, 1998, 2.

16. Senator Jeffords left the Republican Party in May 2001 and declared himself an independent, which gave the Democrats control of the Senate for the first time since 1994.

17. Keller, "Will the Campaign Finance Reformers Finally Prevail in '98?" *Roll Call*, January 26, 1998, A37.

18. See Tiefer, *Congressional Practice and Procedure*, 573–583.

19. Keller, "Senator Snowe Works to Save Campaign Finance Reform on Eve of Senate Vote," *Roll Call*, February 19, 1998, 3.

20. 144 *Congressional Record*, 869 (1998).

21. Melinda Henneberger, "Republican Lawmaker Is Caught in the Middle," *New York Times*, March 31, 1998, A1.

22. For example, one recurrent comment among many Republican staff members was that Shays should become a Democrat; a sentiment that Republican members themselves often would imply as well.

23. David Lightman, "Shays May Pay For His Rebellion," *Hartford Courant*, April 1, 1998. Shays placed his arm around Gingrich as he put this question to him.

Gingrich indicated that he had no problem, but was not pleased with Shays's efforts on campaign finance reform. Shays replied that the next time Gingrich was angry, "Just call me on the phone."

24. Richard Kindleberger, "Newcomer Is Named to Police Securities," *Boston Globe*, December 21, 1990, 77.

25. Roger H. Davidson and Walter J. Oleszek, *Congress and Its Members*, 6th ed. (Washington, D.C.: CQ Press, 1998), 235; Richard S. Beth. "The Discharge Rule in the House: Recent Use in Historical Context (Updated April 17, 2003)." Congressional Research Service Report Order Code 97-856 GOV.

26. Davidson and Oleszek, *Congress and Its Members*, 6th ed., 235.; see also Barbara Sinclair, *Unorthodox Lawmaking: New Legislative Processes in the U.S. Congress* (Washington, D.C.: CQ Press, 1997), 87.

27. House Resolution 259 provided for consideration of the Blue Dog bill, with several amendments that could be offered as a substitute. The rule provided for one hour of debate on the base bill (the Blue Dog bill) and then one hour on each of seven amendments. Those who would be able to offer amendments under this rule were Reps. Scotty Baesler, D-Ky.; Sam Farr, D-Calif.; John T. Doolittle, R-Calif.; Richard A. Gephardt, D-Mo.; Dick Armey, R-Tex.; Asa Hutchinson, R-Ark., and anyone who offered the text of a bill passed by the Senate. The amended rule later introduced by Baesler added Shays and Rick White, R-Wash. A letter to Shays from Baesler and John Tanner, D-Tenn., stated they would ask for unanimous consent to replace the original rule with this substitute. In addition, Baesler agreed that he would offer the Shays-Meehan bill if the discharge petition were enacted. The rule called for any substitute bill that passed to become the base text, and if more than one passed, the one with the highest number of votes would become the base text. There would then be ten additional hours of open debate, during which time any member would be able to offer any germane amendment to the base bill. Staff to Representative Shays, memorandum, April 7, 1998.

28. Press release issued by House Speaker Newt Gingrich's office following the November 13, 1997, press conference.

29. As cited in Joseph E. Cantor, *CRS Issue Brief—Campaign Financing*, report no. IB87020, updated October 16, 1998, i.

30. This state level soft money became known as Levin funds, after Senator Carl Levin (D-Mich.) who brokered the deal to include the provision in the final BCRA bill.

31. The Democratic Caucus is the organization of all Democrats in the House.

32. Steven A. Holmes, "House G.O.P. Shifts on Campaign Bills," *New York Times*, March 28, 1998, A8.

33. "The Ebb and Flow of Reform: Mr. Gingrich Retreats," *New York Times*, editorial, March 27, 1998, A18.

34. Indeed, about 50 percent of the bills passed by the House are considered under suspension of the rules today, whereas only about 8 percent were passed from

the suspension calendar in the 1970s. See Davidson and Oleszek, *Congress and Its Members*, 229.

35. See Henneberger, "Republican Lawmaker Is Caught in the Middle." Common Cause and others pointed out that the Republican bill would not, after all, ban all soft money for federal elections, because it wouldn't touch the use of soft money for issue ads, one way the parties got around the limits.

36. "Hypocrisy on Campaign Funds," *Washington Post*, editorial, April 1, 1998, A18.

37. See Lizette Alvarez, "Campaign Finance Backers Petition to Force House Vote," *New York Times*, April 18, 1998, A8.

38. Ironically, making discharge petitions public was pioneered in an earlier Congress by Newt Gingrich himself. See press release, "Leadership Statement on Campaign Finance Reform," April 22, 1998.

39. By "critical mass" we mean a number sufficient to make the Republican leadership fear that they would lose control of the House floor. As one GOP source close to the leadership noted in mid-April, "Once we get to 10 Republicans [signing the petition], there will be concern." Quoted in Lisa Caruso, "Moderate Republicans Ponder Discharge Petition Route," *National Journal's Congress Daily*, April 16, 1998.

40. Representative Tom Campbell, R-Calif., played an important intermediary role between the Shays-Meehan reformers and the leadership to broker this deal. In addition, meetings with the other Republican discharge petition signers, led by Zach Wamp, pushed the leadership into contemplating such an agreement.

41. Jim VandeHei and Amy Keller, "DeLay Forms Team to Kill Reform Plans," *Roll Call*, May 14, 1998, 32.

42. The Monica Lewinsky story broke in January 1998, and through the rest of the year the allegations against the president, his public denials, and his eventual confession that he had lied about the affair seriously reduced Clinton's credibility and effectiveness. The GOP-controlled House voted to impeach President Clinton on December 19, 1998, for lying under oath about the affair, but the Senate acquitted him on February 12, 1999.

43. Representative Gerald Solomon, R-N.Y., House Rules Committee chair, met with Shays and promised to be fair. The GOP leadership had placed pressure on the committee to make reform difficult, and therefore the definition of fair meant "everyone" would be heard.

44. VandeHei and Keller, "DeLay Forms Team to Kill Reform Plans," 32.

45. The "motor-voter" law was passed in 1993 and required states to give citizens the opportunity to register to vote when they acquired or renewed their driver's license.

46. VandeHei and Keller, "DeLay Forms Team to Kill Reform Plans," 1. The Free Speech Coalition included DeLay and Reps. Anne M. Northup, R-Ky.; Bill Paxon, R-N.Y.; Edward Whitfield, R-Ky.; Roy Blunt, R-Mo.; Roger Wicker, R-Miss; and John Doolittle, R-Calif.

47. A "Dear Colleague" letter is written by a member of Congress to his or her fellow members regarding a particular bill, policy, or position. This is a form of communication used by members of Congress to converse with one another. Some letters are sent to all members; others are targeted to specific delegations, parties, or members.

48. VandeHei and Keller, "DeLay Forms Team to Kill Reform Plans," 32.

49. Peter H. Stone, "Hammering Campaign Reform," *National Journal*, June 13, 1998, 1366.

50. The Democratic Congressional Campaign Committee, or DCCC, is the national political party organization that assists Democrats running for the House of Representatives. The Republican counterpart is the National Republican Congressional Committee (NRCC).

51. This included originally fifteen Democrats and twelve Republicans although the number grew as the process progressed. Briefing books are often used, but the extent of their use as well as their content was much vaster than the standard sort used in congressional debate.

52. Michael Mintrom, "Policy Entrepreneurs and the Diffusion of Innovation," *American Journal of Political Science* 41 (1997): 738-770, 739.

53. By voting "present," the Commission bill sponsors did not have to vote against their own bill. Thus they ensured that the bill would not receive more "yea" votes than the Shays-Meehan bill.

54. The Committee of the Whole has the same membership as the entire House but only 100, rather than 218, members are required for a quorum in order to do business.

55. The Republican reform members were Christopher Shays; Michael Forbes, R-N.Y.; John Edward Porter, R-Ill.; Jim Ramstad, R-Minn.; Sue Kelly, R-N.Y.; Zach Wamp; Nancy Johnson, R-Conn.; Fred Upton, R-Mich.; Jim Greenwood, R-Pa.; Jack Metcalf, R-Wash.; Amo Houghton, R-N.Y.; Jim Leach, R-Iowa; Mike Parker, R-Miss.; and Tom Campbell, R-Calif.

56. A July 1998 letter from L. Anthony Sutin, acting assistant attorney general, to Gingrich stated that the Department of Justice "strongly opposed these amendments": Doolittle Amendment 61, Doolittle Amendment 62, Peterson (of Pennsylvania) Amendment, Wicker Amendment 31, and Goodlatte Amendment.

57. Jack W. Germond and Jules Witcover, "A Flash of Hope for Reformers," *National Journal*, July 11, 1998, 1643.

58. Thomas helped broker a deal that was in part designed to regain some input into the process. As the chairman of the committee of jurisdiction (the House Oversight Committee), he had lost some face with the removal of most of the process from his committee's consideration, his failure to broker an earlier deal that led to the suspension votes, and the sound defeat of his own reform effort.

59. Amendments sponsored by Reps. Bob Barr, R-Ga.; Bob Schaffer, R-Colo.; Fred Upton, R-Mich.; Tom DeLay; and Dan Miller, R-Fla., were not offered.

60. At this point the Shays-Meehan bill had enough votes to be Queen of the Hill. Therefore the Freshman and Doolittle bills were now offered as substitute bills to the Shays-Meehan bill.

61. Helen Dewar, "House Approves Campaign Finance Limits," *Washington Post*, August 7, 1998, A1. Dewar also notes that the House Republican leaders "came to power under a reform banner, but found themselves defending a system that many of their own members described as corrupt."

62. E. J. Dionne Jr., "A Chance for Campaign Reform," *Washington Post*, August 7, 1998, A25.

63. See Sinclair, *Unorthodox Lawmaking*, chap. 6.

64. One of the strategies that supporters of reform tried to use early on in the process in the 105th Congress was to persuade those in the Republican majority who had voted for campaign finance reform while in the minority in 1992 to do so again. Some suggested that the bill that was passed in the 102d Congress and later vetoed by President George Bush be reintroduced or at least used as a base to achieve Republican support. What proponents of this strategy failed to mention is that the 1992 process was filled with its own partisanship, and passage then was called into question as a political ploy by the Democrats in an election year. The Democrats controlled both chambers of Congress in 1992 and passed a bill that reflected their views in part because they expected Bush to veto it, making it a "free vote" for the Democrats and allowing them to claim that the Republican president had killed reform.

65. John W. Kingdon, *Agendas, Alternatives, and Public Policy* (Glenview, Ill.: Scott, Foresman, 1984).

3

CLEARING A PATHWAY THROUGH THE LABYRINTH: PASSING CAMPAIGN FINANCE LEGISLATION

On March 20, 2002, lawmakers who supported the McCain-Feingold/ Shays-Meehan campaign finance legislation and their allied interest groups joined together for a rally on the grounds of the U.S. Capitol, and they had reason to celebrate. Their long quest to revise the nation's campaign finance laws was about to come to fruition. Earlier in the day the Senate had voted 60–40 to pass the same version of the Bipartisan Campaign Reform Act (BCRA) that the House of Representatives had approved a month earlier by a 240–189 vote. All that was needed to complete the long legislative odyssey was for President George W. Bush to make good on his statement that he would sign the bill into law. A week later, despite expressing reservations about BCRA's constitutionality, the president did just that. So, what conditions made this legislation possible in 2002 that did not exist in 1998, when the Senate blocked campaign finance legislation for the third time in the 105th Congress? What had changed between September 1998 and March 2002, when reform legislation won significant majorities in both chambers of Congress?

Part of the explanation lies in the fact that BCRA supporters made inroads in the 105th Congress that laid the groundwork for the bill's ultimate success. In passing the Shays-Meehan bill in the House in 1998, reform proponents charted a pathway through the legislative labyrinth that would serve as a model in future legislative battles. That pathway included:

(1) narrowing the primary focus of the bill and making strategic compromises to broaden the bill's support base; (2) relying on an active issue network led by legislators who could rise above being just issue leaders to become true policy entrepreneurs; (3) effectively using the rules of parliamentary procedure to overcome the inherent advantage that the House majority party leadership possesses; and (4) capitalizing on external events as well as mistakes by their opponents.

Charting the pathway, however, was one thing; actually navigating it was another. The most significant obstacle for BCRA supporters was to obtain the 60 votes in the Senate needed to end a filibuster. Also, initial success in the House did not guarantee that supporters would triumph again in that chamber. Since BCRA's opponents were sure to learn from mistakes they had made in the 105th Congress, the bill's supporters could not expect similar errors in judgment the next time. Finally, with George W. Bush succeeding Bill Clinton as president following the 2000 election, reform proponents lost a well-positioned ally who had stepped in at key moments to keep campaign finance reform legislation alive. Arizona Senator John McCain's emphasis on campaign finance reform in his bid for the Republican presidential nomination in 2000, however, brought attention to the issue and may have led to President Bush's lukewarm support for certain reform principles. The way in which BCRA's supporters continued to seek a way through the legislative labyrinth until they achieved success illustrates both the challenges in achieving legislative success in an inefficient policymaking process and the efforts required to pass such high-stakes legislation as campaign finance reform.

History Repeats Itself in the 106th Congress

As the 106th Congress (1999–2001) began, supporters of the McCain-Feingold/Shays-Meehan campaign finance legislation were faced with a strategic quandary. Certainly they wanted to build off the success they had achieved in the House during the 105th Congress, but taking the same approach in the Senate as they had in the previous legislative session could well lead to the same result. At the heart of the strategy in the 106th Congress, then, was a decision that reform efforts would start first in the House. If the bill's supporters could repeat their success from the previous year there, they might be able to build momentum and put pressure on the Senate to approve the legislation. With this strategy in mind, Representatives Christopher Shays, R-Conn., and Marty Meehan, D-Mass., introduced their Bipartisan

Campaign Reform Act of 1999 on January 19, 1999. The proposal was substantively similar to the version of the bill that had passed the House just a
few months earlier.

When a piece of legislation carries over from one session of Congress to
another, the political actors involved are in a position to learn from past experiences, potentially improving their chances of obtaining the outcome
they desire. But BCRA's supporters were not the only ones who learned
lessons from the 105th Congress and put them into action in the 106th—so
too did the bill's opponents. One of their less successful strategies in the
105th Congress, the bill's opponents came to realize, was the way in which
the House leadership and other reform bill opponents went about trying to
defeat the legislation. From broken promises, to hurried votes, to a barrage of
poison pill amendments, the bill's opponents actually helped keep campaign
finance alive and built momentum in favor of the legislation.

In the 106th Congress, however, the new Speaker of the House, Dennis
Hastert, R-Ill., quickly announced that campaign finance legislation would

Source: Congressional Quarterly

Rep. Dennis Hastert, 59th Speaker of the House, January 1999 to January 2007.

be brought up in September. This decision was designed to limit the threat of a discharge petition. Unlike in the 105th Congress, where a discharge petition was needed to have the issue brought to the floor at all, House leaders could now proclaim that campaign finance legislation would receive consideration in the due course of the House's legislative business. This decision had another strategic aspect to it, of which the bill's supporters were well aware. They wanted the House to address the issue early in the session so the Senate would have plenty of time to take it up. The Speaker's announced plan for consideration by the House in September, near the end of the session and close to the start of the 1999–2000 election season, virtually guaranteed that comprehensive campaign finance legislation would be filibustered again in the Senate.[1] The new Speaker and the bill's opponents realized that they did not have to put up as many procedural roadblocks because, as most observers agreed, regardless of what the House did, comprehensive campaign finance legislation was sure to fail again in the Senate. As it had been in the 105th Congress, a vote on campaign finance legislation in the House would be a *free vote* because it did not matter whether the bill passed in the House; it was likely to be defeated in the Senate.

In addition, changes in the partisan landscape in the House provided a new tool that the legislation's opponents took advantage of as they tried to defeat, or at least slow the momentum of, campaign finance legislation. The Republicans had lost seats in the House following the 1998 midterm elections, further narrowing their already-slim majority position. Dennis Hastert's succession of Newt Gingrich as Speaker made Republican adherence to the party's positions more important.[2] After the Blue Dog Democrats' announcement on April 14th that they intended to pursue a discharge petition similar to the one used in the 105th Congress, Speaker Hastert and other Republican leaders requested that their party members not sign the petition and adhere to the Speaker's plan to bring the bill up in September. Many Republicans, even supporters of the Shays-Meehan bill, were hesitant to challenge their new party leaders so openly, as the GOP leaders had made it clear that signing the Democratic discharge petition would be "a vote of no confidence in the new speaker."[3]

Even Representative Christopher Shays initially did not sign the discharge petition, which put him in an awkward position between his party leaders and supporters of the campaign finance legislation bearing his name. These supporters wanted Shays to continue to push the issue against the wishes of his party leaders, as he had done the year before. "I feel like it's a tightrope," he commented. "I just have to be very careful."[4] Ultimately, Shays decided

bringing campaign finance to the floor earlier in the session was more important than siding with his party's leaders on the issue. In late May 1999, he
and five other Republicans signed the discharge petition.[5] Still, this amount
represented only half of the number of Republicans who had signed the discharge petition the year before.

Speaker Hastert was not the only new face in the campaign finance debate
of the 106th Congress. Interest groups and others outside of Congress had
by this time placed new emphasis on the issue, helping to bring campaign finance legislation more into the political mainstream. For instance, Doris
Haddock, nicknamed "Granny D," was an eighty-nine-year-old great-
grandmother who walked from California to Washington, D.C. to show her
support for campaign finance legislation, attracting much media attention
along the way. The Committee for Economic Development (CED), a nonpartisan, business-oriented public policy and research organization that included many well known executives from America's leading corporations,
supported a ban on soft money, citing the "soft-money shakedown" that
many businesses faced.[6] On the other side of the issue, the National Right to
Life Committee (NRLC) indicated that it would include a House member's

Source: Congressional Quarterly

Doris "Granny D" Haddock at the Capitol in Washington, D.C., on February
3, 2000, after walking across the country to promote campaign finance reform.

vote on the Shays-Meehan bill on its pro-life voter scorecard. Doing so meant
that if a member wanted to maintain a 100 percent NRLC antiabortion rating, he or she would have to vote against Shays-Meehan.[7]

Despite the necessary changes in tactics brought about by the infusion of
new actors and circumstances, once the legislative consideration of Shays-
Meehan started in the 106th Congress, the process looked very similar to
that of the 105th. Since Shays-Meehan supporters were not able to obtain
the requisite 218 signatures for the discharge petition, they had to wait until
September to start debate on the issue. The voting process, much like that in
the 105th Congress, was a complicated endeavor. Proponents of the Shays-
Meehan bill had to defeat amendments that would have increased individual
contribution limits from $1,000 to $3,000, weakened the bill's proposed restrictions on printed attack ads, required candidates to raise at least half of
their contributions from their home states, exempted Internet ads from regulation, and invalidated the entire bill if any part of it were struck down by
the courts (i.e., the severability issue discussed in Chapter 2).[8] Of the eight
amendments on which the House voted, reform supporters classified six as
poison pill amendments that would have broken apart their coalition. All of
these were defeated, showing once again that the extraordinary efforts of the
Shays-Meehan issue network had paid off. Additionally, the reform supporters defeated the three substitute bills that would have replaced the Shays-
Meehan bill altogether. The House did approve two amendments.[9]

On September 15, 1999, the House passed the Shays-Meehan bill for the second straight year by a margin of 252 to 177. Fifty-four Republicans voted to support the measure despite their party leadership's opposition. But thirteen Democrats broke with their party, some of them because of the hard-hitting
campaign against reform waged by the NRLC. The Shays-Meehan supporters in
the House no doubt felt somewhat bittersweet about their victory, though, for
they knew that campaign finance reform faced an uphill battle in the Senate.

Unlike in the House, the 1998 midterm Senate elections did not have any
significant impact on the prospects for campaign finance reform in the Senate. The aggregate partisan numbers stayed the same (55 Republicans to 45
Democrats), and the defeated incumbent senators had not been significant
players in the reform process. Reform efforts in the Senate tracked, but
lagged behind, the Shays-Meehan efforts in the House. Senators John
McCain, R-Ariz., and Russell Feingold, D-Wis., reintroduced their bill, as
modified by the Snowe-Jeffords amendment in the 105th Congress. Nevertheless, the Senate did not take up campaign finance reform until after the
House passed the Shays-Meehan bill.

At this point, McCain and Feingold made the strategic decision to scale back their bill even further in the hope of gaining additional Republican support for a cloture vote to end the inevitable filibuster. They introduced a revised reform bill on September 16, 1999, with the understanding from Majority Leader Trent Lott, R-Miss., that the bill would be considered in October. The new McCain-Feingold bill (S. 1593) contained a complete ban on soft money as well as a provision regarding using union dues for political purposes. The revised bill discarded the new regulations on campaign-like issue advocacy advertisements. If the revised McCain-Feingold bill passed, it would have to go to the House for approval, for all bills must pass in identical form in both chambers before going on to the president for his signature. McCain regarded the revised bill as a compromise that provided a ban on soft money, "the bare minimum of reform," that might bring "additional Senators on board prior to coming to the floor in October." [10] Indeed, McCain said that he was a "realist" and acknowledged that a *comprehensive* reform bill was not likely to pass in the Senate. [11] The pared-down bill was a gamble that reform proponents were willing to take and that interest groups reluctantly supported. Yet the scaled-down bill drew new support from only one additional Senate Republican, Sam Brownback of Kansas, and many Democrats were leery of breaking apart the reform proposal to deal only with soft money.

The issue ad provision had inspired the hard-hitting First Amendment criticisms that derailed McCain's efforts during the last Congress. Yet Senator Mitch McConnell, R-Ky., who began calling himself the "designated spear catcher on this issue," showed no sign that he would drop his opposition even to the scaled-back bill. [12] McConnell, who headed the GOP's Senate reelection committee, the National Republican Senatorial Committee, argued that his party needed large amounts of soft money to counter the issue ads run by labor unions that overwhelmingly favored Democrats. Even McConnell, the champion of the First Amendment argument, was appealing to his fellow Republicans with this more pragmatic partisan argument. Without the issue ad restrictions in the bill, the First Amendment argument was no longer relevant. The foes of reform, facing only the soft money provision, were then forced to rely on their more strategic and partisan arguments to defeat campaign finance reform.

In October, on the first day the Senate considered the revised McCain-Feingold bill, the usually collegial Senate debate turned personal—specifically toward Senator McCain. As before, Senator McConnell led the anti-reform efforts. He responded to McCain's argument that soft money corrupted Congress by asserting "someone must be corrupt for there to be corruption.

How can there be corruption if no one is corrupt? That's like saying the gang is corrupt but none of the gangsters are." [13] McCain retorted "who is corrupted by this system? All of us are corrupted by it because money buys access and access is influence." [14]

Despite the drama of these confrontations on the floor of the Senate, they did not end up playing a decisive role in the eventual outcome. Neither did the First Amendment arguments that reform opponents used to help defeat the McCain-Feingold bill in 1997 and 1998. Instead, the Senate's consideration was driven by the use of parliamentary maneuvers. As issues gave way to process, "the campaign finance debate...simply degenerated into a procedural battle." [15]

For example, Senator McConnell won approval with a voice vote for a "seemingly innocuous amendment" that modified the Senate rules so that Senators had to provide "credible information" regarding corruption. [16] McConnell, in effect, wanted to make the reformers name names and to force them to turn their reform efforts into a witch hunt. Reform supporters worried that this would hamper their endeavors, since they would no longer be able to simply make the generic claim that money in politics is a corrupting force. [17]

Another example of the unusual parliamentary tactics employed was an amendment offered by McCain that would have killed his own proposal. His reason for doing this was to demonstrate the support that a soft money ban would have and to isolate the senators trying to kill the effort. This tactic failed, however, when opponents of this reform bill joined with the proponents, thus rendering the vote meaningless. The opponents could afford to "throw the vote," as Senator Feingold noted, because they knew they would have other chances to defeat the legislation. [18]

In the end, however, campaign finance reform in the 106th Congress once again fell victim to a Senate parliamentary procedure—the filibuster. Not even a late effort by President Clinton, who sent a letter to Senate Democrats supporting the revised McCain-Feingold bill, could provide enough votes to shut down the opponents' filibuster. On a vote that would have allowed the Senate to consider the House (Shays-Meehan) version of the bill, the reform supporters garnered only 52 of the 60 votes needed (again, a supermajority, rather than a simple majority, was needed to proceed). On a second vote that would have allowed the revised McCain-Feingold version to move forward, reform supporters added three new Republican Senators to their ranks. But two regular reform proponents voted no, giving the reform supporters a net increase of only one vote. [19] After these votes, Majority Leader Trent Lott proclaimed campaign finance reform "dead for the year." [20]

Although supporters of campaign finance legislation had been defeated twice in trying to bring about comprehensive changes to the nation's campaign finance laws, one small glimmer of hope emerged out of the 106th Congress. In 2000, McCain and Feingold introduced an incremental reform proposal that addressed the so-called *527 groups*—tax exempt, nonprofit groups formed under Section 527 of the Internal Revenue Code. These secret political groups were permitted to raise and spend unlimited amounts of money without disclosure of contributors or spending as long as their communications did not expressly advocate the election or defeat of candidates. The use of 527 groups in elections gained prominence when a 527 group ran televisions ads that attacked John McCain's environmental record just before the March 7th presidential primaries in which McCain was running.

McCain reported that the idea for the 527 legislation came to him in the middle of the night when, on the evening of June 5th, he decided to try to change the "nature of the campaign finance battle by seizing on one easily definable area to fix." [21] McCain and Feingold hoped that several senators in tough re-election bids might feel compelled to vote with them on this reform issue. They also hoped that the narrow refinement of a single area of the law would give them the momentum needed to pass more comprehensive reform, which would include a ban on soft money. McCain's amendment to tighten controls on 527 groups passed on June 8, 2000, on a voice vote, despite some procedural wrangling trying to defeat the bill. The House ended up passing a compromise version of the bill by a vote of 385 to 39; the Senate subsequently approved the House version 92–6. While President Clinton praised the new law when he signed it on July 1, 2000, remarking "this is a good day and this is a good law," he also noted that it was "a step but not a substitute for comprehensive campaign reform." [22]

The 2000 Elections

Although not apparent at the time, the 2000 elections turned out to be quite crucial in clearing a path through the legislative labyrinth for BCRA's eventual passage. As early as the 105th Congress, Shays and Meehan displayed an ability to take advantage of contemporary events taking place outside of the legislative process. The 2000 elections provided a number of such external events that reform proponents ultimately used to their advantage to get BCRA passed.

The most significant of these stemmed from the actions of one of the bill's leaders. In 2000, John McCain sought the Republican nomination for the U.S. presidency, and he made campaign finance reform one of the core issues of his platform. In doing so, McCain brought the issue of campaign finance further into the political mainstream, helping to make it an issue that mattered to the broader public rather than just a policy debate taking place among members of Congress. Although McCain lost the Republican nomination to George W. Bush, he managed to achieve some early successes, most notably winning the New Hampshire and Michigan primaries. Additionally, McCain enjoyed significant support from voters who identified themselves as *Independents,* that is, people who did not identify themselves as either Republicans or Democrats. [23] Even more significantly, McCain became the first presidential candidate to make the Internet a prominent part of his campaign, investing money and personnel early on to develop the needed infrastructure. In doing so, he reaped substantial benefits. For example, immediately after beating George W. Bush in the New Hampshire primary (the nation's first primary), McCain saw his Web site collect donations at a reported rate of $30,000 an hour. Overall, McCain raised $6.4 million during the 2000 campaign through the Internet. [24]

When he returned to the Senate following the primary season, McCain's standing and influence was bolstered by his new popularity on a national scale. It was, in part, this popularity that allowed him to get the 527 legislation passed through Congress. And it was also the basis on which McCain stepped up his efforts to pass comprehensive campaign finance legislation following the 2000 elections.

Another significant event in the 2000 elections was the substantial increase in money both raised and spent in federal campaigns compared with prior elections. The increases were astronomical: George W. Bush raised over $91 million from individuals prior to the Republican convention in 2000, while Al Gore, Bill Bradley, and John McCain raised $34 million, $29 million, and $28 million, respectively. Just four years earlier, in the 1996 election, Bill Clinton and Bob Dole had raised only about $28 million and $29 million, respectively, in their presidential campaigns. All congressional candidates together raised and spent over $1 billion running for office during the 2000 election cycle, compared to the $791 million they raised collectively in the 1996 election cycle and the $781 million raised in the 1998 election cycle. Perhaps nowhere was the increase in campaign fundraising more dramatic than in the area of soft money for the national political parties. As shown in Chapter 1, the Democrats nearly doubled the amount of soft money raised in the 2000 election cycle when compared to the previous presidential election year of 1996, while the Republicans saw more than an 80% increase during the same period.

The growth of money in elections generally, and soft money in particular, placed more attention on the McCain-Feingold/Shays-Meehan bill. More significantly, though, it also started to change the minds of a small but crucial number of legislators. Shortly after the 2000 elections, Senator Thad Cochran, R-Miss., announced that he was throwing his support behind McCain and Feingold, noting "it became obvious to me that the influence of soft money and independent groups was overwhelming the effort of candidates."[25] The two senators welcomed Cochran's support, and their bill became the McCain-Feingold-Cochran bill (although it was still commonly referred to simply as *McCain-Feingold*). Cochran was the first of the more traditional conservative Republicans to support the campaign finance legislation, and the first of what would eventually be five Republican senators who switched their positions on the legislation. The 2000 elections also resulted in turnover in the composition of the Senate, which included replacing campaign finance legislation opponents with new senators who supported McCain-Feingold. Between the Senate's changed composition and the switch in positions by several Senators, McCain believed that he had the 60 votes needed to be able to end a filibuster in the Senate.

Clearing the Path for Final Passage

Emboldened by the new circumstances surrounding the debate on campaign finance, McCain quickly moved to get BCRA on the legislative agenda in the Senate. But while there was growing momentum behind the bill, barriers remained. Some were obstacles that reform proponents had dealt with before, such as the fact that the leaders in both the House and Senate were opposed to the legislation. Others, however, were new. But when an issue remains on the legislative agenda over an extended period of time, as campaign finance legislation did, both supporters and opponents must be able to adapt to changing circumstances.

At the outset of the 107th Congress (2001–2003), the most significant new event regarding campaign finance was George W. Bush's election to the presidency. As president, Bill Clinton had stepped in at key moments in the legislative process to keep the effort to revise the nation's campaign finance laws moving. During the Clinton presidency, reform supporters knew that if they were able to get a bill through Congress it would be signed into law by the president. With President Bush in the White House, however, the prospect of having to overcome a possible presidential veto became a very real issue that both sides needed to take into account. As one political analyst

George W. Bush, 43rd president of the United States, who signed the Bipartisan Campaign Reform Act into law in 2002, in front of his father, George H. W. Bush, 41st president of the United States, who vetoed campaign finance reform legislation during his term in office.

wrote at the time, "the arrival of Bush as the arbiter of whether campaign finance overhaul becomes law has created an entirely new—and unpredictable—legislative dynamic. No longer must Republicans rely on filibusters to stop advocates of overhaul as they did in 1994, 1996, 1997, 1998, and 1999. But nor do Democrats have a backstop in the White House to block a bill that cuts against them politically." [26]

Shortly after the Senate started debating McCain-Feingold in March 2001, President Bush issued a set of "reform principles" that included a ban on soft money from corporations and labor unions, but not individuals; First Amendment-based support for groups engaging in issue advocacy; and a paycheck protection provision that would apply to political donations from both unions and corporations. By calling these ideas "reform principles" Bush potentially could have changed the terms of the campaign finance debate. Until this time, supporters of the McCain-Feingold/Shays-Meehan legislation—particularly the public interest groups pushing for campaign finance legislation—had been seen as the judges of what constituted true "reform" of the nation's campaign finance laws. If Bush were to successfully alter the terms of the debate, even slightly, he and his allies in Congress could claim that *they* had passed a *true* reform bill, but one that did not reach as far, or raise the same constitutional questions, as McCain-Feingold.

At a minimum, Bush's reform principles threatened to give rise to a compromise bill that might draw support away from the McCain-Feingold bill, making it more vulnerable to legislative defeat. One such compromise bill was offered by Senator Chuck Hagel, R-Neb., whose bill permitted soft money, but would have capped the amount. His bill also increased the amount that individuals could contribute and contained no issue-ad provision. Observers noted that Hagel was poised to be a broker between McCain and President Bush if a campaign finance bill were to eventually become law.[27]

Another new factor legislators had to contend with was that, given Shays-Meehan supporters' past success in the House, and the fact that McCain apparently had enough support in the Senate to defeat a filibuster, campaign finance legislation had a realistic chance of passing both chambers of Congress. As a result, campaign finance was no longer a *free vote*—especially in the House. Many analysts speculated that support for Shays-Meehan in the House was not actually as strong as the margins by which the legislation passed in both the 105th and 106th Congresses. Some members may have voted in favor for the bill for strategic reasons—to appear to be in favor of reform, for example, or (among Democrats) to support their party leaders—and not because they favored passage of the bill. They primarily voted, then, because they knew the bill would be defeated in the Senate. Members now faced a decision: either vote as they had previously or openly change their position on the issue and vote against the campaign finance legislation.

Senator John Breaux, D-La., who previously voted for McCain-Feingold, did in fact come out against the measure. His rationale, though, was a strictly partisan one. Democrats could generally raise soft money as effectively as Republicans, but lagged behind in raising regulated hard dollars. McCain-Feingold's prohibition on soft money was, he reasoned, comparable to "unilateral disarmament" for Democrats.[28] Although many Democrats reportedly shared Breaux's concerns, the campaign finance legislation leaders in both chambers ultimately were able to hold most of their coalitions together. As Representative Christopher Shays acknowledged, "putting people on record was very important."[29] One benefit that legislation supporters gained by having gone through their battles over the years was that a number of members of Congress established a track record on the issue. Certainly, members could change their minds on the issue, as Thad Cochran and John Breaux had. But unless they were willing to do so publicly, members generally were bound to vote as they had before.

Once the campaign finance debate started in the Senate, the McCain-Feingold coalition allowed certain amendments to be made to their legislation to broaden its base of support, such as an amendment offered by Senator Carl Levin, D-Mich., that allowed state parties to raise and spend limited soft money (such funds have since come to be referred to as *Levin funds*) on generic campaign activities as long as certain restrictions were followed (see Box 3-1 on page 87 for additional information). Supporters of the McCain-Feingold bill, though, had to defend it against a series of poison pill amendments, much as Shays-Meehan supporters had done in

Source: Congressional Quarterly

Sen. Carl Levin, D-Mich., sponsored the Levin Amendment to BCRA that permits state parties to raise limited amounts of soft money. His compromise amendment helped gain additional support for BCRA in Congress.

Source: Congressional Quarterly

Sen. Tom Daschle (right), D-S. Dak., with Reps. Shays (far left) and Meehan. Senator Daschle was Senate majority leader during Senate passage of BCRA in 2002.

the House. The Senate coalition generally managed to do so, [30] as well as defeat most of the elements of the Hagel proposal. The most significant issue, though, was a provision in Senator Hagel's proposal that would have increased the maximum amount that an individual could contribute to candidates and parties. The McCain-Feingold bill kept that amount at $1,000, a figure that had been in place since the inception of FECA in the 1970s. Procedural votes involving possibly increasing this amount, however, showed support for the proposal.

Once again, McCain-Feingold supporters made a strategic compromise to shore up support for their bill: they would allow an increase in hard-money contribution limits. Democrats insisted on capping the allowable contribution at $2,000 for individuals, though some coalition members, led by Senator Fred Thompson, R-Tenn., tried to negotiate a higher number. In the end, the vote that added the compromise language—a $2,000 cap for individual contributions with $75,000 in maximum total contributions per election cycle—was an overwhelming 84–16 in favor; it allowed McCain-Feingold supporters to put the issue behind them and added some momentum to their cause. Senate Minority Leader Tom Daschle, D-S.D., captured the sentiment of the bill's supporters when he commented: "I support this compromise reluctantly because it is necessary to keep us moving forward." [31]

As the debate in the Senate over McCain-Feingold neared its conclusion, opponents of the bill received news that undercut an important part of their strategy: President Bush let it be known that he would not veto the legislation. White House spokesman Ari Fleischer laid out the president's position. "The president has sent the signal that he wants to send, that he cannot be counted on to veto it [the McCain-Feingold bill] because he wants to reform the system," he said. "It's too early yet to say precisely what he will sign, but he's sending very clear signals that he does not believe we need to veto campaign finance reform, because he wants to reform the system." [32]

President Bush's apparent change in position may have been for any of several reasons. Perhaps sensing the momentum gathering behind the bill, the president may have decided to conserve his political capital for battles over other issues. At this time, Bush was still in the first 100 days of his first term, having attained the presidency despite losing the popular vote to Al Gore in the 2000 election and having the outcome decided by a 5 to 4 decision in the Supreme Court. Also, Bush may have wanted to avoid restarting the heated intra-party squabble over campaign finance he had engaged in with John McCain during the 2000 Republican primaries. Finally, Bush may not have had much personally invested in the issue because he had already proven during the 2000 elections that he was an effective—indeed record-setting—fundraiser even with a $1,000-per-person contribution limit. Regardless of Bush's reasoning, his role in the legislative dynamic surrounding the campaign finance debate could now be predicted, and the Republican opponents of McCain-Feingold were dismayed by the president's position.

The Senate passed McCain-Feingold on April 2, 2001, by a 59–41 margin, with all but three Democrats voting for the bill. The pressure now was on the Shays-Meehan coalition to successfully lead their bill through the House for a third time. But, in addition to the challenges they had faced before (a House leadership opposed to the bill and the loss of a *free vote* for those who may have voted strategically in the past), the bill's leaders faced a significant substantive hurdle in holding their coalition together: the Senate compromise increasing the maximum contributions by individuals. Representative

Shays bluntly assessed his bill's chances. "If [House Democrats] can't accept [a hard-money increase], the bill is dead," he said. "Ultimately, I'm convinced that we have to accept a hard-money increase in order to pass a bill." [33]

Before House supporters of the bill could even get to vote on the substance of the legislation, though, they had to contend with several delays, some of which were caused by members of their own coalition. The Black and Hispanic caucuses, whose 55 combined members were a necessary component of the Shays-Meehan coalition, wanted to go beyond campaign finance reform and address election-reform issues more broadly, such as voting equipment and other problems that surfaced during the 2000 election. Caucus leaders even floated the idea of tying their support for campaign finance reform directly to action on election reform. This kind of tension in the ranks underscored the need for Shays and Meehan to keep their coalition united behind campaign finance legislation. They could not try to push their bill for a quick vote so long as coalition leaders had continuing concerns about the level of the bill's support; unless the support of the Black and Hispanic caucuses was firmly shored up, the coalition leaders knew that they would likely not be able to pass campaign finance legislation if and when they had the opportunity to do so.

The Shays-Meehan coalition also had to contend with the House leadership, which had the formal power to determine when floor debate on campaign finance would begin. On May 16, 2001—six weeks after the Senate passed the McCain-Feingold bill—Speaker Dennis Hastert sent a letter to Christopher Shays indicating that the House would debate campaign finance following the members' return from their July 4th recess. Although some of the legislation's supporters were irate over the continued delay, Shays indicated that he and his coalition would work within the time frame set forth by the Speaker.

When the House began consideration of campaign finance in July, however, the focus was once again on the procedural rules that would govern the debate rather than on the substance of the bill itself. Seeking to deal efficiently with the many concessions they had made to coalition members to retain their support, Shays and Meehan proposed combining fourteen separate amendments to their bill into a single manager's amendment. The House Rules Committee, however, required that each amendment be considered individually, thereby creating fourteen different opportunities for opponents to weaken the Shays-Meehan coalition. Meanwhile, the House leadership was promoting a bill sponsored by Representative Bob Ney, R-Ohio, chair of the House Administration Committee, that would have capped soft money contributions at $75,000 and required that such contributions be used only for generic voter registration and get-out-the-vote activities—the latter specifically designed to address concerns and draw support from the Black and Hispanic caucuses. Unable to obtain a set of rules for debate, Democrats, together with 19 Republicans, voted against allowing the House to debate campaign finance legislation, gambling that they could obtain a better set of rules in the future. After the vote, however, Speaker Hastert indicated that he had no plans to bring up campaign finance legislation in the future since the House had other matters to address.

In most instances, legislative delay is detrimental (and possibly fatal) to a bill's chances for passage. Much of the House leadership's strategy on campaign finance legislation over the years had been to delay votes on the subject as much as possible. When a bill is delayed it loses momentum, members focus on other matters, and opponents have more opportunities to put new obstacles in the legislation's pathway through the legislative labyrinth. Such was the prospect that campaign finance legislation faced following the vote on the rule for debate. But then an unexpected external event occurred—one that on its face had nothing to do with campaign finance—and provided the necessary impetus to clear the legislative pathway for BCRA.

In the fall of 2001, Enron Corp., one of the nation's largest and most prominent businesses, was in the news headlines with stories of accounting fraud and insider trading that led to the company's collapse and bankruptcy (at the time the company filed for bankruptcy on December 2, 2001, it was the largest bankruptcy ever). Once regarded by investors as one of the most innovative and profitable companies on the stock market, Enron had quickly become a symbol for corporate greed and unscrupulous business practices, as the company's top executives sought to hide significant financial losses through complex legal and tax structures, even as they sold their own stock holdings in the company for sizable profits. Their actions cost many investors and employees their life savings. In the fall of 2001, anything remotely connected with Enron ran the risk of being tainted by the scandal.

Enron was a very active donor of campaign funds, both to parties and individual candidates. The company gave $3.6 million in soft money to the Republican and Democratic parties between 1990 and 2001, and its political action committee contributed more than $1 million to candidates from both parties in both chambers of Congress. Even though the company's contributions were entirely legal, Enron donations became such a political hot-button that many candidates and party organizations either returned Enron contributions or donated them to funds set up to assist employees affected

Kenneth Lay, CEO and Chairman of Enron Corp., was indicted on 11 counts of securities fraud and related charges. The Enron scandal illustrated the problem of unregulated corporate money in campaigns and galvanized support for campaign finance reform.

by the company's collapse. Campaign finance legislation supporters were quick to point out the connection between money contributed by corporate giants like Enron and the objectives reform proponents sought to promote. Marty Meehan argued that "Enron is a textbook study on money's influence in Washington. At a minimum, the taint of big money contributions undermines confidence in government decisions." [34] Christopher Shays went even further, proclaiming, "it's corrupt to have large sums of corporate money in the campaign system. This was an unethical company buying access to decision makers." [35]

The legislative effect of the Enron scandal was most immediately seen in support for a discharge petition that had been introduced following the vote on the rules in July. In January 2002, Democratic and other coalition leaders rounded up the necessary 218 signatures on the discharge petition to bring the issue of campaign finance to the floor under a different set of rules for debate. While not all the signers had committed to voting for the Shays-Meehan bill, the Enron scandal at least convinced them that the issue needed to be openly debated. Twenty Republicans signed the discharge petition against the wishes of their party leaders, including crucial signatories number 215 and 216, Charlie Bass, R-N.H., and Tom Petri, R-Wis.

By the time the Shays-Meehan bill reached the House floor in February 2002, even its staunchest opponents conceded that they were not likely to defeat the legislation outright. Instead, they decided to take an alternative approach once again tied to the procedural rules governing any legislation's passage. For a bill to fully pass Congress and be presented to the president for signature, the House and Senate must pass the same piece of legislation; any differences between the two versions passed by each chamber must be resolved. Reconciling any differences is typically undertaken by a conference committee comprised of members from both the House and Senate appointed by the majority leaders in each body. Representative John Doolittle, R-Calif., summed up the strategy of Shays-Meehan opponents. "We're not going to defeat [Shays-Meehan]," he said. "The only question is can it be amended in such a fashion that it goes to conference. The master strategy is to get it to conference." [36]

If the bill were to go to a conference committee, Speaker Dennis Hastert's control over the membership of the committee could provide opponents with a final opportunity to defeat, or at least limit the scope of, BCRA. Reform supporters did not face a similar prospect with respect to the committee appointees from the Senate, where majority control of that chamber had swung to the Democrats. In May 2001, Senator James Jeffords of Vermont announced that he was leaving the Republican Party to become an Independent who would caucus with the Democrats for organizational purposes. The Senate at the time was split 50–50 with the Republicans considered as the majority; Jeffords's decision effectively changed the balance of the Senate to the Democrats' favor. As a result, Democratic Senator Tom Daschle assumed the role of Senate Majority Leader. Nevertheless, reform legislation supporters could not count on Democratic control of the Senate to counter the threat posed to their bill by the conference committee process.

As Shays and Meehan had done in the past, they defeated the amendments that would have made it most difficult to hold their coalition together. On February 14, 2002, the House passed the Shays-Meehan bill by a vote of 240–189. The version that passed, however, differed from the one that the Senate had passed the previous March. Faced with the prospects of a confer-

Source: Congressional Quarterly

In May 2001, Sen. James Jeffords of Vermont switched from the Republican Party to become an independent who caucused with the Democrats, giving majority control of the Senate to the Democrats and thus changing the outlook for such Democratic priorities as campaign finance reform.

ence committee that would further delay and possibly derail the legislation's prospects of becoming a law, McCain-Feingold supporters in the Senate made one final key strategic decision: they accepted the House's version of the bill in its entirety as an amendment to the Senate's version. To do so they had to appease members who were losing what they believed were key components not included in the House version and hold the coalition together in the face of a threatened filibuster. The legislation's supporters had converted one Democrat who had opposed McCain-Feingold the previous year— Senator Ernest Hollings, D-S.D.—who provided the necessary sixtieth vote to close off any filibuster. When the last set of legislative maneuvering ended, the Senate approved the House's version of BCRA by a vote of 60–40.

As finally enacted, the bill had changed in some significant ways from the one that had first passed in the House in 1998, and it certainly was a far cry from the comprehensive bill that John McCain had first pushed in 1995. Interest groups that had long supported the McCain-Feingold/Shays-Meehan reform efforts criticized the final piece of legislation for being watered down.

Even Senator Mitch McConnell called the bill "a shadow of its former self [as] Reformers kept stripping it back like peeling an onion." [37] Despite the legislative compromises that had taken place in the years before it finally passed, the bill did achieve its primary goals of addressing the *twin evils* of soft money and issue ads. Representative Chris Shays characterized the bill as achieving "eighty-five percent of what we wanted." He noted that "this bill is a result of compromise to get the 60 votes [needed to end debate in the Senate]. But it's a strong bill." [38] See Box 3.1 for a summary of the major provisions of the legislation. When President Bush signed BCRA into law a week later, the bill had completed its journey through the legislative labyrinth.

BOX 3-1 Summary of Major Provisions of the Bipartisan Campaign Reform Act of 2002

Soft Money

BCRA includes several provisions designed to end the use of nonfederal or "soft money" (money raised outside the limits and prohibitions of federal campaign finance law) in connection with any activity affecting federal elections. Among other things, the Act:

- Prohibits national parties from raising or spending soft money.
- Requires state, district, and local party committees to fund certain "federal election activities" with federal funds (i.e., hard money), rather than soft money, and, in some cases, with money raised according to new limitations, prohibitions, and reporting requirements (i.e., *Levin funds* [defined below]), or with a combination of such funds. Federal election activities include voter registration activity within 120 days before an election; generic get-out-the-vote (GOTV) or similar campaign activities in an election where a candidate for federal office is on the ballot; public communication that refers to a clearly identified federal candidate and that promotes, supports, attacks, or opposes any federal candidate; and services provided by an employee of a state or local party committee who spends more than 25% of that person's time on activities in connection with a federal election.
- Limits fundraising by federal and nonfederal candidates and officeholders on behalf of party committees, other candidates, and nonprofit organizations.

Box *continued*

National Parties

Beginning November 6, 2002, national party committees may not solicit, receive, direct to another person, or spend soft money. Limitations were placed on the national party committees soliciting funds for or making donations to tax-exempt 501(c) organizations and so-called 527 organizations.

State, District, and Local Parties

There are three categories of funding available to state, district, and local parties:

- Federal funds (hard money) raised under federal limitations and prohibitions may be used in connection with a federal election.
- Nonfederal funds are those outside the limits and, in many cases, the prohibitions of federal law but which are permitted by state law. These may not be used for federal election activity (unless they qualify as *Levin funds*).
- *Levin funds* are soft money donations allowable under state law, raised directly by the specific state or local party that intends to use them, and limited to no more than $10,000 in a calendar year from any "person" (a "person" can include a corporation or union, but not a foreign national, if state law allows). State and local parties in some cases can use *Levin funds* for a portion of voter registration activity or for voter identification, GOTV, or generic campaign activity as long as they do not refer to a clearly identified federal candidate and the funds are not used for radio or television communications (unless they are exclusively state and local candidates).

Federal Candidates and Officeholders

BCRA places limits on the amount and type of funds that can be raised by federal candidates and officeholders for both federal and state candidates. These restrictions apply to the candidates and/or officeholders, their agents, and entities directly or indirectly established, maintained or controlled by, or acting on behalf of, any such candidate or officeholder. These persons may not solicit or disburse funds in connection with an election for federal office unless they are federal funds; however, they may solicit or disburse funds in connection with any nonfederal election if those funds are consistent with state law and also do not exceed the contribution limits in FECA and are not from sources prohibited

continued

Box *continued*

under FECA. Federal candidates or officeholders may, however, attend, speak, or be a featured guest at a fundraising event for a state, district, or local party organization at which nonfederal or *Levin funds* are raised.

Electioneering Communications (Issue Ads)

BCRA and FEC rules contain provisions related to television and radio ads that refer to a clearly identified federal candidate and are distributed to the relevant electorate within a particular time period before an election. These are often referred to as "issue ads" because they typically discuss candidates in the context of certain issues without specifically advocating a candidate's election or defeat. Subject to certain exemptions, such ads are now considered "electioneering communications" and as such may no longer be funded by corporations or labor organizations. Other individuals or groups who pay for these ads must report the activity and the sources of funds if the payments exceed a specific threshold.

The defining characteristics of an "Electioneering Communication" are:

- The communication refers to a clearly identified candidate for federal office.
- The communication is publicly distributed on radio or television, including broadcast, cable, or satellite (with certain statutory exceptions and exemptions under regulations promulgated by the Federal Election Commission).
- The communication is distributed during a specific time period before an election—within 30 days prior to a primary election or 60 days prior to a general election.
- The communication is targeted to the relevant electorate—i.e., it can be received by 50,000 or more people in the district or state where the candidate is running for federal office. For presidential campaigns this means 50,000 or more people in a state holding a primary within 30 days or within 30 days of the start of the nominating convention.

Coordinated and Independent Expenditures

New rules define when a communication is considered coordinated between a candidate or political committee and a person making a communication. The new regulations provide for a three-part test (looking at source of payment, content standards, and conduct standards) to determine coordination. Satisfaction of all three justifies the conclusion that a communication is coor-

Box *continued*

dinated and is for the purpose of influencing an election. If that is shown, the person with whom coordination takes place is deemed to have made an in-kind contribution or made a coordinated expenditure (in the case of party committees) on behalf of the candidate.

Contribution Limitations and Prohibitions

BCRA increases limits on contributions made by individuals and some political committees; indexes certain contribution limits for inflation; prohibits contributions by minors to federal candidates and parties; and prohibits contributions, donations, expenditures, independent expenditures, and disbursements by foreign nationals.

New contribution limits for individuals—beginning January 1, 2003:

- Contributions to candidates—$2,000* per election (was $1,000).
- Contributions to state, district, and local party committees—$10,000 (combined) per year (was $5,000).
- Contributions to national party committees—$25,000* per year (was $20,000).
- Overall limit on contributions from one person now $95,000* every two years (was $25,000 per year). Within this limit, however, only $37,500 may be contributed to candidates and no more than $37,500 to other committees that are not national parties.
- National party committees may now contribute up to a total of $35,000* to Senate candidates per six-year campaign (was $17,500).

*Amounts with an asterisk are indexed for inflation. Increases will be implemented during odd-numbered years starting in 2005 and will be in effect for a two-year period.

Disclaimers

The new law requires a statement whether a candidate authorized a particular advertisement to accompany radio, television, print, and other campaign communications.

Millionaire Candidates

BCRA may raise the individual contribution limits for Senate and House candidates who are competing for office with self-financed candidates if the self-

continued

Box *continued*

financed candidate spends more than a specified amount of their own funds
on the campaign. The increase depends on the amount that the self-financed
candidate spends from personal funds along with some other factors. The law
also removes the limitation on national and state party committee expenditures on behalf of a candidate if the opposing self-financed candidate's expenditures exceed a threshold amount and other conditions are met.

Source: Federal Election Commission, "Major Provisions of the Bipartisan Campaign Reform Act of 2002." Available at http://www.fec.gov/press/bkgnd/bcra_overview.shtml.
Original material edited and condensed by the authors.

Lessons from BCRA's Passage through the Legislative Labyrinth

Although most bills do not travel the extraordinary path through the legislative labyrinth that BCRA did, its journey provides insights into the use of unorthodox policymaking that are helpful in understanding the modern legislative process. One of most significant lessons from BCRA's passage
underscores the importance of policy entrepreneurs in pursuing legislation
generally, but particularly when the legislation's supporters are not working
from a position of institutional leadership. Leadership can come in many
shapes and forms—many of which were displayed in Congress's consideration of campaign finance reform. Certainly, both House members and senators empower the majority party's formal leaders to shape the legislative
process in their respective chambers. Yet leadership in Congress also can
come from policy entrepreneurs, those issue leaders who forge strong legislative coalitions and effective issue networks around specific proposals.

The increasingly decentralized nature of Congress helps explain why
issue leaders are now freer and more likely to endure the high cost of pursuing legislation without the benefit of holding a formal position of power, or
at least being supported by those in such positions. Being a policy entrepreneur remains risky, particularly if one goes against his or her own party's
leaders. For Christopher Shays and John McCain, opposing the leaders of
their own party may have made it more difficult to lead the campaign finance reform effort in their chambers, but support from other lawmakers
and from groups and citizens outside of Congress helped insulate them
from the potential consequences of working at odds with their party. Policy
entrepreneurs commit a great amount of their time, energy, and resources

to a single issue, perhaps at the expense of other matters, some of which may need their attention in order to maintain electoral security back home. This is probably why most policy entrepreneurs tend to be electorally secure and therefore free to pursue issues that may not directly affect the folks back home. This necessarily limits the number of lawmakers willing to become policy entrepreneurs, since almost no member of Congress believes his or her reelection is assured no matter how big the margin of victory may have been in the last election. [39]

Despite these pitfalls, being a policy entrepreneur does have its possible rewards—particularly in a hostile political climate. Certainly, seeing legislation one deeply believes in become law is a reward in itself. Even more, a successful policy entrepreneur can leverage his or her success in one policy area into others. John McCain's rise to national prominence is one example. During the initial rounds of debate, Shays and Meehan appeared to be the more effective issue leaders and policy entrepreneurs on campaign finance. They were the ones who harnessed their internal and external issue network into a cohesive coalition that not only kept campaign finance on the policy agenda but got it passed in their chamber despite opposition from the majority party leadership—something that McCain had not been able to accomplish. Their persistence and success gained them national media attention.

McCain, though, solidified his position as a policy entrepreneur with his 2000 presidential run and his resulting ability to make campaign finance a more visible issue in the political mainstream. Whereas Shays and Meehan were clearly the leaders of a coalition, McCain successfully positioned himself so that the issue was connected to him personally. His prestige in the wake of the 2000 presidential primaries forced the issue on the Senate's agenda early in the 107th Congress. When he successfully steered McCain-Feingold through the Senate for the first time in March 2001, his clout had grown. Senator Mike DeWine, R-Ohio, commented that McCain's influence in the Senate "clearly will go beyond campaign finance reform, and any issue that John decides to focus on and concentrate on and use his enhanced stature to highlight, he's going to have the ability to have an impact. It's clear that he has an enhanced ability to affect public policy. It's abundantly clear." [40] While not all legislators will be able to catapult themselves to the heights that McCain did, the promise of being able to exert a greater influence on legislation may be enough to encourage some members of Congress to pursue roles as issue leaders and policy entrepreneurs.

Another key lesson that BCRA's passage highlights is the incremental nature of policymaking. For all the talk throughout the years of McCain-

Feingold/Shays-Meehan being a comprehensive campaign finance reform bill, it was in effect an incremental (albeit substantial) piece of legislation that addressed only a portion of the potential issues affecting the financing of elections. Immediately after it passed, BCRA supporters were talking about the other issues they wanted to address: provisions that were stripped out of BCRA during the legislative process; the presidential campaign finance system; and overhauling the Federal Election Commission (FEC), to name a few. Also, although BCRA's passage in Congress may have marked the end of the bill's journey through the legislative labyrinth, it was just beginning its trip through the policy labyrinth. Senator McConnell had already promised to be the lead plaintiff in a case challenging BCRA's constitutionality (see Chapter 4). Further, the legislation needed to be implemented by the FEC (see Chapter 5), as well as put into practice to see what its effects, consequences, and loopholes might be (see Chapter 6). The nature of the policy cycle ensured that campaign finance would remain an active issue on the political agenda for quite some time.

This incremental approach to policymaking may appear inefficient, and at times it certainly is. But it is also the product of a political system designed to ensure that any new law has sufficient support from a variety of interests in the nation, while at the same time protecting the rights of the minority. Most issues are multifaceted; high stakes issues like campaign finance that implicate fundamental tenets of our political system are sure to evoke strong and divergent opinions.

In examining BCRA, however, one can say that each side of the issue could point to some provision they liked or could at least accept, as well as find something about the law—either a provision in BCRA itself or something that BCRA did not address—they did not like. Reform supporters may have believed that the bill was watered down, but at least it addressed the twin evils that had come to be seen as the most significant problems in the system. First Amendment advocates could take heart that BCRA did not ban issue ads outright, but only subjected them to additional regulation as electioneering ads. Republican partisans could support doubling the maximum individual contribution to $2,000, with that amount then being indexed for inflation. BCRA may not have been a bill that anyone specifically wanted, but it was one that a majority in both chambers of Congress and the president could accept in the political climate of early 2002. The incremental nature of policymaking in our nation's political system also allows all sides to continue to make their case to other members of Congress and the general public in an effort to lay the groundwork for future changes in the law. Yes, the policymaking process may be inefficient, but it is one designed to ensure careful deliberation over our nation's public policies.

In many ways, the incremental nature of the policymaking process is a reflection of the governmental structure that the Founders created to protect a minority interest against tyranny of the majority. But if that is so, does BCRA's passage through the legislative labyrinth indicate that the system can still be manipulated by those in power to thwart the principle of majority rule? If so, is this not a form of tyranny of the minority? In a most narrow sense, one could legitimately argue this case. As early as 1998, the McCain-Feingold and Shays-Meehan bills appeared to have majority support in both chambers of Congress, yet they remained blocked by a minority of legislators, particularly those in leadership positions in both the Senate and House. Assuming that the votes in the Senate and House truly reflected the preferences of the legislators (instead of being strategic votes cast for other reasons), then the will of the majority could be seen as having been thwarted in that instance.

Viewed from a different perspective, however, one sees that the principles of our political system were not distorted. In the end, campaign finance legislation passed by a majority in both chambers of Congress. The fact that BCRA had to be refined to win the votes necessary for passage (including having enough votes to secure cloture on a filibuster in the Senate) perhaps shows that the 1998 and 1999 versions of the bill did not truly have majority support.

Another way to examine the issue involves considering the nature of representation as envisioned by James Madison and the other Founders. The elected representatives, in Madison's view, were supposed to divorce themselves from the passions of their constituents and, instead, make decisions for the benefit of the nation as a whole. Throughout the period under study here, the nation's voters elected Republican majorities in both the House and Senate (the Democrats took control of the Senate in 2001 only after Senator James Jeffords left the Republican Party). From this perspective, the focus is not on the majority will with respect to any specific issue, but the broader perspective of the nation's interest as a whole. In this regard, one could argue that the Republican leadership was expressing the majority will in protecting individuals' First Amendment rights by trying to defeat campaign finance legislation. Conversely, one might argue that the partisan factions were using this opportunity to exert their own understandings of how this issue needed to be remedied.

A third approach focuses on the strategic use of parliamentary procedures and legislative rules that characterized the debate over campaign finance legislation. Congress operates under a complex set of rules and procedures designed to facilitate passing legislation in an orderly manner. With the array of matters that Congress addresses each year, the institution could easily get bogged down in the minute details of the legislative process unless a system was established and followed. Nevertheless, these rules sometimes do have a substantive impact on public policy. Further, they can be utilized, some may even say manipulated, in one's favor to secure a desired result.

As reform legislation proponents encountered, the majority party leadership—which generally determines what rules will govern the debate on any particular issue—has a distinct advantage in trying to use legislative rules in its favor. But even this advantage does not necessarily thwart the majority rule principle. Certainly, alternative parliamentary devices enable a majority of legislators to come together to overcome any roadblocks that the majority party leadership has raised—most notably during the campaign finance debate, the threat and actual use of the discharge petition allowed reform legislation proponents to bring their bill to the floor in the House when they otherwise had no chance to do so. Another approach is to utilize the parliamentary rules as well as or better than the majority party leadership, such as the Shays-Meehan issue network did so effectively in the 105th Congress. Furthermore, one or more policy entrepreneurs could exert enough pressure on the leadership to force debate on the issue, such as John McCain did shortly after the 2000 elections.

The debate over campaign finance legislation in the 105th–107th Congresses that culminated with BCRA's passage shows the difficulty in trying to balance fundamental values of our political system when they come into conflict. No one approach is necessarily better than another; reasonable people can and will have differing opinions about how to resolve the conflict. The only thing that most people might agree on, though, is that when the conflict between two sets of fundamental principles becomes too great, some resolution acceptable to a majority of people must be found. The legislative process may seem inefficient, but it does provide a forum for all voices to be represented and heard. Additionally, it offers a mechanism by which the most fundamental problems can be addressed, even if only on an incremental basis until the next great conflict arises or if the compromise reached is no longer effective.

NOTES

1. Alison Mitchell, "6 Republicans Break Ranks on Campaign Finance Issue," *New York Times*, May 27, 1999.
2. Following the 1998 elections, Gingrich was held publicly accountable, even by key colleagues in the House, for the party's loss of seats in the election. After Representative Bob Livingston, R-La., the chair of the House Appropriations Committee, announced that he would challenge Gingrich for the Speakership and a number of Republican House members reportedly told Gingrich that they would not vote for him in any race for the Speakership, Gringrich made a surprise announcement on November 6, 1998, that not only would he not seek the Speakership but he would also be resigning his seat in the House of Representatives. Livingston was subsequently nominated without opposition to serve as the next Speaker. But before the 106th Congress opened, Livingston withdrew his name from consideration as Speaker when news of his marital infidelities came to light, just as the House was embroiled in debate to impeach President Clinton related to matters connected with the president's extramarital relationship with White House intern Monica Lewinsky. The Republican Party then chose Hastert as its Speaker.
3. Mitchell, "6 Republicans Break Ranks on Campaign Finance Issue."
4. Frank Bruni, "Tightrope for Republicans on Campaign Finance," *New York Times*, April 23, 1999.
5. The six Republican signers were: Michael N. Castle, Del.; Michael P. Forbes, N.Y.; Greg Ganske, Iowa; Nancy L. Johnson, Conn.; Constance A. Morella, Md.; and Christopher Shays, Conn. As an aside, Michael Forbes later switched to the Democratic Party.
6. This term was used by Edward Kangas, chairman of the global board of directors of Deloitte Touche Tohmatsu, in a *New York Times* op-ed piece explaining the CED's views. Edward A. Kangas, "Soft Money and Hard Bargains," *New York Times*, October 22, 1999.
7. For example, Representative James Barcia, D-Mich., admitted that he did not sign the Blue Dog discharge petition in part to maintain his 100 percent rating. Michael Grunwald, "Campaign Finance Issue Divides Abortion Foes," *Washington Post*, September 14, 1999. Representative Chris Shays estimated that the NRLC's position could cost the bill ten votes.
8. Helen Dewar, "Campaign Reforms Pass House," *Washington Post*, September 15, 1999.
9. One amendment had passed in the 105th Congress prohibiting foreign-born lawful permanent residents from contributing to federal campaigns. The second would "require non-officeholders—such as New York Senate hopeful

Hillary Rodham Clinton—to pay the full cost of travel when they fly on government planes to campaign." Dewar, "Campaign Reforms Pass House."

10. Robin Tone, "The 'Designated Spear Catcher' on Campaign Finance," *Washington Post*, July 19, 1999.

11. Senator John McCain, "McCain, Feingold Introduce Revised Campaign Finance Reform Bill for October Debate," press release, September 16, 1999.

12. Tone, "The 'Designated Spear Catcher' on Campaign Finance."

13. *Congressional Record*, October 14, 1999, p. S12585–S12586.

14. *Congressional Record*, October 14, 1999, p. S12592.

15. Alison Mitchell, "McCain Outmaneuvered in Vote on Campaign Finance Change," *New York Times*, October 19, 1999.

16. Alison Mitchell, "Republicans Pillory McCain in Debate over Soft Money," *New York Times*, October 15, 1999.

17. Further complicating the process was the additional burden that filibusters regarding rule changes require a two-thirds vote (67) for cloture instead of the normal three-fifths vote (60) required to end a filibuster during normal debate.

18. Mitchell, "McCain Outmaneuvered in Vote on Campaign Finance Change."

19. On Roll Call vote #330, taken on October 9, 1999, a "Motion to Invoke Cloture on Daschle Amdt. No. 2298," was rejected by a vote of 52 Yeas to 48 Nays. Senate Roll Call Vote #331, a "Motion to Invoke Cloture on Reid Amdt. No. 2299" taken on October 19, 1999, was rejected by a vote of 53 Yeas to 47 Nays. Senators Brownback, R.-Kans., Hutchinson, R-Ark., and Roth, R-Del., all voted for cloture on vote #331, but not on vote #330. Conversely, Senators Chafee, R-R.I., and Specter, R-Pa., voted against cloture on vote #331 and for cloture on vote #330.

20. Quoted in Jim Drinkard, "Campaign Reform 'Dead' for Another Year," *USA Today*, October 20, 1999.

21. "McCain Catches Leaders Off Guard with Campaign Finance Victory," *CQ Weekly*, June 10, 2000.

22. Lawrence L. Knutson, "Banning Secret Money: Clinton Signs Law Closing Campaign Finance Loophole," http://www.ABCNEWS.com, July, 1, 2000.

23. For example, in California and Washington, voters unaffiliated with either party can cast an unaffiliated ballot in the primaries. In 2000, McCain overwhelmingly won in this voting.

24. Michael Cornfield and Jonah Seiger, "The Net and the Nomination," in *The Making of the Presidential Candidates 2004*, ed. William G. Mayer (Lanham, MD: Rowman and Littlefield Publishers, Inc., 2004), 209. See also, Victoria A. Farrar-Myers, "Emerging Trends in Presidential Campaign Finance: The 2004 Campaign," (paper presented at the annual meeting of the Southern Political Science Association, New Orleans, 2005).

25. Matthew Tully and Derek Willis, "Cochran's Decision to Back McCain on Campaign Finance Overhaul Signals a Break in GOP Opposition," *CQ Weekly*, January 13, 2001.

26. Andrew Taylor and Derek Willis, "As Campaign Finance Debate Nears, Maneuvers and Worries Intensify,"*CQ Weekly,* March 17, 2001.

27. Ibid.

28. Ibid.

29. Karen Foerstel, "Campaign Finance: Passage Ends a Political Odyssey," *CQ Weekly,* March 23, 2002.

30. One interesting exception was an amendment offered by Senator Paul Wellstone, D-Minn., one of the most liberal members in the Senate at the time. Wellstone's amendment sought to ban certain interest groups from broadcasting political ads. Senators McCain and Feingold opposed adding the amendment to their bill because of concerns about its constitutionality. Senator McConnell, however, supported the amendment *because* he thought it was unconstitutional. McConnell proclaimed, "I thought a bill that's already unconstitutional ought to be made a little more unconstitutional. ...This bill, if it ever becomes law, is going to end up in court, and you're looking at the plaintiff." Quoted in Andrew Taylor, Derek Willis, and John Cochran, "McCain-Feingold Survives Hard Fight over Soft Money,"*CQ Weekly,* March 31, 2001. Although the Wellstone amendment received enough votes to be added to McCain-Feingold, its supporters did not see the addition as detrimental so long as the severability provision remained intact (meaning that even if the Supreme Court struck down the Wellstone amendment, the rest of the bill would survive).

31. Taylor, Willis, and Cochran, "McCain-Feingold Survives Hard Fight over Soft Money."

32. Ibid.

33. Quoted in Karen Foerstel and John Cochran, "House Democrats' Tepid Response May Imperil McCain-Feingold," *CQ Weekly,* April 7, 2001.

34. Quoted in Karen Foerstel, "Campaign Finance Bill Finds New Energy in Enron Ruins,"*CQ Weekly,* January 19, 2002. See also, Allan J. Cigler, "Enron, a Perceived Crisis in Public Confidence, and the Bipartisan Campaign Reform Act of 2002," *Review of Policy Research* 21 (2004): 233–252.

35. Quoted in Foerstel, "Campaign Finance Bill Finds New Energy in Enron Ruins."

36. Quoted in Karen Foerstel, "Opponents of Shays-Meehan Bet It All on a Conference,"*CQ Weekly,* February 9, 2002.

37. Foerstel, "Campaign Finance: Passage Ends a Political Odyssey."

38. Ibid.

39. See Thomas E. Mann, *Unsafe at Any Margin: Interpreting Congressional Elections* (Washington, D.C.: American Enterprise Institute, 1978).

40. Quoted in Taylor, Willis, and Cochran, "McCain-Feingold Survives Hard Fight over Soft Money."

4

FROM THE HALLS OF CONGRESS TO THE SUPREME COURT: THE IMPACT OF JUDICIAL INTERPRETATION ON PUBLIC POLICY

The universe of campaign finance regulation is one this Court has in part created and in part permitted by its course of decisions.

U.S. Supreme Court, *Randall v. Sorrell* (2006)
(Justice Anthony M. Kennedy, concurring).

As the debate on the Bipartisan Campaign Reform Act of 2002 (BCRA) was reaching its conclusion, Republican Senator Mitch McConnell of Kentucky repeatedly promised that he would be the lead plaintiff in a court case challenging the constitutionality of the Act. Within hours of President Bush signing BCRA into law, McConnell made good on that promise and filed a lawsuit in the United States District Court for the District of Columbia. This challenge to the constitutionality of the new law came as no surprise to its supporters. In fact, the bill contained a unique provision that called for expedited handling of any court challenge and appeal.

In the clash of fundamental values underlying campaign finance reform—that of fair and open elections versus an individual's First Amendment right to freedom of speech—the bill's supporters promoted the former while believing that BCRA did not place any unconstitutional restrictions on the latter. Its opponents, however, sought to move their fight against BCRA's limitations on political expression from the legislative branch to the judiciary. The lawmakers knew that questions about BCRA's constitutionality would plague the new law until the Supreme Court provided what they hoped would be a final determination putting the issue to rest. The need for a decision by the Court was even more imperative as candidates and parties throughout the nation needed to know what rules would govern their actions in the upcoming 2004 election. On December 10, 2003, approximately 21 months after BCRA's passage, all interested parties received their answer. The Supreme Court issued a splintered ruling in *McConnell v. Federal Election Commission* that found certain portions of BCRA unconstitutional, but upheld the primary provisions of the law, including those regulating issue ads and prohibiting soft money at the federal level.[1] The core of BCRA would remain the law of the land. All federal candidates and the national parties now knew that they would need to work within the regulatory framework that the new law established.

The *McConnell* decision was just one in a series of cases in which the Supreme Court has helped define the nation's campaign finance laws and shaped the terms of the debate on this important issue. The Court's decisions on campaign finance demonstrate in a broader sense the role that the judiciary plays in the policymaking labyrinth. After a bill completes its journey through the legislative process and becomes law, that law may still need to be interpreted, particularly when it touches upon core values embedded in the Constitution and underlying our nation's political system. Judicial interpretation of any piece of legislation can significantly impact how the public policy decisions made by the legislature are carried out. Therefore, the impact that the judiciary can have in our nation's policymaking process ought to be well understood.

The Founders' View of the Judiciary

The founders recognized a certain inherent weakness in the judiciary in that it had no independent means to enforce its decisions. Alexander Hamilton wrote in *Federalist* No. 78 that the judiciary "may truly be said to have neither FORCE nor WILL, but merely judgment; and must ultimately depend upon the aid of the executive arm even for the efficacy of its judgments."[2] Further, Hamilton noted that "in a government in which [the government's powers] are separated from each other, the judiciary, from the nature of its functions, will always be the least dangerous to the political rights of the Constitution; because it will be least in a capacity to annoy or injure them." [3] Accordingly, the judiciary is sometimes referred to as "the least dangerous branch." [4]

Nevertheless, in our system of checks and balances the judiciary does provide a powerful check on the actions of the legislative and executive branches—namely, the power to declare acts of Congress that the president has signed into or allowed to become law to be unconstitutional. Although the seminal case of *Marbury v. Madison* [5] (1803) was needed to cement this power of judicial review, the framers of the Constitution foresaw the important role of the judiciary in ensuring that actions of the legislature did not conflict with the basic tenets of the Constitution. As Alexander Hamilton wrote, "it is far more rational to suppose, that the courts were designed to be an intermediate body between the people and the legislature, in order, among other things, to keep the latter within the limits assigned to their authority." [6] Federal judges and justices, armed with this power and granted lifetime tenure to encourage their independent and deliberative reflection on issues presented to them, would provide a further check in our political system against the passions of the people and their tendency "to occasion dangerous innovations in the government, and serious oppressions of the minor party in the community." [7] The judiciary's duty, therefore, was to adhere to the fundamental principles embodied in the Constitution even if the present passions of the people (or their elected representatives) deviated from those principles.

In order to fully exercise its power to determine the constitutionality of a piece of legislation, the judiciary is required to interpret the laws that Congress passes. In Hamilton's words, "[t]he interpretation of the laws is the proper and peculiar province of the courts." [8] Perhaps the judiciary's most significant impact on the policymaking process lies in its ability to interpret laws in order to judge their constitutionality. How a court interprets a law in deciding its constitutionality dictates what interpretation will be used going forward as that law is implemented. In other words, if a court interprets a piece of legislation one way in order to find the act constitutional, then that is how the law must be interpreted by the executive branch in administering it and by the legislature if it seeks to craft subsequent revisions to the law. Similarly, if a court interprets a law differently and as a result finds it to be unconstitutional, then the court's interpretation and rationale subsequently shapes how Congress must structure any new law for it to be constitutional.

The Judiciary and Campaign Finance

Following the passage of the Federal Election Campaign Act (FECA) in 1971 and its major amendment in 1974, the Supreme Court addressed the fundamental constitutional issues raised by the legislation in the seminal case of *Buckley v. Valeo,*[9] 424 U.S. 1 (1976), with subsequent decisions filling in some of the unanswered questions that emerged over time. Similarly, the Supreme Court addressed BCRA's constitutional questions in *McConnell* with a stream of cases at the Supreme Court and lower appellate levels already filling in the remaining gaps. These cases, *Buckley* in particular, have shaped the terms of the campaign finance debate as well as helped give rise to and sustained continuing conflict between the competing values of fair and open elections and freedom of speech.

Buckley and Its Progeny

Of the Supreme Court's substantive conclusions in *Buckley,* the one with the most significant long-term impact was the distinction the Court made between contributions to a candidate and expenditures (whether by a candidate, party, group, or individual). The Court ruled that FECA's limitations on contributions to candidates were permissible, but that restrictions on expenditures violated the Constitution (except for limitations tied to a presidential candidate's receipt of public funding, in which case such limitations were a permitted condition to receiving such funding). As a result of this determination, not only were FECA's expenditure limitations struck down, but the landscape of campaign finance legislation was changed. Those looking to modify the nation's campaign finance laws could not expect to have limitations on expenditures sustained if challenged in court.

The impact of the *Buckley* decision, however, goes beyond what regulations were constitutionally permitted. In many ways, the fundamental clash of values between free speech and promoting fair and open elections untainted by corruption or the appearance of corruption can be traced directly to the Supreme Court's *Buckley* decision. The Court's interpretations of FECA and its amendments in light of the then-current campaign finance practices effectively eliminated a number of possible viewpoints and alternative rationales toward campaign finance regulation. As a result, such alternative approaches could no longer be used as a basis for accepting or rejecting future changes to the nation's campaign finance laws. This reduced the complex issue of campaign finance down to the two competing core values of freedom of speech and fair and open elections.

Consider, for example, the Court's consideration of the reasons that were offered in support of campaign finance regulation. FECA's supporters claimed that the extensive regulatory system would (1) prevent corruption or the appearance of corruption, (2) "equalize the relative ability of all citizens to affect the outcome of elections," and (3) check skyrocketing campaign costs to "open the political system more widely to candidates without access to sources of large amounts of money." [10] The Court deemed these last two as "ancillary" and concluded that they were insufficient to justify the restrictions found in FECA. Instead, the Court concluded that the only governmental interest that supported upholding FECA's limitations on contributions was "the prevention of corruption and the appearance of corruption spawned by the real or imagined coercive influence of large financial contributions on candidates' positions and on their actions if elected to office." [11]

The two rationales rejected by the Supreme Court are tied to a notion of equality of opportunity—namely, that each citizen should have the same opportunity to affect an election and each candidate should have an equal opportunity to be victorious respectively. Recall, however, from Chapter 1 that James Madison distinguished between a system of equal political rights and equality of property, recognizing that an inherent inequality in property is a result of our system of liberty and freedom. In the world of campaign finance generally and the *Buckley* decision specifically, an inequality in outcomes is specifically connected to an inequality in property. Some citizens and some candidates will have greater resources to have a greater impact on the outcome of an election. Just as Madison pointed out, though, the Supreme Court effectively acknowledged that the fundamental value of liberty needs to take precedence over the related effects resulting from the exercise of that liberty, even if it may be somewhat undesirable. In this case, the undesirable result is that some citizens have a greater ability to influence the outcomes of elections than others.

As a result of the *Buckley* decision, supporters of campaign finance regulations must base their arguments for reform on the notion that the use of money in elections corrupts the electoral process or at least would appear to corrupt it. On the one hand, this rationale is very broad and can be made to apply in many different contexts. In that regard, supporters of reform would seem to be able to justify a wide array of regulations so long as they can fit such regulations in the argument that the system is corrupted or appears to be corrupted absent the regulation. On the other hand, this broad rationale becomes vulnerable when specific examples of corruption are required.

Remember in Chapter 3, where Senator McConnell challenged reform supporters to demonstrate which of the members of the Senate had been corrupted by the presence of money in their elections. McConnell's rhetorical
question of "how can there be corruption if no one is corrupt" exposes a
weakness in the rationale that reform supporters must use following *Buckley:*
other than occasional cases of bribery or other improper actions taken by
members of Congress tied to campaign finance contributions, reform supporters have difficulty proving that the system is corrupted by the presence of
exorbitant funds in and around elections.

First Amendment advocates and other opponents of campaign finance
regulations are in a similar predicament. The Supreme Court's rationale
in *Buckley* for rejecting limitations on expenditures as unconstitutional
was based on a key assumption that equated money with speech itself. As
noted in Chapter 1, the Court believed that "a restriction on the amount
of money a person or group can spend on political communication during
a campaign necessarily reduces the quantity of expression by restricting
the number of issues discussed, the depth of their exploration, and the size
of the audience reached." [12] The Court drew the analogy that FECA's expenditure limitations were like driving a car on a tank of gas: "Being free
to engage in unlimited political expression subject to a ceiling on expenditures is like being free to drive an automobile as far and as often as one desires on a single tank of gasoline." [13] In the end, the Court concluded,
"[t]he First Amendment's protection against governmental abridgment of
free expression cannot properly be made to depend on a person's financial
ability to engage in public discussion." [14] By comparison, though, FECA's
limitations on contributions were upheld because the fundamental First
Amendment right involved in making a political contribution was the
symbolic act of the contribution itself and not necessarily the specific
amount given.

By equating the expenditure of money with the expression of speech,
the Court made such expenditures a fundamental constitutional right that
could be restricted only under strict scrutiny. [15] This interpretation, however, was not universally accepted at the time of the *Buckley* decision, nor
has it been fully accepted since. Specifically, one could look at limits on
spending money in elections not as an impermissible restriction of speech,
but instead as a permitted regulation of conduct. This was the approach
taken by the United States Court of Appeals for the District of Columbia
Circuit in *Buckley* when it upheld FECA's expenditure restrictions prior to
the Supreme Court's decision. In addition, Justice Byron White dissented

in *Buckley* from that portion of the Court's opinion that struck down expenditure limits:

> Proceeding from the maxim that "money talks," the Court finds that the expenditure limitations will seriously curtail political expression by candidates and interfere substantially with their chances for election. ... As an initial matter, the argument that money is speech and that limiting the flow of money to the speaker violates the First Amendment proves entirely too much. ... In any event, as it should be unnecessary to point out, money is not always equivalent to or used for speech, even in the context of political campaigns. ... The judgment of Congress was that reasonably effective campaigns could be conducted within the limits established by the Act and that the communicative efforts of these campaigns would not seriously suffer. In this posture of the case, there is no sound basis for invalidating the expenditure limitations, so long as the purposes they serve are legitimate and sufficiently substantial, which in my view they are. [16]

If the Supreme Court had not decided to equate money with speech, or subsequently decided that its original interpretation was not correct, supporters of more vigorous campaign finance regulation would be able to develop a much broader range of permissible campaign finance regulations.

Following *Buckley*, the courts continued to interpret the issues surrounding campaign finance regulations, including several cases that reached the Supreme Court. [17] After *Buckley* but prior to *McConnell*, much of the Supreme Court's "campaign finance jurisprudence has been based in large part on [the] distinction between contributions and expenditures." [18] In these cases, the Supreme Court generally followed the framework established in *Buckley*, striking down certain limitations on expenditures (e.g., *Colorado Republican Federal Campaign Committee v. Federal Election Commission* in 1996 [19]) while upholding limitations on contributions (e.g., *Nixon v. Shrink Missouri Government PAC* in 2000 [20]). Even the justices of the Supreme Court, though, were neither able nor willing to escape the continuing debate over the fundamental values at stake in campaign finance regulations.

Justice Clarence Thomas has been perhaps the most outspoken critic of the *Buckley* decision, arguing on multiple occasions that the Court should overturn *Buckley*. [21] His opinions have targeted what he sees as impermissible restrictions on freedom of speech and criticized the Court's reasons for upholding such restrictions. For example, in *Colorado Republican Federal Campaign Committee v. Federal Election Commission*, a 1996 case that dealt with limitations on expenditures made by political parties to their candidates, Thomas argued:

> The Government [as a party to the case defending the constitutionality of the law in question] does not explain precisely what it means by "corruption," however; the closest thing to an explanation the Government offers is that "corruption" is "the real or imagined coercive influence of large financial contributions on candidates' positions and on their actions if elected to office."...As applied in the specific context of campaign funding by political parties, the anticorruption rationale loses its force. ...For instance, if the Democratic Party spends large sums of money in support of a candidate who wins, takes office, and then implements the Party's platform, that is not corruption; that is successful advocacy of ideas in the political marketplace and representative government in a party system. ...[T]he Government, which bears the burden of demonstrating that the recited harms are real, not merely conjectural, has identified no more proof of the corrupting dangers of coordinated expenditures than it has of independent expenditures. And insofar as it appears that Congress did not actually enact [the provision of the law in question] in order to stop corruption by political parties but rather for the constitutionally insufficient purpose of reducing what it saw as wasteful and excessive campaign spending, the statute's ceilings on coordinated expenditures are as unwarranted as the caps on independent expenditures. [22]

In other words, Justice Thomas contended that no definitive proof of corruption had been offered.

Justice Anthony Kennedy also took a pro-First Amendment approach in his dissenting opinion in the *Shrink Missouri* case. He offered a perspective, though, that could bridge the gap between the apparently competing values of fair and open elections and the right to freedom of speech. For Kennedy, these values are not necessarily in conflict with each other; instead, the best way to ensure fair and open elections is to have unrestricted expression of political ideas. Kennedy wrote that "[w]hether our officeholders can discharge their duties in a proper way when they are beholden to certain interests both for reelection and for campaign support is, I should think, of constant concern not alone to citizens but to conscientious officeholders themselves. There are no easy answers, but the Constitution relies on one: open, robust, honest, unfettered speech that the voters can examine and assess in an ever-changing and more complex environment." [23]

Expressions by Supreme Court justices who want to overturn the *Buckley* decision have not been limited solely to those who believe that campaign finance restrictions should be eliminated. Justice White elaborated on his argument from *Buckley* in such cases as *Federal Election Commission v. Massachusetts Citizens for Life, Inc.* (1986) and *Federal Election Commission v. National Conservative Political Action Committee* (1985). In the latter case, he wrote:

> The First Amendment protects the right to speak, not the right to spend, and limitations on the amount of money that can be spent are not the same as restrictions on speaking. I agree with the majority that the expenditures in this case "produce" core First Amendment speech. But that is precisely the point: they produce such speech; they are not speech itself. ...The burden on actual speech imposed by limitations on the spending of money is minimal and indirect. All rights of direct political expression and advocacy are retained. Even under the campaign laws as originally enacted, everyone was free to spend as much as they chose to amplify their views on general political issues, just not specific candidates. The restrictions, to the extent they do affect speech, are viewpoint-neutral and indicate no hostility to the speech itself or its effects. [24]

Justice John Paul Stevens has followed the line of reasoning of Justice White and extended it to criticize the key assumption in *Buckley* that equated money with speech. Bluntly addressing the issue in his concurring opinion in *Shrink Missouri*, Stevens argued, "[m]oney is property; it is not speech. ... Speech has the power to inspire volunteers to perform a multitude of tasks on a campaign trail, on a battleground, or even on a football field. Money, meanwhile, has the power to pay hired laborers to perform the same tasks. It does not follow, however, that the First Amendment provides the same measure of protection to the use of money to accomplish such goals as it provides to the use of ideas to achieve the same results." [25]

The strong language that Justices Thomas, Kennedy, White, and Stevens employed demonstrates that campaign finance is not just a divisive political or legislative issue. It also is a complex constitutional question that evokes positions as strongly held by the justices of the Supreme Court as those possessed by the members of Congress. Like congressional lawmakers, however, the justices must be able to find a position and rationale that a majority—or in some cases at least a plurality—of the members of the Court can support in order to issue a decision. [26] In addition, the Court's reliance on judicial precedent in deciding cases in which similar points have been previously litigated—the doctrine of *stare decisis*—results in judicial rulings remaining in effect and continuing to be followed despite criticisms levied against the original decision.

Such is the nature of the Court's *Buckley* decision and the cases that followed in its wake. The Court issued a *per curium* opinion in *Buckley*, meaning that the author(s) of the opinion were not specifically named as they are in most of the Court's decisions. Although the decisions and the rationales underlying the *Buckley* decision were not always internally consistent, the Court managed to find a basis on which a sufficient number of justices could come together to render a decision in the case. In the end, the Court upheld some of FECA's regulations governing campaign finance while striking down others. This framework, in addition to structuring the legislative debate over campaign finance in the years that followed the *Buckley* decision, established the basis on which the Court would make its campaign-finance decisions after *Buckley*. But despite *Buckley*'s continuing influence, a persistent question in nearly all of the post-*Buckley* Supreme Court cases has been whether *Buckley* should remain the law of the land on campaign finance or be overruled.

McConnell and Its Progeny

Section 403 of BCRA contained unusual special rules for expedited judicial review if the legislation were challenged on constitutional grounds. Specifically, any such action had to be filed in the United Stated District Court for the District of Columbia and would be heard by a three-judge panel convened particularly for the case. Further, any appeal from the District Court had to be commenced within 30 days after the final decision by the trial court and would go directly to the Supreme Court, bypassing the customary intermediate appeal to the U.S. Court of Appeals. BCRA also expressly permitted members of Congress to bring an action challenging BCRA's constitutionality. Senator Mitch McConnell did just that, fulfilling his promise to be the named plaintiff in the case.

The District Court rendered its opinion in *McConnell v. Federal Election Commission*[27] on May 1, 2003, striking down some parts of BCRA as unconstitutional, but upholding others. But the court's opinion raised more questions than it answered. Some observers speculated that the District Court knew that whatever it decided, the Supreme Court would weigh in and decide *McConnell* for itself. In some ways, the District Court could be said to have had a *free vote* of its own.

As for the Supreme Court's decision in the case, it ruled that certain portions of BCRA were unconstitutional,[28] but allowed the legislation's primary components—those addressing soft money and issue ads—to stand. The Court had a difficult time finding a single position that a majority of the justices could support. For example, Justice Stevens and Justice O'Connor wrote the governing opinion with respect to BCRA Titles I (dealing with soft money) and II (addressing issue ads and electioneering communications), and they were joined by Justices Souter, Ginsburg, and Breyer. Chief Justice Rehnquist wrote the opinion with respect to miscellaneous provisions in BCRA Section III (miscellaneous provisions) and IV (severability, effective date, and judicial review), while Justice Breyer wrote with respect to Section V (additional disclosure provisions). Interestingly, though, Chief Justice Rehnquist, Justice Scalia, Justice Thomas, Justice Kennedy, and Justice Stevens (joined by Justice Ginsburg and Breyer) each dissented with respect to at least one portion of the Court's opinion.

In the end, *McConnell* did not overturn *Buckley*. Instead, the Court perpetuated the underlying rationales found in the *Buckley* decision. Most notably, the Stevens and O'Connor opinion propped up the underlying argument in support of federal regulation of campaign finance, specifically the issue of the potentially corruptive force associated with large amounts of money in elections. In upholding BCRA's prohibition on soft money, Stevens and O'Connor wrote that "[t]he evidence connects soft money manipulation of the legislative calendar, leading to Congress's failure to enact, among other things, generic drug legislation, tort reform, and tobacco legislation. ...To claim that such actions do not change legislative outcomes surely misunderstands the legislative process."[29] The opinion cited statements by sitting and former Senators that were introduced as evidence at the trial-court level. These statements indicated that soft money contributions had influenced the outcomes of proposed legislation in these areas. Critics of campaign finance regulation such as Senator Mitch McConnell and Justice Thomas had previously demanded evidence that money in elections led to corruption; in *McConnell*, the Court's decision was grounded in such evidence. Stevens and O'Connor observed that "[j]ust as troubling to a functioning democracy as classic quid pro quo corruption is the danger that officeholders will decide issues not on the merits or the desires of their constituencies, but according to the wishes of those who have made large financial contributions valued by the officeholder."[30]

As noted in Chapter 1, money can be seen as a corrupting force if it distorts the representational relationship between the electorate and elected officials by giving a greater voice to a minority faction with greater financial resources. This conception of corruption—based on the "corrosive and distorting effects of immense aggregations of wealth"—is much broader than a quid pro quo exchange with individual members of Congress; it is a much more systemic conception of "corruption in the political arena." [31] While the Court may have implicitly adopted such a conception in *Buckley,* Stevens and O'Connor in *McConnell* expressly based their opinion on it.

What Stevens and O'Connor pointed to as evidence of the corruptive influence of money in elections, however, Justice Thomas continued to see simply as the successful promotion of ideas within the political marketplace. "Apparently, winning in the marketplace of ideas is no longer a sign that the ultimate good has been reached by the free trade in ideas or that the speaker has survived the best test of truth by having the thought get itself accepted in the competition of the market," Thomas wrote in dissent. "It is now evidence of corruption. This conclusion is antithetical to everything for which the First Amendment stands." [32] For his part, Justice Kennedy attacked the Stevens and O'Connor opinion for its use of a broader conception of corruption— one that he considered to be a "quick and subtle shift, and one that breaks new ground." [33] He argued that:

> Favoritism and influence are not…avoidable in representative politics. It is in the nature of an elected representative to favor certain policies, and, by necessary corollary, to favor the voters and contributors who support those policies. It is well understood that a substantial and legitimate reason, if not the only reason, to cast a vote for, or to make a contribution to, one candidate over another is that the candidate will respond by producing those political outcomes the supporter favors. Democracy is premised on responsiveness.[34]

The Stevens and O'Connor section of the opinion also undercut some of the theoretical basis of the First Amendment arguments that Justices Thomas and Kennedy had advanced in prior cases. Without going as far as concluding that money is not speech, as Justice Stevens previously argued, the *McConnell* opinion recognized that the *Buckley* "magic words" test "was an endpoint of statutory interpretation, not a first principle of constitutional law" [35] and was "functionally meaningless." [36] As a result, restrictions on electioneering communications that did *not* expressly advocate the election or defeat of a candidate were not necessarily impermissible limitations on an individual's First Amendment rights. Justices Stevens and O'Connor concluded that "*Buckley*'s express advocacy line, in short, has not aided the legislative effort to combat real or apparent corruption, and Congress enacted BCRA to correct the flaws it found in the existing system." [37] This conclusion implicitly gives greater weight to the value of having fair and open elections untainted by corruption or the appearance of corruption over the restrictions on speech associated with BCRA's regulations related to electioneering communications.

The Stevens/O'Connor opinion also took issue with the view that Justice Kennedy expressed in his dissent in *Shrink Missouri* that the key to having fair and open elections was to permit unfettered political speech unhampered by regulations or restrictions. They wrote, "[c]uriously, Plaintiffs [i.e., McConnell and the other parties challenging BCRA's constitutionality] want to preserve the ability to run these advertisements while hiding behind dubious and misleading names. ...Given these tactics, Plaintiffs never satisfactorily answer the question of how uninhibited, robust, and wide-open speech can occur when organizations hide themselves from the scrutiny of the voting public." [38] Chief Justice Rehnquist and Justices Scalia, Thomas, and Kennedy each countered the Stevens/O'Connor opinion on First Amendment grounds, with Thomas providing the most direct response to the issue of anonymous political speech:

The historical evidence indicates that Founding-era Americans opposed attempts to require that anonymous authors reveal their identities on the ground that forced disclosure violated the freedom of the press. Indeed, this Court has expressly recognized that the interest in having anonymous works enter the marketplace of ideas unquestionably outweighs any public interest in requiring disclosure as a condition of entry, and thus that an author's decision to remain anonymous is an aspect of the freedom of speech protected by the First Amendment. The Court now backs away from this principle, allowing the established right to anonymous speech to be stripped away based on the flimsiest of justifications. [39]

In many key ways, the *McConnell* decision favors the approach of promoting fair and open elections over the concerns about allowing impermissible restrictions on an individual's freedom of speech. The decision upheld BCRA's core provisions focusing on the *twin evils* of soft money and issue ads and bolstered—perhaps even broadened—the Court-approved rationale that the government has a compelling interest in promoting fair and open elections free from corruption or the appearance of corruption. From the Stevens/O'Connor perspective, banning soft money and regulating electioneering communications did not amount to unconstitutional restrictions on freedom of speech. The *McConnell* decision, however, turned out not to be indicative of a permanent swing toward the pro-regulation perspective, but was instead just a small shift in the ongoing balancing of the competing values at stake.

The major campaign-finance cases decided since *McConnell* have continued to provide a mixed approach, all the while working within the framework established by *Buckley*. The first major campaign finance case to reach the Supreme Court after *McConnell* was *Randall v. Sorrell*[40] (2006), a case addressing Vermont's limitations on both candidate expenditures and contributions to candidates. The outcome of the *Randall* case mirrored many of the cases that preceded it, featuring: (1) a fractured opinion on which a majority of the court could not agree to a unified approach, although six different members were able to reach similar conclusions albeit based on different rationales, (2) continued calls for overruling *Buckley* from both pro-First Amendment advocates like Justice Thomas and Justice Kennedy, as well as from regulation supporter Justice Stevens, and (c) a substantive decision that retained and applied *Buckley*'s finding with respect to unconstitutional restrictions placed upon expenditures. Perhaps the most notable aspect of the *Randall* opinion is that it struck down the Vermont law's limits on contributions, even though the Supreme Court had allowed limitations on contributions in *Buckley*. As Justice Breyer, joined by new Court members Chief Justice John Roberts and Justice Samuel Alito, wrote:

> *Buckley* recognized that contribution limits...unlike expenditure limits...involve little direct restraint on the contributor's speech...[and] are permissible as long as the government demonstrates that the limits are closely drawn to match a sufficiently important interest. ...[W]e have no scalpel to probe each possible contribution level...[and] cannot determine with any degree of exactitude the precise restriction necessary to carry out the statute's legitimate objectives....Nonetheless, as *Buckley* acknowledged, we must recognize the existence of some lower bound. At some point the constitutional risks to the democratic electoral process become too great. After all, the interests underlying contribution limits, preventing corruption and the appearance of corruption, directly implicate the integrity of our electoral process. Yet that rationale does not simply mean the lower the limit, the better. That is because contribution limits that are too low can also harm the electoral process by preventing challengers from mounting effective campaigns against incumbent officeholders, thereby reducing democratic accountability.[41]

In other words, limits on contributions are not permissible per se, but must be proportionate to the governmental interest of reducing corruption or the appearance of corruption.

Other post-*McConnell* cases decided at the appellate level have had mixed results. Some cases have upheld certain regulations on campaign finance activity (e.g., *Alaska Right to Life Committee v. Miles*[42] in 2006), while others have struck down restrictions on First Amendment grounds (e.g., *American Civil Liberties Union of Nevada v. Heller* in 2004[43]). Perhaps the most telling comment made by an appellate court was in the Seventh Circuit United States Court of Appeals case *Majors v. Abell*[44] (2004), where Judge Richard Posner concluded, "Reluctant, *without clearer guidance from the [Supreme] Court,* to interfere with state experimentation in the baffling and conflicted field of campaign finance law without guidance from authoritative precedent, we hold that the Indiana statute [that requires advertisements that expressly advocate the election or defeat of a candidate to include a disclaimer giving notice of the identity of the person who paid for the communication] is constitutional."[45] Judge Posner's statement about the need for clearer guidance from the Supreme Court suggests that the nature of the issue of campaign finance is one in which such clarity may not ever be reached, and the courts—just like legislators in Congress and state legislatures—will constantly be seeking ways to balance the competing values at stake in any campaign finance legislation.

Such an approach to judicial analysis—namely, that of balancing competing values—underlies much of the Supreme Court's decision in *Federal Election Commission v. Wisconsin Right to Life* in 2007.[46] On first blush, the decision appears to strongly rebuff BCRA's attempt to prohibit a corporation from using its general treasury funds to pay for any electioneering communication within 30 days prior to a federal primary election or 60 days before a federal general election where an identified candidate is running. Along these lines, the Court concluded that issue ads, or at least advertisements that could reasonably be interpreted to be issue ads, could not be subject to BCRA's regulations. But the Court also did not overturn the portion of the *McConnell* decision which concluded that BCRA's relevant provisions (BCRA §203) dealing with express advocacy and its functional equivalents were *facially constitutional,* instead specifically focusing on BCRA's provisions *as-applied* to certain advertisements in question. Further, the court implied support for BCRA's regulation of *sham* issue ads—that is, ads that are electioneering in nature but do not use any of *Buckley*'s magic words such as "vote for"—that were of the greatest concern for BCRA's sponsors in Congress.

Like a number of the cases discussed above, the *Wisconsin Right to Life* decision failed to bring a simple majority of the Court together behind a single rationale. The official opinion of the Court was adopted by only two justices,

Chief Justice John Roberts and Justice Samuel Alito. Justice Antonin Scalia, joined by Justices Clarence Thomas and Anthony Kennedy, concurred in part and concurred in the judgment (meaning that Scalia reached the same conclusion as did Chief Justice Roberts but for different reasons), thus providing majority support for the judgment itself. Whereas the Roberts opinion reached its conclusion by working within the framework established by the *McConnell* decision, Scalia contended that part of the Court's decision in *McConnell* as it related to BCRA §203 should be overturned. Justice Souter dissented from the Court's opinion, and was joined by Justices Stevens, Ginsburg, and Breyer. Justice Alito even wrote a short concurring opinion noting that if the Court's decision proved to be unworkable, the Supreme Court might once again have to reconsider the issues in the case at hand as well as its decision in *McConnell;* a conclusion that Justice Souter also reached, albeit for different reasons. [47]

The *Wisconsin Right to Life* case focused on whether BCRA's regulations on express advocacy and its *functional equivalent* (i.e., communications that were electioneering in nature, but did not expressly advocate the election or defeat of a candidate) were permissible when applied in certain contexts. The issue specifically concerned whether certain ads that Wisconsin Right to Life conceded were otherwise prohibited by BCRA §203 (given their timing and the corporation's general treasury funds being used to pay for the ads) were the functional equivalent of express advocacy or issue advocacy. If the former, the ads would be subject to BCRA's restrictions; if the latter, the Court concluded that the ads could be run without having to comply with BCRA's regulations (the Court decided that the government did not have a sufficiently compelling interest to warrant regulation of this form of political speech). In order to "give the benefit of any doubt to protecting rather than stifling speech," the Court indicated that "the proper standard for an as-applied challenge to BCRA §203 must be objective." [48] To this end, the Court identified such an objective standard and, in applying this standard to the ads in question, laid out the characteristics it believed distinguished issue advocacy from express advocacy:

> In light of these considerations, a court should find that an ad is the functional equivalent of express advocacy only *if the ad is susceptible of no reasonable interpretation other than as an appeal to vote for or against a specific candidate.* Under this test, [Wisconsin Right to Life's] three ads are plainly not the functional equivalent of express advocacy. First their content is consistent with that of a genuine issue ad: The ads focus on a legislative issue, take a

position on the issue, exhort the public to adopt that position, and urge the public to contact public officials with respect to the matter. Second, their content lacks indicia of express advocacy: The ads do not mention an election, candidacy, political party, or challenger; and they do not take a position on a candidate's character, qualifications, or fitness for office.[49]

A compromise position is often subject to criticisms from both sides of the debate on an issue, and the balancing-of-interests approach that Chief Justice Roberts took in *Wisconsin Right to Life* is no exception. Justice Scalia contended that the objective standard set forth above was too vague, basing his argument on the clear distinction that the *Buckley* "magic words" test offers: "[T]he way to indulge [the instinct that the distinction between issue advocacy and political advocacy is often difficult to determine] is either to eliminate restrictions on independent expenditures altogether or to *confine* them to one side of the *traditional line*—the express-advocacy line, set in concrete on a calm day by *Buckley,* several decades ago. [BCRA] Section 203's line is bright, but it bans vast amounts of political advocacy indistinguishable from hitherto protected speech."[50] To that end, Justice Scalia concluded that the Court's opinion did not go far enough in resolving the problem he saw, and believed that "[t]oday's cases make it apparent that...*McConnell*'s holding concerning §203 was wrong"[51] and should be overturned.

On the other side of the issue, Justice Souter's dissent criticized the Court's opinion for effectively overturning the portion of the *McConnell* decision addressing §203: "There is neither a theoretical nor a practical basis to claim that *McConnell*'s treatment of §203 survives. ...The price of *McConnell*'s demise as authority on §203 seems to me to be a high one. The Court (and, I think, the country) loses when important precedent is overruled without good reason."[52] Souter contended that BCRA still offers corporations numerous avenues for engaging in issue advocacy without violating BCRA's prohibitions, and the result of the case would facilitate "easy circumvention" of federal campaign finance regulations.[53]

Despite these criticisms from Scalia and Souter, the balancing-of-interests approach in Chief Justice Roberts's opinion prevailed and will provide the determinative guidance on the issue of corporate spending on issue advocacy versus express advocacy and its functional equivalent. As a result, BCRA, as-applied, may still prevent the most egregious examples of *sham issue ads,* which are susceptible to no reasonable interpretation other than being the functional equivalent of express advocacy, but will not prohibit as large of a scope of advertisements as BCRA's legislative sponsors originally envisioned. Moreover, in reaching its conclusion, the Court also signaled an important point to be kept in mind in balancing the competing interests of freedom of speech and having fair and open elections: "Where the First Amendment is implicated, the tie goes to the speaker, not the censor." [54]

Extending the Labyrinth: Implications of Judicial Interpretation

In our system of government the influence of the judiciary is limited to the issues contained in the cases brought before it. Unlike the legislature, which is free to choose the areas of policy it wants to affect, the judiciary exercises power only when litigants with a dispute choose to resolve that dispute in the courts. Despite the limited purpose of this "least dangerous branch" (and notwithstanding any argument over the extent to which judges should be policymakers, if at all), [55] judicial decisions have a substantive impact on the policymaking process. The quotation from Justice Kennedy at the start of this chapter—that the Supreme Court helped create and permit the universe of campaign finance regulations that exists today—succinctly captures this reality.

When Congress first enacted the Federal Election Campaign Act (FECA) in 1971 and broadened it in 1974, its members sought to implement a comprehensive regime of campaign finance regulation. The Supreme Court's *Buckley* decision, however, segmented that comprehensive approach, upholding certain restrictions on political contributions while striking down limitations on expenditures as unconstitutional. In doing so, the Court defined the parameters that have shaped the campaign finance debate ever since. The *Buckley* decision required any campaign finance restriction to be tied to preventing corruption or the appearance of corruption in order for that restriction to be permissible. Similarly, the Court's decision to equate money with speech placed the First Amendment in the middle of the debate and heightened the level of judicial scrutiny that must be used when assessing whether any infringement on the freedom to make political expenditures—and thus, the freedom of speech—could be permitted.

Since *Buckley,* interested parties have used the courts to try to reach a definitive conclusion regarding campaign finance regulations. Looking to the courts for answers when a legislative solution cannot be found is a form of *politics by other means.* In politics by other means, we refer to situations where proponents of a particular issue or view seek to promote their position or resolve conflicts outside the normal legislative process. In the case of BCRA, the policy labyrinth was extended beyond the halls of Congress into the judiciary. Both proponents and opponents of the law expected their side to prevail in the courts and provided a means to obtain an expedited resolution. The Supreme Court's splintered decision in *McConnell*, however, did not provide clear guidance about what BCRA meant for conducting campaigns. More significantly, the decision demonstrated the limitations in using the courts to find an authoritative solution to the issue of campaign finance regulation.

If anything, the campaign finance cases since *Buckley*, including *McConnell*, mirror the difficulties that Congress has had in trying to reach definitive conclusions on the issue. These difficulties start with multiple viewpoints, some of them very strongly held, that perpetuate the tension between the core values of freedom of speech and ensuring fair and open elections. Like legislators trying to hold together a coalition to win passage of a new law, the nine justices on the Supreme Court must reach some sort of consensus in order to issue a ruling. Also, much as a bill's sponsor in Congress may need to make strategic concessions to broaden support for a piece of legislation, Supreme Court justices have been known to moderate their positions to garner majority support for their opinions. Consider, for example, Justice Stevens's assertion that money was not speech in his concurring opinion in *Shrink Missouri* (a position he reiterated in his dissenting opinion in *Randall*). When it came to the opinion he authored with Justice O'Connor in *McConnell*, Justice Stevens did not employ that position. More than anything, however, the *politics by other means* approach of looking to the courts for answers regarding campaign finance is not likely to yield any definitive results, because the Court is working within the confines of the framework that the *Buckley* decision provided.

One thing the Supreme Court can do, however, is to overturn *Buckley*. Certainly, a number of members of the Court, including Justices Thomas, Kennedy, and Stevens, have advocated this, albeit for different reasons. According to Justice Kennedy, one benefit of doing so would be to give legislators a clean slate. "I would overrule *Buckley* and then free Congress or state legislatures to attempt some new reform, if, based upon their own considered view of the First Amendment, it is possible to do so." [56] In other words, if the Court were to strip away the framework that *Buckley* created, the members of Congress would not be required to formulate any new legislation within the parameters that they currently must follow. Freed of such restraints, Congress could take a fresh look at the issue of campaign finance and seek to develop a new approach toward having a comprehensive and constitutional approach to campaign finance.

Overturning *Buckley,* though, would require the members of Congress to engage in a complete reassessment of the priorities of how elections should function in our political system. The debate would not focus just on the issues of fair and open elections and free speech, but would include other core values that have not been included in the campaign finance debate in the wake of the *Buckley* decision—values like equality of the exercise of political rights, one person–one vote, and the nature of political representation. Undertaking such a debate would require an exercise of political will on the part of all three branches of government—legislative, executive, and judicial. Actors in each branch would need to determine what new framework we as a nation would want and can accept given our constitutional system.

The alternative would be to keep the *Buckley* framework in place, imperfect and unsatisfying as it may be. But it is a known framework within which legislators, candidates, political parties, and interest groups have grown accustomed to operating. For example, the Court acknowledged in *McConnell* that BCRA was structured based on the environment created in part by *Buckley:* "We are also mindful of the fact that in its lengthy deliberations leading to the enactment of BCRA, Congress properly relied on the recognition of its authority contained in *Buckley* and its progeny." [57]

The *Buckley* framework has been in place for over 30 years, but has proved able to incorporate incremental policymaking that addresses the most problematic issues at any given time, such as shown with BCRA. In doing so, the *Buckley* framework has provided a shortcut through the policy labyrinth, allowing such problems to be addressed without directly confronting the multiple competing values at stake in campaign finance policymaking. The fundamental policy question thus becomes whether it is best to continue to operate within an imperfect but familiar framework, or delve into the unknown and start over to develop a truly comprehensive approach to campaign finance policy.

NOTES

1. *McConnell v. Federal Election Commission,* 540 U.S. 93 (2003).
2. *Federalist* No. 78.
3. Ibid.

4. See, e.g., Alexander M. Bickel, *The Least Dangerous Branch: The Supreme Court at the Bar of Politics* (New Haven: Yale University Press, 1986).

5. *Marbury v. Madison,* 1 Cranch 137 (1803). *Marbury* institutionalized the Supreme Court's power of *judicial review*—that is, the power to strike down a law as unconstitutional.

6. *Federalist* No. 78.

7. Ibid.

8. Ibid.

9. *Buckley v. Valeo,* 424 U.S. 1 (1976).

10. *Buckley,* 424 U.S. at 26.

11. Ibid.

12. Buckley, 424 U.S. at 19.

13. *Buckley,* 424 U.S. at 19 (footnote 18)

14. *Buckley,* 424 U.S. at 49.

15. When the Supreme Court reviews a law that restricts an individual's exercise of a fundamental constitutional right, the Court applies a *strict scrutiny* test. Strict scrutiny requires the government to have a *compelling interest* in restricting the fundamental right and for the law in question to be *narrowly tailored* to that governmental interest. Because of these high standards, many laws examined under the strict scrutiny test are held to be unconstitutional.

16. *Buckley,* 424 U.S. at 262-264 (White, J., concurring in part and dissenting in part).

17. These cases include: *California Medical Association v. Federal Election Commission,* 453 U.S. 182 (1981); *Federal Election Commission v. National Conservative Political Action Committee,* 470 U.S. 480 (1985); *Federal Election Commission v. Massachusetts Citizens for Life, Inc.,* 479 U.S. 238 (1986); *McIntyre v. Ohio Elections Comm'n.,* 514 U.S. 334, 354, 131 L. Ed. 2d 426, 115 S. Ct. 1511 (1995); *Colorado Republican Federal Campaign Committee v. Federal Election Commission,* 518 U.S. 604 (1996); *Nixon v. Shrink Missouri Government PAC,* 528 U.S. 377 (2000); and *Federal Election Commission v. Colorado Republican Federal Campaign Committee,* 533 U.S. 431 (2001).

18. *Colorado Republican Federal Campaign Committee v. Federal Election Commission,* 518 U.S. 604, 635 (1996) (Thomas, J. dissenting).

19. *Colorado Republican Federal Campaign Committee v. Federal Election Commission,* 518 U.S. 604 (1996).

20. *Nixon v. Shrink Missouri Government PAC,* 528 U.S. 377 (2000).

21. See, for example, *Colorado Republican Federal Campaign Committee v. Federal Election Commission,* 518 U.S. 604 (1996); *Nixon v. Shrink Missouri Government PAC,* 528 U.S. 377 (2000); and *McConnell v. Federal Election Commission,* 540 U.S. 93 (2003).

22. *Colorado Republican Federal Campaign Committee,* 518 U.S. at 645-647 (Thomas, J., concurring in part and disssenting in part; internal quotations and citations omitted).

23. *Shrink Missouri*, 528 U.S. at 409 (Kennedy, J. dissenting).

24. *National Conservative Political Action Committee*, 470 U.S. at 508-509 (White, J., dissenting).

25. *Shrink Missouri*, 528 U.S. at 398 (Stevens, J. concurring).

26. As a general premise, Supreme Court cases are decided on a majority-rule basis, in which a single opinion obtains the support of a majority of the justices. Sometimes, however, in complex cases, no single opinion and rationale may obtain majority support, but a specific outcome does. In other words, five or more justices may reach the same determination of what they believe the result of the case should be, but they do so based on two or more different rationales. In this situation, the opinion that garners the greatest number of votes (among those that comprise the majority outcome) is referred to as a plurality opinion and would become the opinion of the Court. All other opinions that support the majority outcome become concurrences, while those that would reach a different outcome would become dissenting opinions. As a hypothetical example, suppose five justices all believe that a case should be decided for X. Justice A writes an opinion supported by Justices B and C, and based on Rationale I. Justice D writes an opinion supported by Justice E, and based on Rationale II. In this example, the outcome of the case is decided in favor of X, Justice A's opinion—referred to as the plurality opinion—becomes the opinion of the Court, and Rationale I establishes the precedent for the Court to consider in future cases. Justice D's opinion employing Rationale II becomes a concurring opinion. Even if the remaining justices all join a single opinion that would decide the case for Y (instead of X), that opinion would become a dissent. Understanding the difference between a majority and plurality opinion is important in the context of campaign finance because many important cases (for example, *McConnell* and *Wisconsin Right to Life*) have been decided on the basis of a plurality opinion.

27. *McConnell v. Federal Election Commission*, 251 F. Supp. 2d 176 (D.D.C. 2003); *McConnell v. Federal Election Commission*, 251 F. Supp. 2d 948 (D.D.C. 2003).

28. The provisions of BCRA that the Court found unconstitutional included (1) a ban on contributions to candidates and donations to parties by people under the age of 18; and (2) a prohibition on political parties, after the date on which a candidate receives a party's nomination, (a) from making coordinated expenditures for a candidate if the party previously made independent expenditures in support of that candidate, and (b) from making independent expenditures for a candidate for whom the party previously made coordinated expenditures.

29. *McConnell*, 540 U.S. at 150.

30. *McConnell*, 540 U.S. at 153.

31. *Austin v. Michigan Chamber of Commerce*, 494 U.S. 652 at 660 (1990); quoted in part in *McConnell*, 540 U.S. at 205.

32. *McConnell,* 540 U.S. at 274 (Thomas J., concurring in part and dissenting in part; internal quotations omitted).

33. *McConnell,* 540 U.S. at 295 (Kennedy J., concurring in part and dissenting in part).

34. *McConnell,* 540 U.S. at 297 (Kennedy J., concurring in part and dissenting in part).

35. *McConnell,* 540 U.S. at 190.

36. *McConnell,* 540 U.S. at 193.

37. *McConnell,* 540 U.S. at 194.

38. *McConnell,* 540 U.S. at 197 (internal quotations omitted).

39. *McConnell,* 540 U.S. at 275-6 (Thomas J., concurring in part and dissenting in part; internal quotations omitted).

40. *Randall v. Sorrell,* 126 S.Ct. 2479 (2006).

41. *Randall,* 126 U.S. at 2491-92 (internal quotations and citations omitted).

42. *Alaska Right to Life Committee v. Miles,* 441 F.3d. 773 (9th Cir. 2006).

43. *American Civil Liberties Union of Nevada v. Heller,* 378 F.3d 979 (9th Cir. 2004).

44. *Majors v. Abell,* 361 F.3d 349 (7th Cir. 2004).

45. *Majors,* 361 F.3d at 355 (emphasis added).

46. The Court's decision in *Wisconsin Right to Life* was announced on June 25, 2007, as this book was in its final stages before being published but in enough time for the authors to take the decision into consideration. Citations to *Wisconsin Right to Life* shall be to the slip opinion made available through the Supreme Court's Web site: http://www.supremecourtus.gov.

47. Souter wrote near the end of his dissent: "The facts are too powerful to be ignored, and further efforts at campaign finance reform will come. It is only the legal landscape that now is altered, and it may be that today's departure from precedent will drive further reexamination of the constitutional analysis; of the distinction between contributions and expenditures, or the relation between spending and speech, which have given structure to our thinking since *Buckley* itself was decided. *Federal Election Commission v. Wisconsin Right to Life, Inc.,* Slip Opinion (Dissent), J. Souter, pp. 34–35.

48. *Wisconsin Right to Life,* Slip Opinion, C.J. Roberts, p. 16.

49. Ibid.

50. *Wisconsin Right to Life,* Slip Opinion (Concurring in part and concurring in the judgment), J. Scalia, p. 18 (emphasis in the original).

51. *Wisconsin Right to Life,* Slip Opinion (Concurring in part and concurring in the judgment), J. Scalia, p. 18.

52. *Wisconsin Right to Life,* Slip Opinion (Dissent), J. Souter, p. 32.

53. *Wisconsin Right to Life,* Slip Opinion (Dissent), J. Souter.

54. *Wisconsin Right to Life,* Slip Opinion, C.J. Roberts, p. 21.

55. Typically, the issue of whether judges should be policymakers is framed in terms of a debate between judicial activism (involving overturning precedent,

utilizing judicial review, and making decisions that shape government policy) and judicial restraint (a view that adheres strictly to *stare decisis* and rejects any active lawmaking by courts). For additional discussion, see Robert Dahl, "Decisionmaking in a Democracy: The Supreme Court as a National Policy Maker," *Journal of Public Law* 6(1958): 279–295; Jonathan D. Casper, "The Supreme Court and National Policy Making," *American Political Science Review* 70(1976): 50–63.

56. *Shrink Missouri*, 528 U.S. at 409-410 (Kennedy, J. dissenting).

57. *McConnell*, 540 U.S. at 137.

5

THROUGH THE REGULATORY WRINGER: THE FEDERAL ELECTION COMMISSION TAKES ON BCRA

"The happy warriors are back at work, and we will prevail...we will not be thwarted by an unelected group of bureaucrats," proclaimed Senator John McCain at a June 26, 2002 news conference.[1] Senator McCain was reacting to regulations proposed by the Federal Election Commission (FEC) to implement and enforce the Bipartisan Campaign Reform Act of 2002 (BCRA). The BCRA lawmakers accused the FEC of ignoring the intent of the law and of replacing Congress's goals with its own political agenda. McCain and his colleagues were determined to make sure that what they intended to do with their landmark campaign finance legislation would not be changed, watered down, circumvented, or undermined in the rulemaking process by the very officials who are charged with implementing and enforcing the law.

Passage of a law by Congress is not a measure's last step in the policymaking labyrinth. As we saw in Chapter 4, by exercising the power of judicial review the courts can interpret a law passed by Congress to determine whether it is constitutional. Likewise, executive branch agencies write rules and regulations to implement and enforce laws, and these rules and regulations have the force of law themselves. In our system of *separated institutions sharing powers,*[2] rules and regulations promulgated by bureaucratic agencies are a continuation of the lawmaking process, one that can be just as important and influential as the congressional legislative process itself. In the case of

BCRA, lawmakers on both sides of the campaign finance reform debate, and their allied groups, played a major role in trying to influence and shape this rulemaking process.

As Clear as Mud

Legislators are keenly aware that they have to make the laws they craft as clear and specific as possible if they want to ensure that, when the law is implemented by an agency, the agency will follow the legislation's intended goals. Congress, however, does not always pass clear and highly specific legislation. Further, congressional lawmakers may afford bureaucrats a good deal of discretion in interpreting and implementing the laws they pass. But why?

One explanation frequently offered is that Congress does not have the specialized knowledge and expertise to authoritatively prescribe the details of complex laws. This is especially true when legislation deals with a complex scientific issue such as pollution control or nuclear power. For example, the 1970 amendments to the Clean Air Act directed the Environmental Protection Agency (EPA) to establish primary air-quality standards for protecting human health by 1975 and secondary standards for protecting vegetation, buildings, etc. within "a reasonable time." [3] Neither the desired standards nor the timeline for secondary standards were defined by Congress in its legislation, leaving it to the EPA to fill in these specifics.

Yet expertise did not seem to be lacking in Congress when lawmakers were debating campaign finance reform. Indeed, every member of Congress is an expert of sorts, for they have all been candidates for federal office and have first-hand experience with campaign finance laws and regulations. However, attempting to pass comprehensive and highly specific campaign finance legislation when 535 *experts* each have a vote is no easy task. In fact, this abundance of experts probably contributed to making passage of BCRA so prolonged and difficult. For one thing, the members of Congress are not necessarily objective experts when it comes to campaign finance reform, since any decisions that the lawmakers make collectively may directly impact them individually. As we saw in Chapters 2 and 3, congressional lawmakers at times made expressly partisan arguments about why a proposed provision in BCRA or the bill as a whole would help or hurt legislators or their party. These arguments had an impact on BCRA's final language and on it subsequently becoming law.

Lawmakers also might pass legislation that is not highly specific and prescriptive in order to gain the necessary support for their proposals from their colleagues; sometimes it may be better to pass an imperfect and imprecise bill than fail in reaching a legislative solution by trying to come to agreement on the specifics. Legislators face a *collective action problem* in trying to merge individual lawmakers' goals into collective or group achievements. [4] So, they bargain and compromise with one another to get a bill that will gain enough support to pass. Indeed, as lawmakers for centuries have known, and as former Senator Alan K. Simpson, R-Wyo., declared, "you cannot legislate without the ability to compromise." [5]

Senators John McCain, R-Ariz., and Russell Feingold, D-Wis., and Representatives Christopher Shays, R-Conn., and Marty Meehan, D-Mass., toiled for seven years to get their reform bill passed and signed into law. As we saw in Chapters 2 and 3, getting from the original proposal to the final product involved a series of twists and turns that included a number of compromises and adjustments to the legislation. For example, the original bill contained provisions such as free television and radio time for candidates in exchange for campaign spending limits, reduced political action committee contribution limits, and prohibitions on bundling. None of these provisions survived through final passage of BCRA.

Another reason lawmakers might not always pass clear and detailed laws is that they are constantly aware, and sometimes quite concerned about, the impact that their votes in Congress will have on their chances for reelection. David Mayhew's characterization of legislators as consumed with and driven by the *electoral connection* of everything that lawmakers do may seem overly instrumental to some. Yet it is certainly true that concern for reelection must be a lawmaker's *proximate* concern—that is, the requirement that must be satisfied first before other goals, such as forging good public policy, can be pursued. [6] Campaign finance reform legislation is somewhat unique in this respect, for lawmakers must consider not only their constituents' possible response to how they vote on such a bill, but also the content of the legislation itself since it could affect the conduct and outcome of their own campaigns.

Given the many factors that can influence the final language of a bill, it is not surprising that what BCRA's sponsors may have intended (i.e., the Act's *legislative intent*) was not necessarily what the FEC *did* in writing regulations to implement the law. Lawmakers often think that their legislative language and intent are perfectly clear, but bureaucrats who write the rules and regulations for those laws may not see it that way. In fact, some of the FEC commissioners did not support the new law and had worked against its passage. Indeed, the rulemaking process for BCRA's implementation was quite politically charged and as much of a labyrinth of unorthodox procedures as the measure's legislative and judicial processes.

The Politics of Regulation

As BCRA was making its way through the many judicial decisions to which it was subjected (see Chapter 4), the FEC began its rule-making process. BCRA passed on March 20, 2002, and was signed into law (PL 107-155) a few days later on March 27. On April 10, the four chief sponsors of the law, Senators McCain and Feingold and Representatives Shays and Meehan, sent a letter asking FEC Chairman David Mason and Commissioner Bradley Smith to recuse themselves from implementing the new law. The reform lawmakers said that the two FEC officials had engaged in "inappropriate and ill-advised conduct" by actively opposing the bill while it was being debated in Congress. The two commissioners refused to step aside. [7]

The FEC is a decidedly political agency that deals with a highly contentious, and often partisan, issue. FEC commissioners are appointed by the president and confirmed by the Senate, and serve six-year terms; they may be reappointed for subsequent six-year terms and also may stay in office following the expiration of the term until such time as a successor is appointed and confirmed. The FEC has six commissioners, three Democrats and three Republicans. The nomination and confirmation of FEC commissioners is often politically charged. For instance, in 2000, Bradley Smith, a Republican, was nominated to be an FEC commissioner, but he was not confirmed for more than three months as Senate Democrats would not allow a confirmation vote until the Republicans agreed to hold confirmation votes for some of President Bill Clinton's judicial nominees. Senator McCain likewise acted to hold up George W. Bush's judicial picks in 2002 until the president named a pro-reform Democrat to the FEC.

Much like BCRA's legislative history, the process of writing and enacting rules and regulations to implement the new campaign finance law was also highly politically charged. These functions became a new battleground for all sides of the debate, as reform advocates worked to ensure that the FEC's regulations were consistent with what they intended in the Act, and BCRA's opponents worked to soften and weaken the statute's effect as the FEC translated the law into practice.

Lost in Translation or Purposely Undermined?

The FEC issued its first proposed BCRA regulations on May 20, 2002, dealing with soft money. Public comments on the proposed regulations were due by May 29. In a May 29 letter to the FEC, the four cosponsors of the law said that the proposed regulations would "create loopholes through which the existing system could continue to operate. ... Only if the Commission adopts the recommendation we make in these comments will the final regulations reflect the will of the people...that soft money be banned."[8] The lawmakers were determined to make sure that the *intent* of BCRA was not thwarted in the rulemaking process. The final regulations addressing soft money were released and published in the *Federal Register* on July 29, 2002 ("the *Federal Register* is the official daily publication for rules, proposed rules, and notices of Federal agencies and organizations, as well as executive orders and other presidential documents"[9]). The FEC has continually promulgated additional rules stemming from BCRA, including rules on electioneering communication (issued October 23, 2002), coordinated and independent expenditures (issued January 3, 2003, and corrected February 7, 2003), and modifying its rules related to Levin funds (issued November 17, 2005).

After the FEC issued its soft money regulations in July of 2002, BCRA's four main cosponsors launched a plan of multiple assaults against the FEC that included a lawsuit challenging the new regulations, an effort to block the president's confirmations in the Senate, an attempt in Congress to overturn the new regulations, and possible elimination of the FEC. GOP congressional leaders, who had worked hard to defeat the legislation, got into the mix as well with their own offensive, including delaying a Democratic nomination to the FEC.[10] These varied techniques illustrate how congressional lawmakers can get involved in the executive branch's implementation of the laws they pass; that is, how some powers are shared in our separated institutions. Also, what happened with respect to the FEC's implementation of BCRA shows how the rulemaking process can be as politically charged as the lawmaking that created the need for regulations.

In the Administrative Procedures Act of 1946 and subsequent changes to it, Congress established standards that government agencies must follow in the rulemaking process. In addition, the Act directed Congress to exercise *continuous watchfulness* over the agencies and programs. In this case McCain, Feingold, Shays, and Meehan were exercising that responsibility of watchfulness in very concrete ways.

Take 'em to Court!

Representatives Shays and Meehan sued in U.S. District Court on October 8, 2002, to overturn the new soft-money rules written by the FEC. Senate ethics rules restrict senators from joining lawsuits as a plaintiff, so the lawsuit was brought only by the House sponsors of BCRA. Shays and Meehan argued that the FEC's regulations "contravene the language" of the BCRA and "will frustrate the purpose and intent of the BCRA by allowing soft money to continue to flow into federal elections and into the federal political process." [11] They said that the FEC's regulations to implement the BCRA's ban on soft money donations to the national parties were "flawed and corrupt" because they would allow the parties to circumvent the ban on soft money. [12] Senator McCain, commenting at the time that his House colleagues commenced the lawsuit, proclaimed that the four FEC commissioners who voted for the regulations were corrupt, "because anyone who willingly and knowingly violates their constitutional responsibilities is corrupt." [13]

Almost two years later, on September 18, 2004, about six weeks before election day, U.S. District Court Judge Colleen Kollar-Kotelly struck down 15 of the 19 FEC regulations that Shays and Meehan had challenged. Judge Kollar-Kotelly previously sat on the three-judge panel of the U.S. District Court for the District of Columbia that issued the initial ruling in the *McConnell* case in 2003 before it moved to the Supreme Court (see Chapter 4). She ruled that the FEC had acted contrary to Congress's intent; that one of the regulations ran "completely afoul of the law;" that another would "foster corruption;" and another "would render the statute largely meaningless." [14]

Judge Kollar-Kotelly struck down the FEC's exemption from coordinated-communication rules of certain communications made more than 120 days before an election, as well as the agency's exemption of all Internet communications from those rules. She found that the FEC's definitions of the terms "solicit" and "agent," as they related to the ban on soft money and coordination (for agents), could be too easily circumvented. She also threw out the FEC's exemption of 501(c)(3) charity groups from the provisions that govern electioneering communications, which the FEC had argued the Internal Revenue Service regulated. [15] Party campaign committee officers and others criticized her ruling for its timing (six weeks before a presidential election) as well as its content, and some of the commissioners moved to appeal.

In October 2005, an appellate court denied the FEC's request to hear the appeal, and the pressure was on to craft acceptable regulations to implement the 2002 law. Although Judge Kollar-Kotelly wrote that the new rules should be written with "reasonable expediency," a year later (and nearly three years after BCRA went into effect) only one of the fifteen invalidated regulations had been reissued. [16] Moreover, the six-member Commission was now down to five members, following the departure of Commissioner Bradley Smith, a strong critic of BCRA and of Judge Kollar-Kotelly's ruling. Three of the remaining commissioners were serving in expired terms, awaiting appointments to replace them. A *Roll Call* editorial noted that the FEC had "slow-walked the process," and because a majority of commissioners presumably would soon vacate their positions, the situation "gives the three holdover commissioners little incentive to work hard to undo the damage they've done. It also means the new commissioners, when appointed, will spend some time getting up to speed on the issues." [17]

Representatives Shays and Meehan went back to court in July 2006 to challenge the FEC's new, re-written rule governing candidate coordination under BCRA. In the new complaint filed in the U.S. District Court for the District of Columbia, the lawmakers argued that the new coordination rules "create an immense incentive for candidates and political parties to engage in massive, unregulated coordination with corporations, unions, wealthy individuals, and interest groups—free from any contribution limitations, source restrictions or even disclosure requirements." [18] FEC Chairman Michael Toner took strong exception to the complaint, and he was confident the new regulations would be upheld by the court.

The Legislative Approach

In addition to pursuing litigation, BCRA's sponsors also attacked the FEC through the legislative process. For instance, after the FEC issued its first regulations in July 2002, Senators McCain and Feingold threatened to undo the proposed rules using the Congressional Review Act (CRA), which was enacted in 1996. The CRA gives Congress 60 days to disapprove rules and regulations issued by an agency with passage of a joint resolution by a simple majority in each chamber (the CRA's process of congressional review limits Senate debate and forbids filibusters, but requires no expedited review in the House). Congress had used the CRA only once before, in March 2001, when Republicans and some centrist Democrats overturned workplace ergonomics regulations issued in the final days of the Clinton administration. [19] In the end, though, the lawmakers did not fully pursue this legislative remedy and left their chances of striking the rules to the Shays-Meehan lawsuit.

Some of BCRA's congressional supporters also called for a major reorganization or even complete elimination of the FEC, for they saw the Commission as ineffectual and too weak to properly implement the new campaign finance law. BCRA's four main co-sponsors threatened to abolish the FEC altogether. Senator McCain said, "There is now compelling and overwhelming evidence that the FEC is incapable institutionally of imposing the reform. ...The FEC has to be abolished and replaced by a responsible body." [20] Senator Feingold noted that the FEC "is the poster child for the failure of a regulatory agency. ...We didn't work for seven years to fix this system only to have it break again."[21] The lawmakers were particularly critical of Commissioner Bradley Smith and FEC Chairman David Mason, who they had asked to recuse themselves from the BCRA rulemaking process because the commissioners had publicly opposed the law while it was being considered in Congress. Indeed, Representative Christopher Shays called for the resignation of the FEC commissioners. Commissioner Smith responded, "I am very disappointed by the level of debate. ...They are engaged in something that's not constructive. It would be more constructive to provide funding to the FEC so it can do its job."[22]

Because the FEC is evenly divided between Republicans and Democrats, the agency's deliberations often end in deadlock, and it often does not take action against those who break campaign finance laws. In many cases, the Commission does not even investigate a complaint because they are unable to reach an agreement to do so. Moreover, Feingold and others blamed the FEC for creating the soft money loophole in the first place (pursuant to a regulation issued in 1979 in an effort to promote the political parties' get-out-the-vote and other party-building efforts), and they questioned the body's ability to carry out BCRA's ban on these funds. Critics of the FEC have called for a stronger and more independent agency, but "convincing lawmakers they need a more aggressive agency to scrutinize their campaigns [has been and] will be a very tough sell."[23]

BCRA's primary sponsors proposed a three-member panel that would have two commissioners, one from each party, and a strong chairperson with significant administrative powers. The chair would serve a 10-year term, which the sponsors argued would elevate him or her above politics, much like the leaders of such other agencies as the FBI. FEC commissioners and others criticized the plan, saying such a design would give one party a 2-to-1 advantage. Moreover, even with a strong chairperson heading up the agency, it would only be as strong and independent as the politicians who created it would permit. As one journalist noted, "No matter the number of commissioners or their powers, it will still fall to the president to nominate them and the 100 members of the Senate to confirm. And since those are the very players whose campaigns the FEC regulates, the temptation to stack the deck by nominating the pliant and the partisan will continue to be enormous."[24] To date, there has been no reshaping or overhaul of the FEC.

It Matters Who Writes the Rules

The changing membership of the FEC posed additional challenges to BCRA's post-passage journey through the policy labyrinth. As noted above, FEC commissioners can stay in office after the expiration of their terms until their replacements are appointed by the president and confirmed by the Senate. This was the situation that existed in the early summer of 2002, when Democratic Commissioner Karl Sandstrom remained in office even though his term in the FEC had officially expired. In May, soon after passage of BCRA, Senate Majority Leader Tom Daschle, D-S.D., had submitted to the White House the name of Ellen Weintraub, a former counsel for the House Ethics Committee, to fill a vacancy on the FEC. BCRA supporters from both parties were anxious to get Weintraub, who was regarded as a supporter of the Act, confirmed quickly so that she could be actively involved in establishing the Commission's BCRA-related rules and regulations. [25]

On June 24, 2002, Senator McCain told Senate Republican Leader Trent Lott of Mississippi that he would attempt to delay holding confirmation votes on all of George W. Bush's other nominees until the president appointed a new Democratic commissioner to the FEC. [26] McCain proclaimed, "I'm not going to allow some bureaucrat whose term expired to emasculate the legislation I worked so hard to pass." [27] McCain wanted President Bush to make a *recess appointment* in August. Such an appointment is one where the president fills a vacant federal government position while the Senate is out of session (i.e., in recess). The appointment must be approved by the Senate by the end of the next session or the position becomes vacated once again. If Bush were to make a recess appointment, it would expedite the process of getting Weintraub's service on the Commission started since she would not have to undergo the normal advice-and-consent approval process in the Senate. McCain pointed out that President Bush had exercised his recess appointment power earlier that year by naming Republican Michael Toner as an FEC commissioner.

Responding to McCain's statement, the White House announced through an aide that the president would not exercise his recess appointment power and that Weintraub's nomination would have to go through "the standard process." [28] Further, her nomination was "in the very early stages of what can be a lengthy process." [29] Senate Republican leaders also observed that the Democrats in the Senate had set a precedent two years earlier when Republican nominee Bradley Smith's confirmation to the FEC had been stalled for months. The GOP Senate leaders further urged President Bush to hold off on sending Weintraub's nomination to the Senate for confirmation until the Democrats voted to confirm some of President Bush's judicial and other picks. GOP Senator Mitch McConnell, R-Ky, the chief opponent of the McCain-Feingold bill in the Senate, said "If I were the president, I would say the price to pay for the nomination is eight hearings and eight votes on circuit court nominees." [30] McConnell noted that, "there is not likely to be a lot of nominations made or nominations confirmed anytime soon." [31] A stalemate seemed to have taken hold.

Majority Leader Tom Daschle was anxious to get confirmations back on track, especially the Democrats' nominations to other bipartisan agencies and boards. The Bush Administration had been ignoring Democrats' suggestions for nominations and was instead appointing people with whom the Democrats were not familiar. [32] In early July, Daschle worked out a deal with the White House and with Senate Minority Leader Trent Lott. Daschle would push through President Bush's judicial nominees, and the president would nominate the Democrats' picks to a number of bipartisan panels.

Bush, however, did not agree to expedite the vetting process for Weintraub, who had yet to be cleared by the FBI. For his part, McCain fully intended to continue blocking the president's nominations. He noted that the FEC appeared to be accelerating its rule-making for BCRA. The longer it took for the president to appoint Weintraub and the Senate to confirm her, the less influence she was likely to have on the rules being written by the FEC. [33] The logjam continued until July 25, when Senator McCain was assured by the White House that Weintraub would be on the FEC by October. In the end, however, Bush did not actually appoint Weintraub until a recess appointment on December 6, 2002 (after which she was renominated and approved in early 2003). By that time, the FEC had already issued its initial set of BCRA-related rules on soft money and electioneering communication.

The Politics of Little or No Action: 527s and the FEC

After BCRA's passage, a number of observers expected that at least some of those who had contributed large sums of soft money to the parties were likely to find other outlets to satisfy their desire to influence federal elections. [34] As one avenue for influence was closed off, the argument went, big spenders would find others. The most likely channel for large sums of money was 527 groups. As noted in Chapter 3, 527s are tax exempt, nonprofit groups formed under Section 527 of the Internal Revenue Code. These organizations can accept unlimited contributions, even from corporations and unions; spend unlimited amounts of money on voter mobilization and issue-advocacy advertising; and operate with little regulation or oversight. [35] Perhaps the most well-known and controversial 527 group to date has been the Swift Boat Veterans for Truth, a group of almost 200 Vietnam War veterans that formed to defeat 2004 Democratic presidential nominee John Kerry after being offended by Kerry's focus on his service in Vietnam and by his anti-war activities after returning home from the war. [36]

The FEC, through both its action and inaction on the issue, contributed to the growth of 527 groups following BCRA. Some of the most controversial 527s that emerged were partisan in nature—a phenomenon due in part to the new campaign finance landscape that followed BCRA's passage and the FEC's implementation of the law. The FEC's impact on the role that 527 organizations play in the world of campaign finance and elections can be traced to rules the Commission issued in July 2002. Among them was a rule that allowed the creation of independent nonprofit partisan groups that would not be considered party committees and would, therefore, not be subject to BCRA's ban on soft money. As a result, in the final weeks before election day 2002, partisan activists on both sides established a number of these non-party partisan groups as section 527 organizations. They were dubbed "shadow" parties and "quasi" parties by some critics who pointed out that unlimited soft money could be filtered through these partisan 527s, even if the official party committees could no longer raise and spend soft money. [37]

The 2004 election featured a large increase in the number of 527 organizations. The sheer magnitude of fundraising and spending by 527 groups was reason for concern for some. During the 2003–2004 election cycle, federal 527 groups raised an estimated $426 million, [38] up from $151 million for the pre-BCRA 2002 election (the first election for which reliable 527 data are available). [39] Approximately two-thirds of the 527 groups active in 2004 were new ones that focused on the presidential election. [40] Democratic-oriented 527 groups far outspent Republican-oriented 527s in 2004: the Democratic groups spent about $320 million, while the GOP groups spent an estimated $109 million (see Box 5-1). [41]

Reform advocates pushed for strict regulation of 527s by the FEC, arguing that these groups should be brought under the same hard money regulations as parties and PACs because of their election-related activities. The FEC, however, dealt with 527-related complaints from the 2004 election slowly and refused to issue regulations for the groups. In May 2004, Republican Commissioner Michael Toner proposed a rule that "would have required many of the 527 organizations to register with the FEC as political committees, which would have then subjected them to the law's strict hard-money contribution limits." [42] After the commissioners rejected his proposal by a 2-to-4 vote, Toner said, "no one should be surprised if 527 soft-money spending in '06 and '08 becomes one of the driving forces in determining which candidates

BOX 5-1 Spending by Top Federal
527 Organizations Active in the 2004 Election

Organization	Expenditures (in dollars)
Democratic-leaning groups	
America Coming Together	78,040,480
Joint Victory Campaign 2004 *	72,588,053
Media Fund	57,694,580
Service Employees International Union Political Fund	46,726,713
AFSCME Special Account	22,332,587
MoveOn.org Voter Fund	21,346,380
New Democratic Network—Nonfederal Account	12,524,063
Citizens for a Strong Senate	10,228,515
1199 SEIU Nonfederal Committee	8,115,937
EMILY's List Nonfederal	8,100,752
Republican-leaning groups	
Progress for America Voter Fund	35,631,378
Swift Boat Vets and POWs for Truth	22,565,360
College Republican National Committee	17,260,655
Club for Growth	9,629,742
Club for Growth.net	4,039,892
National Federation of Republican Women	3,462,507
November Fund	3,124,718
National Association of Realtors	2,989,377
California Republican National Convention Delegation	1,612,595
Republican Leadership Coalition, Inc.	1,440,479

Source: Campaign Finance Institute, "527 Group Fundraising Grew More Slowly in First Quarter of 2006 than 2004," news release, May 19, 2006, www.cfinst.org/pr/051906 .html, Table 2.

*Note that Joint Victory Campaign 2004 served as the fundraising arm for America Coming Together (ACT) and the Media Fund; therefore, it transferred most of its funds to ACT and the Media Fund.

are elected." [43] Senators McCain and Feingold commented that the FEC vote illustrated "why it is necessary to fundamentally restructure that ineffective and irresponsible bureaucracy." [44]

Opponents of Toner's proposal, such as Republican Commissioner Bradley Smith, argued that neither Congress nor the Supreme Court, in upholding BCRA, authorized the FEC to regulate 527 organizations. This argument highlights an important fact about regulatory organizations like the FEC, which can exercise only the type and amount of powers and authority that Congress has delegated to them. Although the FEC and other agencies are sometimes given broad discretionary powers that allow them to play an active role in forming and interpreting public policy, they must work within the guidelines that Congress established.

Interestingly, House Minority Leader Nancy Pelosi, D-Calif., and approximately 140 other House Democrats, some who were the strongest supporters of the Shays-Meehan bill, actually requested that the FEC *not* regulate nonparty 527 organizations. [45] Since Democratic-leaning 527 organizations ended up raising and spending far more in the 2004 election than those 527s supporting the GOP, the Democrats did not want to lose the advantage they had with this rich source of funding and support for their candidates. Republican leaders, however, warned that they, too, would become big 527 players. Republican National Committee chairman Ed Gillespie said: "The 2004 elections will now be a free-for-all. ... Thanks to the deliberate inaction by the Federal Election Commission, the battle of the 527s is likely to escalate to a full-scale, two-sided war." [46] Indeed, the role of 527s in the electoral process was one of the major stories that emerged from the 2004 presidential election, both because of the level of 527 activity and because much of this activity was conducted independently from the candidates and political parties.

On September 14, 2004, Representatives Shays and Meehan filed yet another lawsuit against the FEC, charging that the agency had failed to issue "legally sufficient regulations" for 527 organizations, and that the FEC's inaction "invited widespread circumvention of the law." [47] The George W. Bush–Dick Cheney campaign also sued the FEC to force the agency to rein in 527s, and the two lawsuits were consolidated into one case. By July 2005, there were two competing 527 bills in Congress to address the problem, one from Shays and Meehan that would ban large unlimited contributions to 527s, and the other co-sponsored by Representatives Mike Pence, R-Ind., chairman of the conservative House Republican Study Committee, and Democrat Albert Wynn of Maryland, a member of the Congressional Black Caucus. The Pence-Wynn bill sought to significantly increase the amounts that donors could give to parties and candidates and unleash party spending on candidates in order to, as Representative Wynn argued, give "political parties...parity with 527s."[48] Reform lawmakers strongly opposed the Pence-Wynn bill. Representative Meehan declared at a June 23, 2005 press conference that "several of the reforms that this bill would eviscerate were enacted not three years ago, but 30 years ago in the wake of the Watergate scandals."[49] In the Senate, Senators McCain and Feingold introduced the 527 Reform Act, which was identical to the Shays-Meehan bill in the House. Both the Shays-Meehan and McCain-Feingold bills, however, failed to gain key Democratic support in their chambers, and neither of the 527 bills passed.

In March 2006, U.S. District Court Judge Emmet G. Sullivan ordered the FEC to reconsider its decision not to regulate 527 organizations. Judge Sullivan, however, did not *order* the FEC to issue 527 rules. Instead, he required that the Commission better explain its decision not to issue regulations (instead, the Commission had elected to review complaints on a case-by-case basis), or to issue a rule that would apply to all 527 groups. In 2007 the FEC reached settlements with a few 527 organizations that it says acted as political action committees by advocating the election or defeat of a federal candidate, but did not abide by the fundraising and spending regulations governing PACs. For example, in February 2007, the FEC fined the conservative Progress for America Voter Fund $750,000, the third-largest fine in the agency's history, because it said the group violated campaign finance laws in 2004 by spending more than $30 million on mailings and ads supporting President Bush's re-election, and accepting corporate money and contributions that far exceeded the caps on individual contributions.[50] FEC Chairman Robert Lenhard said of the settlement that "the agency is very serious about regulating both the solicitations and the advertisements that these groups do, to try to discern whether their purpose is to influence federal elections."[51]

Of course, critics still called for regulation of *all* 527s rather than this case-by-case approach, which Judge Sullivan had called "a total failure."[52] In a December 16, 2006 editorial, the *New York Times* said:

> The Commission—ever the enabler, rarely the watchdog, of big money politics—declined in the 2004 campaign to rein in the unlimited financing of such obviously partisan efforts. ...But now, with a skeptical federal judge breathing down its neck and the election long over, the Commission finds that, well, yes, there were grounds to levy fines of several hundred-thousand dollars. ...This dedication to doing next to nothing allowed various stealth

partisans to pollute the last two elections with more than $950 million in 527 financing.[53]

As of summer 2007, there are no 527 regulations in place. Unless Congress or the FEC act to regulate their activities, 527-funded activity is likely to continue and grow during the 2008 election and beyond.

An Ongoing Process

The regulatory process is much like case law in the judicial area, in that the rules evolve as the interpretation of the law is refined by an ongoing process of rule making, resolution of complaints investigated by the agency, legal challenges to the agency's actions, and the agency's legal actions against others. The FEC is a bipartisan body that deals with an incredibly political, and often partisan, issue, and this clearly influences its regulatory activities and decisions. Often its inaction is more consequential than its actions, and the changing membership of the Commission can have a great impact on its decisions. Implementation of BCRA continues as regulations are issued, as some are challenged in court, as complaints about violations of the law are filed with the agency, and as the law itself is challenged in court.

The FEC, like other regulatory agencies, is supposed to provide the necessary technical expertise to fill in the gaps left open by the campaign finance legislation that Congress passes. But in a policy area as politically charged as campaign finance, even "technical interpretations" and other Commission decisions in implementing BCRA and other laws can have a significant substantive impact on the way in which elections are financed and conducted. Similar to what we saw in Chapter 4 with respect to the judiciary, politicians will sometimes look to the FEC for a *politics-by-other-means* resolution to complex and difficult matters. But like the judiciary, the FEC is not an effective place to resolve the underlying tensions in our nation's campaign finance laws; instead, what often happens is that the FEC serves to amplify the ongoing debate and to perpetuate the issues. In fact, the FEC is often the source of additional debate as its implementation of the nation's campaign finance laws may highlight unforeseen consequences of the laws that the members of Congress had not considered. In this regard, the FEC plays an important role in the campaign finance policy labyrinth by directly or indirectly keeping campaign finance an ever-changing matter, even during the times that Congress is not in the midst of debating the issue.

NOTES

1. Karen Foerstel, "Sponsors of Campaign Finance Law Unleash Torrent of Anger Against FEC," *CQ Weekly Report,* June 29, 2002.
2. Richard Neustadt, *Presidential Power* (New York: Macmillan, 1986), 33.
3. B. Guy Peters, *American Public Policy: Promise and Performance,* 6th ed. (Washington, D.C: CQ Press, 2004), 381. See Chapter 13 for a thorough discussion of environmental policy making.
4. Roger H. Davidson and Walter J. Oleszek, *Congress and Its Members,* 10th ed. (Washington, D.C.: CQ Press, 2006), 295. See also John H. Aldrich, *Why Parties? The Origin and Transformation of Political Parties in America* (Chicago: University of Chicago Press, 1995).
5. Davidson and Oleszek, *Congress and Its Members,* 296.
6. David R. Mayhew, *Congress: The Electoral Connection,* 2nd ed. (New Haven: Yale University Press, 2004).
7. Karen Foerstel, "FEC Members Won't Step Aside in Setting Campaign Rules," *CQ Weekly Report,* April 13, 2002.
8. Karen Foerstel, "FEC Regulations Snubbed,"*CQ Weekly Report,* June 1, 2002.
9. Description from the Web site of the National Archives and Records Administration (http://www.gpoaccess.gov/fr/about.html), which is responsible for publishing the *Federal Register.*
10. Karen Foerstel, "GOP Vows to Hold up FEC Nominations until Senate Votes on Pending Judges," *CQ Weekly Report,* May 18, 2002.
11. Quoted on the FEC's Web site of *Shays and Meehan v. FEC* (available at http://www.fec.gov/law/litigation_CCA_S.shtml#shays_02; last visited June 5, 2007).
12. Derek Willis, "Soft-Money Rules Challenged by Campaign Finance Sponsors," *CQ Weekly Report,* October 12, 2002.
13. Ibid.
14. Suzanne Nelson, "FEC Must Rewrite Regulations," *Roll Call,* October 25, 2005.
15. Amy Keller, "Judge Upends FEC Guidelines; Election Agency to Appeal," *Roll Call,* September 21, 2004.
16. Suzanne Nelson, "FEC Must Rewrite Regulations," *Roll Call,* October 25, 2005.
17. "The FEC's Third Strike," *Roll Call,* editorial, October 26, 2005.
18. David Drucker, "Meehan, Shays File BCRA Suit," *Roll Call,* July 12, 2006.
19. Karen Foerstel, "Review Act Seldom Used," *CQ Weekly Report,* June 29, 2002.
20. Foerstel, "Sponsors of Campaign Finance Law Unleash Torrent of Anger against FEC," *CQ Weekly Report,* June 29, 2002.
21. Foerstel, "GOP Vows to Hold up FEC Nomination until Senate Votes on Pending Judges."

22. Foerstel, "Sponsors of Campaign Finance Law Unleash Torrent of Anger against FEC."

23. John Cochran, "Lawsuits, Legislation Take Aim at Election Commission's 527 'Loophole,'" *CQ Weekly Report*, September 1, 2004.

24. John Cochran, "The Once and Future FEC: Revamp or Retread?" *CQ Weekly Report*, September 25, 2004.

25. Foerstel, "GOP Vows to Hold up FEC Nominations until Senate Votes on Pending Judges."

26. Foerstel, "Sponsors of Campaign Finance Law Unleash Torrent of Anger against FEC."

27. Ibid.

28. Ibid.

29. Ibid.

30. Foerstel, "GOP Vows to Hold up FEC Nomination until Senate Votes on Pending Judges."

31. Foerstel, "Sponsors of Campaign Finance Law Unleash Torrent of Anger against FEC."

32. Emily Pierce, "McCain's Hold on Nominations Spurs Bush and Senate Leaders To Agree on Timely Action Plan," *CQ Weekly Report*, July 13, 2002.

33. Emily Pierce, "McCain Deal Speeds up Nominations," *CQ Weekly Report*, July 27, 2002.

34. For example, see the report by Public Citizen, a good government group organized by Ralph Nader as "an independent voice for citizens in the halls of power," released in April 2002, *Déjà Vu Soft Money: Outlawed Contributions Likely to Flow to Shadowy 527 Groups that Skirt Flawed Disclosure System*, April 5, 2002, at http://www.citizen.org/congress/campaign/issues/nonprofit/articles.cfm?ID=7372.

35. This section on 527 organizations draws significantly from Diana Dwyre, "527s: The New Bad Guys of Campaign Finance," in *Interest Group Politics*, 7th ed., ed. Allan J. Cigler and Burdett A. Loomis (Washington, D.C.: CQ Press, 2007).

36. During the Vietnam War, John Kerry served on a *swift boat*, which is a heavily armed patrol boat. According to the organization's Web site, the Swift Boat Veterans for Truth (later changed to Swift Vets and POWs for Truth) "consists of and is limited to former military officers and enlisted men who served in Vietnam on U.S. Navy 'Swift Boats' or in affiliated commands," and was formed "to counter the false 'war crimes' charges John Kerry repeatedly made against Vietnam veterans who served in our units and elsewhere, and to accurately portray Kerry's brief tour in Vietnam as a junior grade Lieutenant." (See http://horse.he.net/~swiftpow/index.php).

37. See Amy Keller, "McCain Takes Aim at 'Shadow' Groups," *Roll Call*, 18 November 2002. The term "shadow Democratic party" was first coined by GOP critics,

but it was soon used by the media. See *"Washington Post* Again Labeled Progressive Groups with Political 'Foes' Term" at http://mediamatters.org/items/20040514004 (June 7, 2005).

38. Campaign Finance Institute, "527 Group Fundraising Grew More Slowly in First Quarter of 2006 than 2004," news release, May 19, 2006 at http://www.cfinst.org

39. Steve Weissman and Ruth Hassan, "BCRA and the 527 Groups," in *The Election after Reform,* ed. Michael J. Malbin (Lanham, MD: Rowman and Littlefield, 2006), 81.

40. Anthony Corrado, "The Future of Campaign Finance: Congress, the FEC, and the Courts," Brookings Institution presentation on October 20, 2005, Washington, D.C., quotation from transcript at http://www.brookings.edu/comm/events/20051020campaign.htm, 6–7.

41. Campaign Finance Institute, "527 Group Fundraising Grew More Slowly in First Quarter of 2006 than 2004," news release, May 19, 2006 at http://www.cfinst.org/pr/051906.html, Table 2.

42. Gregory L. Giroux, "FEC Passes for Now on Regulating '527' Political Organizations; Congress to Hold Oversight Hearing," CQ *Weekly Report,* May 15, 2004.

43. Kate Phillips, "Election Panel Won't Issue Donation Rules," *New York Times,* June 1, 2006.

44. Giroux, "FEC Passes for Now on Regulating '527' Political Organizations."

45. Ibid.

46. Ibid.

47. Matthew Murray, "Stymied on Hill, Critics of 527s Petition Court," *Roll Call,* September 11, 2006.

48. Eliza Newlin Carney, "Congress—Payback Time for '527' Groups?" *National Journal,* July 9, 2005.

49. Ibid.

50. Kate Phillips, "Settlements Including Fines Are Reached in Election Finance Cases of Three Groups," *New York Times,* March 1, 2007. Settlements including fines were reached in December 2006 with the Swift Boat Veterans for Truth, the League of Conservation Voters, and MoveOn.org's Voter Fund (see Kate Phillips, "Settlements with Fines are Reached in Election Finance Cases of Three 527 Groups," *New York Times,* December 14, 2006).

51. Phillips, "Group Reaches Settlement with FEC over 2004 Campaign Advertising."

52. Phillips, "Settlements Including Fines Are Reached in Election Finance Cases of Three Groups."

53. "And This Just in on Elections," editorial, *New York Times,* December 16, 2006.

6

ELECTIONS IN
THE POST-BCRA WORLD

Before and after passage of the Bipartisan Campaign Reform Act of 2002 (BCRA), critics warned of its possible negative consequences: BCRA would weaken and undermine the political parties, favor one party over the other, reduce competition, suppress free speech, and strengthen special interest groups. Others voiced concern that BCRA did not go far enough, and that big money would find ways around the law and other routes to influence federal elections. Moreover, as with most new laws and particularly with this one, the lawmaking process does not end with congressional passage and presidential approval (as we saw in the last two chapters). Lastly, given the history of campaign finance reform, there is always the possibility that *unintended* consequences may result, such as the tremendous increase in the number and influence of political action committees (PACs) following passage of the Federal Election Campaign Act (FECA) and its amendments in the 1970s.

In the final weeks of the 2004 election, some political analysts criticized the new law for failing to meet its objectives:

This was supposed to be the year Big Money would be driven out of presidential politics—or at least wrestled under control. Don't kid yourself. The McCain-Feingold campaign-reform law may have succeeded in drying up the political parties' soft money slush funds. But that money—and more— has simply found a new home in the murkier world of 527s.[1]

Senators McCain and Feingold countered that such critics did not understand the goals of the new law:

> The McCain-Feingold law was never about reducing money in politics. Its goal was to reduce the corrupting influence of unlimited "soft money" contributions to the political parties, usually solicited by federal candidates and officeholders...Ending the practice of the president, party leaders, and members of Congress soliciting huge donations from corporations, unions, and wealthy individuals improved the system. And, despite predictions to the contrary, the parties have thrived in the new hard-money world. [2]

Although BCRA's impact will continue to play out in future elections, we can evaluate the performance and impact of the new law in the first two election cycles after its enactment and consider its possible long-term effects on future elections and on the political actors and organizations involved in those contests.

Political Parties

The passage and implementation of BCRA directly affected political parties more than any other organizations involved in federal elections. Indeed, the law was designed to end the unlimited soft money contributions to the national party committees and address the problems associated with those contributions, namely corruption or the appearance of corruption in federal elections. However, the new law also included provisions to partially offset the loss of funds the parties would experience as a result of the soft money ban: BCRA increased party contribution limits and created a new type of federally regulated state and local limited party soft money known as *Levin money,* after Sen. Carl Levin, D-Mich., who proposed the amendment to establish the new kind of funds. (Senator Levin's amendment allowed state and local parties to raise up to $10,000 in soft money from corporations and unions if state law permits such contributions.) So, how have the parties fared in this new regulatory environment?

National Party Committees
The national political parties had relied heavily on soft money before passage of BCRA (see Figure 1-5 in Chapter 1). Indeed, soft money constituted almost half of their receipts from 1999 to 2002. Some observers predicted that the soft money ban in BCRA would severely weaken the political par-

ties and put them at a financial disadvantage against the growing influence of special interest groups.[3] Some who feared that BCRA would weaken parties also argued that the law would discourage coordination between the national party organizations and state and local parties, which had contributed to robust party-building activities in recent years. Others forecasted that the parties would be motivated to raise more hard money, particularly from small donors, and would find new ways to thrive in the changed campaign finance regime by, for example, enhancing their grassroots organizational efforts.[4]

Another issue was how BCRA might affect interparty competition. Most observers, even some supporters of BCRA, noted that banning soft money would benefit the Republican Party but disadvantage the Democratic Party. Some even called BCRA the "Democratic Party Suicide Bill."[5] Indeed, Republican national party committees had almost always been more successful at raising funds than the Democratic national party organizations,[6] and since passage of FECA in 1974, the GOP had raised more hard money than the Democrats. Some analysts feared that without soft money, the Democratic Party would not be able to compete against the GOP. Recall that then–chairman of the Democratic Congressional Campaign Committee, Rep. Martin Frost of Texas, opposed BCRA for these very concerns.

However, both parties fared well in the first post–BCRA election, and national Democratic Party committees actually surprised many by collecting more in hard money in 2004 than they raised in hard *and* soft money in both the 2000 and 2002 election cycles, as Figure 6-1 shows. Democratic committees raised almost as much hard money for the 2006 midterm elections ($392.1 million) as they had raised in hard *and* soft money for the 2002 midterms ($408.4 million), while GOP committee totals in 2006 declined when compared to 2002 hard and soft dollars combined.[7]

Yet, when we break down party fundraising by committee, we see some unevenness. Figure 6-2 shows each national party committee's receipts: the Democratic National Committee (DNC), the Democratic Senatorial Campaign Committee (DSCC), the Democratic Congressional Campaign Committee (DCCC), the Republican National Committee (RNC), the National Republican Senatorial Committee (NRSC), and the National Republican Congressional Committee (NRCC). The national party committees, the DNC and RNC, generally collect more money during presidential election cycles, and the congressional campaign committees raise more funds during midterm congressional elections; this pattern is reflected in the zig-zag graph lines in Figure 6-2.

Figure 6-1   National Party Committee Receipts, 2000–2006

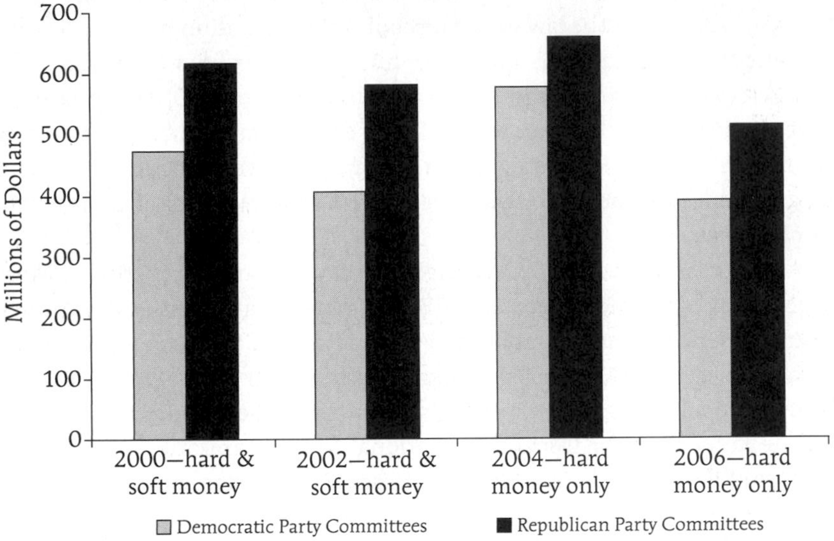

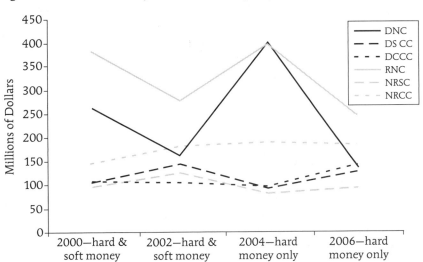

Source: Federal Election Commission, "Party Financial Activity Summarized for the 2006 Election Cycle." News Release, March 7, 2007, 1.

Figure 6-2   National Party Committee Receipts by Committee, 2000–2006

Source: Federal Election Commission, "Party Financial Activity Summarized for the 2006 Election Cycle." News Release, March 7, 2007.

The DNC and RNC actually exceeded fundraising expectations in 2004, including their own projections; they collected more in hard money than they had in hard and soft money for the 2000 presidential election cycle, and as such the national party committees were the driving forces behind the aggregate totals discussed above. Moreover, in 2004 the DNC reached fundraising parity with the RNC for the first time since the Federal Election Commission (FEC) began keeping track in the 1970s. In 2006, however, both the DNC and RNC totals fell below their 2002 midterm election receipts, with the DNC losing ground to the RNC.

The Democratic Hill committees (the DSCC and DCCC) seem to have recovered well from the loss of soft money, falling a bit behind in the first post–BCRA election in 2004 but bouncing back up for the 2006 election, which undoubtedly helped the Democrats to take control of the House and Senate from the Republicans in that election. The DCCC in particular appears to have successfully adapted in the post–BCRA hard money world. As for the GOP Hill committees (the NRSC and NRCC), the NRCC has held fairly steady and still been out-raising any other congressional committee. The NRSC, however, appears to have lost ground without soft money and has not adapted as well as the other committees. These party differences in congressional campaign committee fundraising are somewhat surprising, for most observers predicted that the Democrats, who relied more heavily on soft money prior to BCRA, would be more negatively impacted by the loss of soft money. So, what accounts for such differences?

All the national party committees stepped up their fundraising from individuals, and the committees all collected much more in hard money contributions from them.[8] The committees all added many new donors, with small contributions making up a much larger portion of the parties' total receipts than before. Perhaps the most important, and somewhat unexpected, source of new hard money for the Hill committees post–BCRA was their own federal candidates. House candidates contributed almost 44 percent more from their personal campaign committees to their parties' committees in 2004 than they had in 2002, while senators gave a whopping 174 percent more to their parties in 2004 than in 2002.[9] The Democrats accounted for most of this increase, particularly Democratic senators. Moreover, most of the money—90 percent of House members' party contributions and 69 percent of senators' party contributions—went to the Hill committees.[10] Figure 6-3 shows the increase in federal candidates' contributions to their congressional campaign committees from 2000 to 2006. (The figure incorporates

Figure 6-3   Federal Candidate Contributions to Congressional Campaign
              Committees, 2000–2006

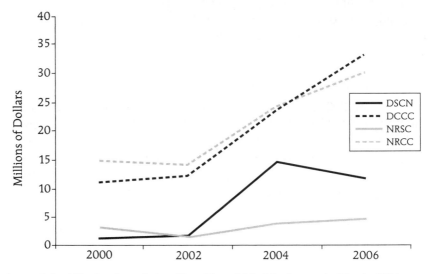

Source: Federal Election Commission, "Party Financial Activity Summarized for the 2006
Election Cycle." News Release, March 7, 2007.

two pre–BCRA and two post–BCRA elections.) The House campaign committees, the DCCC and the NRCC, in particular, have seen tremendous increases in contributions from their party's candidates, with the DCCC moving ahead of all the other Hill committees on this front.

   This increased giving by federal candidates to their parties is due in part to
the enhanced ability of federal candidates to raise campaign funds after
BCRA, which increased the amount individuals can donate to federal candidates from $1,000 (constant since 1974) per person per election to $2,000
(now indexed for inflation) per person per election. As Diana Dwyre and
Robin Kolodny note, "individual donors are motivated more by their personal connection to candidates than to the broader concept of party majorities, [so] it is not a surprise that members would have an easier time raising
money for elections than the party committees." [11] Indeed, most incumbents,
particularly committee chairs, ranking members, and party leaders, tend to
raise far more money than they need for their own reelections. Understand-
ably many transfer some of that money to their party committees to achieve
or maintain their party's collective goal of majority status. Since federal
candidates may transfer unlimited amounts from their personal campaign

accounts to a party committee, this is a rich source of party funding. [12] As long as partisan control of Congress is up for grabs in future elections, we expect that federal candidates will continue to help their parties gain or maintain majority status.

The parties also spent their money differently after BCRA. All of the national party committees spent far more in independent expenditures (i.e., expenditures spent for or against a candidate without the candidates' knowledge or consent) than they had in previous election cycles and less in direct contributions and coordinated expenditures—both of which are limited. Because independent expenditure communications are paid for with hard (regulated) money only, they may expressly advocate the election or defeat of a specific candidate. Further, ads of this nature became the parties' method of choice for helping their candidates, since such express advocacy is likely more effective than issue ads that cannot include such phrases as "vote for" or "vote against."

Yet, in the most recent elections both before and after BCRA, the parties concentrated their efforts on a very small number of the most competitive races in the nation. For example, in 2004 Senate campaign committees spent $38 million in independent expenditures in only twelve races, and House committees directed over $80 million in independent expenditures to about thirty races. [13] Both advocates and opponents of BCRA observed that parties are the campaign players most likely to enhance competition by giving to competitive candidates rather than sure winners, as interest groups and wealthy individuals generally do. Unless the parties spread their campaign resources around more to help create more competitive races, however, they are unlikely to live up to such expectations, even if they do allocate their resources in a more desirable fashion than interest groups and wealthy individuals.

Since the mid-1990s control of the House and Senate has been legitimately up for grabs after decades of mostly Democratic control, and both parties have become more strategic and efficient in allocating resources to maximize the chance of maintaining or gaining control of Congress. [14] The parties shifted resources from safe incumbents, who used to receive the lion's share of party campaign money, to challengers and open-seat candidates in competitive races. House Republicans were quite successful with a highly orchestrated effort to create a GOP farm team by supporting Republican candidates for state and local office and then recruiting them to run for the House after they had established a track record and some name recognition in state or local office. This shift in strategy, along with changes in the political environment (e.g., the mobilization of GOP voters and perceived ineffective policies promoted by the Democratic Party), helped create more competition and led to the GOP taking control of the House in 1994 for the first time in forty years.

Yet neither party has used its resources to support candidates who are not *already* in contests that appear competitive even with changes in the political climate, an incumbent in trouble, or some other indicator that signals a chance to pick up a seat. If the parties engaged in *sustained* efforts to build farm teams and support candidates in somewhat less competitive districts, then we might see more competition in congressional elections and more turnover in House and Senate membership. Of course, other factors, such as how congressional district lines are drawn and overarching national issues, are likely to have the greatest effect on the level of competition in any given election.

State and Local Parties

More than the national party organizations, the state and local political parties felt the effects of BCRA's ban on national party soft money fundraising. Prior to BCRA, the national parties had channeled millions of dollars in soft money through state and local parties to mix with hard money to run issue ads in federal elections. The national parties sent this mix of hard and soft money to the states because many state and local parties operated under more generous soft money spending rules. After BCRA, the state and local parties no longer received millions from the national parties, but this appears to have had very little effect on their own activities. Political scientist Raymond La Raja reports that the "national parties did not transfer as much money to the states in 2004 as in the previous election because, lacking soft money, they had no incentive to fund ads through the state parties."[15] However, state parties "spent about as much in federal elections as they had in previous elections, *minus* the spending on advertising," which they had paid for with national party money.[16] Indeed, the state parties no longer ran ads for federal elections once the flow of soft money from the national parties halted.

In the post–BCRA world, both parties' state and local committees, but especially the Republicans', spent more on grassroots efforts (ground operations such as volunteer activities and rallies, and distributing campaign paraphernalia such as lawn signs, buttons, and bumper stickers) and on voter mobilization (getting voters to the polls) than they had in previous elections. The Democrats tended to use outside groups, such as America Coming Together (a partisan 527 organization), while the Republicans relied more on traditional party-sponsored grassroots and mobilization efforts. Indeed both parties have stepped up their grassroots and voter mobilization efforts in recent years, activities thought to be more desirable than running ads because they promote participation. If BCRA motivated the increase in these more positive electoral activities, then this should be counted as a beneficial consequence of the new law on the state and local levels.

To encourage such activities and to minimize potentially negative effects of BCRA on state and local parties, particularly the loss of national party soft money, lawmakers increased the limits on contributions to state parties for federal election activity from $5,000 to $10,000 and raised the aggregate limit on total political giving for federal elections. Also, in an effort to encourage grassroots state party activity after BCRA, lawmakers agreed to Senator Levin's amendment to allow state and local parties to raise up to $10,000 in soft money from corporations and unions if state law permits such contributions. Yet in the first post–BCRA election in 2004 few state parties raised Levin soft money. Only 17 percent of state party receipts reported to the FEC qualified as soft money in 2004, down from 62 percent in 2000. [17] Big donors were reluctant to give Levin funds to state parties in the first post–BCRA election, with some noting that the rules for such giving were not very clear and were certainly untested. Yet given the significant increase in grassroots and mobilization activity, the state and local parties clearly had little trouble raising the money to fund these activities without much soft money. We may see more extensive use of Levin funds in future elections as donors become more comfortable with the new regulations and parties take advantage of the opportunity to collect this relatively easy-to-raise money.

A New Frontier:
The Rise of 527s and Other Nonprofit Groups

The previous chapter described how 527 groups increased in number and financial influence in federal elections after the passage of BCRA. These tax-exempt, nonprofit groups formed under Section 527 of the Internal Revenue Code were used extensively in the 2004 presidential election. While BCRA was making its way through Congress, critics warned that big-moneyed interests that had given soft money to the political parties—corporations, unions, and wealthy individuals—would seek new outlets for political influence, and they generally pointed to 527s as the most likely outlet. This criticism articulates the *hydraulic theory* of campaign finance—like water, money would find its way around any obstacle [18]—with the claim that big money givers would undermine BCRA by merely shifting their giving to these loosely regulated political organizations with euphemistic names such as America Coming Together (a Democratic 527) and Progress for America (a Republican 527).

The IRS defines a section 527 political organization as:

> a party, committee, association, fund, or other organization...organized and operated primarily for the purpose of directly or indirectly accepting contributions or making expenditures, or both, for...influencing or attempting to influence the selection, nomination, election, or appointment of an individual to a federal, state, or local public office or office in a political organization. [19]

These tax-exempt organizations may accept unlimited contributions, even from corporations and unions; spend unlimited amounts of money on voter mobilization and issue advocacy advertising; and operate with less regulation and oversight than PACs and traditional party committees. Indeed, recall from Chapter 5 the FEC's reluctance to forcefully regulate the activities of 527 groups. However, 527s may not coordinate their activities with candidates.

Congress added Section 527 to the IRS code in 1974 to exempt political organizations from federal income and gift taxes. Lawmakers assumed that such political entities were already registering and reporting their contributions and expenditures to the FEC or to state agencies, so they did not create any registration or disclosure rules for 527 groups. Section 527 organizations were required only to file a (confidential) tax return with the IRS. In fact, it was not until the 2000 presidential election cycle, after 527 groups ran a series of ads with no paper trail to identify their source, that section 527 groups were required to disclose their activities (see Chapter 3). [20] The secrecy surrounding these 527 groups led critics to dub them *stealth PACs* during the 2000 election, and in the midst of the election season, Congress imposed some reporting obligations on 527s. While 527 groups must now comply with the BCRA ban on electioneering communications that are broadcast thirty days before a primary or sixty days before a general election and paid for with soft money, much of what these groups do during elections remained unchanged. For example, get-out-the-vote (GOTV) activities, phone, mail, e-mail, and Internet voter contact are not considered broadcast communications under BCRA and may be paid for with unlimited 527 soft money. [21] If 527s run ads, they either run them before the statutory deadlines

or broadcast issue ads rather than spots that would be considered electioneering communications (although, as shown in Chapter 4, the *Wisconsin
Right to Life* decision gives 527 groups more flexibility with respect to the second option).

Section 527 Organizations after BCRA

As we saw in Chapter 5, the FEC issued a rule in 2002 after passage of BCRA
that permitted the creation of independent nonprofit partisan groups that
would not be considered party committees, and therefore would not be subject to the party soft-money ban in BCRA. This rule motivated party opera-
tives to create a number of these so-called *shadow* or *quasi parties* as 527
organizations in the final weeks before election day in 2002. Critics pointed
out that unlimited soft money could be filtered through these partisan 527s
even if the official party committees could no longer raise and spend soft
money. [22] Yet 527 activity was still fairly limited in 2002.

The 2004 presidential election saw a rise in 527 activity. In the 2003–2004
election cycle, federal 527 groups raised an estimated $426 million, [23] up
from $151 million for the 2002 pre–BCRA election (the first election for
which reliable data are available). [24] Most of this 527 activity was conducted
by new groups formed to influence the presidential election. There were far
more Democratic-leaning 527 groups that far outspent Republican-oriented
groups in 2004: Democratic 527s spent approximately $320 million; and
GOP groups spent about $109 million. [25] See Box 5-1 in Chapter 5 for a list
of the top 527 groups in the 2004 election. Democratic 527s concentrated
extensively on grassroots GOTV efforts. For example, America Coming Together (ACT), the largest effort to mobilize Democratic voters in 2004, spent
an estimated $78 million, more than any other 527 group.

Much of the controversy over 527 activity in 2004 concerned the sources
of funding for many of these groups. For example, international financier
George Soros and Progressive Car Insurance chairman Peter Lewis each contributed $20 million to get the anti-Bush 527 groups started, Bob Perry of
Perry Homes gave $8.1 million to GOP 527s in 2004, and labor unions con-
tributed $94 million to 527s in 2004, up from $55 million in 2002. [26] But
was there really the general transfer of soft money from the national parties,
which could no longer raise it, to 527 groups as many critics of BCRA had
feared?

While there was indeed an increase in 527 activity in 2004, it did not represent a wholesale shift of party soft money to 527 groups. Political scientists
Stephen Weissman and Ruth Hassan analyzed the activities of 527 organiza-

tions both before and after enactment of BCRA. They found that most of the now-banned party soft money did not find its way to 527 groups in 2004:

> [P]ost-BCRA *levels* of giving are not simply explained by the "hydraulic theory." ...*Most* former individual soft money donors have not given large donations to 527s. But for those who did in 2004, one may say that a river of party soft money has turned into an ocean of 527 money. [27]

Individuals who gave $200,000 or more to federal 527s in 2004 generally gave far less soft money to parties in the 2000 and 2002. For example, George Soros contributed $208,000 in soft money to the Democratic Party in 2000 and 2002, but he gave $24 million to Democratic-leaning 527s in 2004. Bob Perry donated only $140,000 in soft money to Republican party committees in the two previous elections, but in 2004 he gave $8.1 million to 527s. [28] In total, "73 former soft money donors provided $157 million to 527s—three times the combined amount they had given to parties in 2000 and 2002 and [to] 527s in 2002...a vast escalation in their total donations." [29] Stated differently, almost half of the money contributed to 527s in 2004 (about $194 million) came from only 77 individuals. [30] Individual contributions to 527s accounted for most of the increase in fundraising by 527 groups, jumping from $37 million in 2002 to $256 million in 2004. [31] However, other former party soft money givers, corporations in particular, did not jump on the 527 bandwagon in 2004. These data suggest that many former party soft money donors did not gravitate to 527s, but those who did significantly increased their contributions.

Corporations contributed far less soft money to 527s in 2004 than they had given to the parties in previous elections. Prior to BCRA, some business donors quietly complained that they were subjected to a party "shakedown" for soft money, and corporations were probably relieved to give less soft money now that the parties no longer had this leverage over them. [32] Also, many corporate leaders were reluctant to give soft money in the first post–BCRA election, for their lawyers had advised against giving to 527s until there was more certainty about the legality of doing so. [33] Corporate contributions to 527 groups declined from $32 million in 2002 to $30 million in 2004, far less than the $216 million in soft money that corporations had given to the national parties in 2002. [34] Since corporations had given more soft money to Republican Party committees in the past, their lack of enthusiasm for 527s (coupled with the fact that labor unions gave far more soft money to 527s in 2004 than they had given to the Democratic Party in 2002) hurt GOP-leaning groups more than Democratic-oriented groups.

These donation patterns partially explain the somewhat unexpected financial success of Democratic 527s over their Republican counterparts in 2004.

There was far less 527 activity during the 2006 election than in 2004. Federal 527 groups raised $117 million for the 2006 midterm election, down significantly from the $424 million that 527s raised for the 2004 presidential and congressional elections, but about the same as the $114 million raised for the 2002 midterm election, the last election before BCRA.[35] Democratic 527s continued to outspend Republican groups, $88 million to $55 million, and as in 2004 large donors accounted for a considerable portion of contributions (almost half) to 527s in 2006. For instance, fifteen individuals gave between $600,000 and $9.75 million to 527s in 2006. Addressing this decline in 527 activity from 2004 to 2006, Weissman and Ryan explain that there was more 527 action in 2004 because that election was:

> the first under…BCRA, which banned unlimited soft money to political parties and candidates, but not to 527s and other politically minded nonprofits. Also Democratic Party operatives and interest groups were looking for ways to help their eventual presidential nominee supplement the low spending limits in the presidential public financing system in order to compete with Republican George W. Bush, who spurned public financing for the primaries. They rushed to exploit the "527 loophole." And the Republicans responded in kind.[36]

A good deal of 527 activity also shifted to the states in 2006. State-focused 527s spent about 41 percent more in 2006 than they had in 2004.[37] Some of this shift is due to labor unions' focus on state campaigns during the 2006 midterm election. The biggest state 527s also increased their spending in 2006: the Republican Governors Association spent $34.3 million in 2004 and $43.1 million in 2006; the Democratic Governors Association spent $24.1 million in 2004 and $28.7 million in 2006.[38]

Box 6-1 lists the top federal 527 spenders in 2006, broken down by partisan orientation. Compare this list to the list of 2004's top 527 spenders in Box 5-1. There were some new players in 2006 but also some familiar groups. Yet the most striking difference between the two lists is the significantly lower expenditure totals of the top 527s in 2006. Moreover, some of the biggest 527 contributors from 2004 gave less in 2006 and some gave more: George Soros gave $3.9 million in 2006, about one-fourth of what he contributed two years earlier; Bob Perry increased his 527 donations in 2004 by $1.5 million to $9.6 million in 2006.

BOX 6-1 Spending by Top Federal 527 Organizations Active in the 2006 Election

Section 527 Committee	Expenditures (dollars)
Democratic-leaning groups	
Service Employees International Union Political Ed & Action Fund	$22,825,753
EMILY's List Non Federal	11,128,005
America Votes, Inc.	9,563,549
America Coming Together—Nonfederal Account	6,998,238
September Fund	4,950,861
America Votes 2006	4,389,203
Heartland PAC	3,039,146
Grassroots Democrats	2,584,756
1199 SEIU Non Federal Committee	2,257,502
UFCW Active Ballot Club Education Fund	1,927,431
Republican-leaning groups	
Progress for America Voter Fund	12,457,683
College Republican National Committee	10,260,343
Club for Growth	7,427,414
The Presidential Coalition, LLC	7,256,082
Economic Freedom Fund	4,835,805
National Federation of Republican Women	3,028,197
Americans for Honesty on Issues	2,830,148
Softer Voices	1,266,000
Free Enterprise Fund Committee	1,231,630
America's PAC	971,747

Source: Stephen R. Weissman and Kara D. Ryan, "Soft Money in the 2006 Election and the Outlook for 2008: The Changing Nonprofits Landscape," A CFI Report, Washington, D.C.: The Campaign Finance Institute, 2007, Appendix, Table 1, 20–21.

Moving on to Other Nonprofits

Big givers also found other outlets for their large dollar contributions in 2006, and some 527 groups found more flexible types of nonprofit organizations from which to operate. Increased FEC 527 regulations, investigations, and civil settlements since the 2004 election seem to have led contributors and groups to look for other ways to spend large sums of loosely regulated money on federal elections, such as 501(c) committees. 501(c) committees are social welfare organizations that are permitted to use unlimited soft money contributions to conduct election activities as long as those efforts are not their primary activity, and, moreover, these groups' contributions and expenditures are largely undisclosed. The social welfare organizations used for federal election activity are the 501(c)(4), 501(c)(5), and 501(c)(6) nonprofit corporations, named for the section of the tax code under which each operates.

On one front, the FEC ruled that any fundraising solicitation indicating that any portion of a 527's receipts would be used to support or oppose the election or defeat of a clearly identified candidate would be considered a contribution, and the group would therefore be subject to FECA limitation and reporting requirements. For example, in 2005, the FEC sued the Republican-oriented Club for Growth in part for its 2004 solicitation activities, and in 2007 the Club for Growth decided to replace its 527 with a new 501(c)(4) group, the Citizens Club for Growth. The Citizens Club told its members in an email that the new Club will "have a significant new ability to run advertisements that directly call for the election or defeat of candidates for Congress...[and] unlike in the past, your donations to the Club will not be disclosed to the public, except in very limited circumstances." [39]

Similarly, the Democratic-leaning League of Conservation Voters reached a 527 settlement with the FEC and then shifted its activities to its 501(c)(4) nonprofit corporation in 2006. Likewise, large contributors began to diversify their contributions more after the 2004 election and the FEC actions that made giving to 527s less attractive. For example, Republican Carl Lindner, Jr., chairman of American Financial Groups, contributed $99,800 in hard money to candidates, parties and PACs, $800,000 to 527 groups, and $479,224 to a 501(c)(4), Common Sense Ohio. [40]

Since there is no comprehensive public disclosure, it is impossible to know just how much 501(c) committees raise and spend, but it appears that 501(c) activity increased in the 2006 federal elections. Such 501(c) activity is likely to increase in future elections as groups look for less restrictive outlets for raising and spending large sums of unregulated money in federal elections. And as groups and individuals seeking to influence federal elections shift money to 501(c)s and away from the more regulated and disclosed outlets, such as PACs and even 527 committees, the less we will know about the sources and amounts of that money. This situation may potentially lead to calls for more regulation of these nonprofit organizations and renewed efforts to bring the money thus raised and spent to influence federal elections within the scope of federal regulation.

The Next Frontier: Taxable Corporations

The 2006 election featured a completely new approach for groups and individuals seeking to influence elections. As nonprofits such as 527 and 501(c) committees have come under increased scrutiny and do not offer the most flexible rules of operation (e.g., the requirement that the primary purpose of 501(c) organizations may not be election activities), powerful partisan players have turned to corporations that are *not* tax exempt but require neither reporting to the IRS or FEC nor disclosure to the public. Notre Dame Law School professor Lloyd Hitoshi Mayer warns that "the use of [nonprofit] tax categories in order to eliminate 'stealth' 527s could lead to the creation of a new category of 'stealth' taxable entities." [41] Two of these new vehicles for influencing elections, Catalist and the Democracy Alliance, appeared for the first time in 2005, and both are Democratic-oriented efforts funded and run by some of the same people who, in the past, have been active in party, PAC, and nonprofit efforts to get Democrats elected.

Catalist, a trademark of Data Warehouse, is a limited liability company formed by Harold Ickes in 2005. Ickes headed two big Democratic 527s during the 2004 election, America Coming Together and the Media Fund. He had served as President Clinton's deputy chief of staff, campaign manager for Bill Clinton's 1996 reelection, and for Hillary Clinton's 2000 Senate campaign, and has long served as a member of the Democratic National Committee's Executive Committee. Ickes's new venture, Catalist, provides data and information, such as voter contact information, voting history, and consumer preferences, from its sophisticated voter database to liberal organizations. [42] On its Web site, Catalist notes that its mission is "[t]o help progressive organizations realize measurable increases in civic participation and electoral success by building and operating a robust national voter database of every voting-age American" [43] Catalist had nineteen clients in 2006, including EMILY's List, the Sierra Club, and the AFL-CIO. [44]

The Democracy Alliance, started in 2005 by former Clinton Treasury official Rob Stein, is a financial clearing-house for large donors that directs funds to various progressive advocacy groups and think tanks in an effort to compete with the extensive and well-established network of conservative policy institutes, watchdog groups, and training organizations. Groups the Alliance has supported include ACORN, Air America Radio, EMILY's List, the Sierra

Club, and Catalist. Donors to the Democracy Alliance include George Soros and his son Jonathan Soros; Colorado software entrepreneur Tim Gill; Peter Lewis of Progressive Insurance; Bernard Schwartz, retired CEO of Loral Space and Communications Inc.; and Hollywood director Rob Reiner.

Partners, as the donors are called, agree to pay a $25,000 entry fee and annual dues of $30,000, and to spend at least $200,000 on Alliance-endorsed organizations; and many donors gave far more: "45 percent of the 95 partners gave $300,000 or better in the initial round of grants last October [2005]." [45] Democracy Alliance Chairman Steven Gluckstern said that in spite of the millions poured into Democratic 527s for the 2004 election, President Bush still won reelection over Democrat John Kerry. This made many contributors look for a new approach: "Among the lessons learned was that to bring back the progressive majority in this country is not just a periodic election strategy." [46]

Indeed, one of the biggest 527 donors from 2004, George Soros, gave large but undisclosed amounts to both Catalist and the Democracy Alliance for 2006. Because they are not tax-exempt, neither of these new organizations discloses its fundraising and spending to the public. Moreover, since they have little or no profit to report, they pay little or no taxes. The Democracy Alliance requires its funded organizations to sign agreements that shield the identity of donors, and most of the think tanks and nonprofit organizations supported by the Alliance are not subject to public disclosure laws. [47] These new for-profit election-oriented organizations thus operate without much public scrutiny. Sheila Kurmholz of the Center for Responsive Politics noted that "all kinds of Democrats and liberals were complaining that corporations and individuals were carrying on these stealth campaigns to fund right-wing think tanks and advocacy groups. Just as it was then, it is a problem today." [48]

More or Less Free Speech?

The Bipartisan Campaign Reform Act prohibited corporations and unions from making or financing electioneering communications (those that refer to a clearly identified federal candidate) within sixty days of a general election or thirty days of a primary. This provision of the law aimed to bring so-called issue ads that featured federal candidates under the same funding, disclosure, and source restrictions as other campaign ads. Pro-reform lawmakers argued that these *sham issue ads* were a serious loophole in the campaign finance regulations that allowed corporations and unions to spend unlimited amounts of unregulated money to influence elections just days before voters cast their ballots. As passed by Congress, BCRA would allow corporations and unions to still run television and radio ads naming a candidate within the black-out period as long as they used funds from their PACs, which are financed by individuals' contributions and are limited and disclosed.

Did this restriction on corporate and union sponsored campaign ads limit free speech, as many opponents of BCRA had argued it would? Senator Mitch McConnell, R-Ky, and others in Congress attacked the bill as a violation of the First Amendment and an assault on free speech in democratic elections, and they were fairly confident that the BCRA electioneering ban would be struck down by the Supreme Court. Some BCRA supporters even thought it might be as well. Yet the Court found the electioneering ban to be constitutionally sound on its face under the First Amendment in its 2003 decision, *McConnell v. the Federal Election Commission.*

Did this restriction on corporate and union electioneering communications have a chilling effect on free speech? Robert Boatright, Michael Malbin, Mark Rozell, and Clyde Wilcox found that "there were almost as many electioneering ads within the [60 day] window in 2004 as in 2000." [49] The ads run within the 60 days were funded by individuals rather than by corporations and unions, while ads run before the 60 day window were funded by all these sources. One new development was that "most of the electioneering ads in 2004 were bought by the newer 527 groups, funded mostly by contributions from individuals." [50] For example, the Swift Boat Veterans formed a 527 organization to fund their ads attacking 2004 Democratic presidential nominee Senator John Kerry for his criticism of the Vietnam War when he returned home from combat and for his service awards, which they claimed were undeserved. This trend suggests that while there were some changes in who ran ads and when ads ran, there was no lack of political speech after BCRA.

As we saw in Chapter 4, though, in 2007 the Supreme Court again considered the blackout period for corporate and union issue ads in *Federal Election Commission v. Wisconsin Right to Life.* As a result of this case, corporations and labor unions likely will have greater flexibility in running what could be considered *quasi-issue advocacy/quasi-express advocacy* advertisements during BCRA's blackout periods. Recall that under the objective standard that the Supreme Court set forth in *Wisconsin Right to Life,* an advertisement would be considered the functional equivalent of express advocacy only if it is susceptible to no reasonable interpretation other than as an appeal to vote for or against a specific candidate. Thus, creative organizations may find ways to frame their advertisements to provide an alternative reasonable interpretation consistent with the indicia or features of an issue ad (e.g., methods like those the Court identified, such as focusing on a legislative issue, taking a position on the issue, exhorting the public to adopt that position, and urging the public to contact public officials with respect to the matter), yet still seek to influence the outcome of one or more elections.

So, Where Are We and Where Are We Going?

The corrupting influence of federal lawmakers soliciting large sums of soft money from unions, corporations, and wealthy individuals was eliminated by BCRA, for it is now illegal for lawmakers to ask for soft money and for parties to accept it. Yet, even without soft money, the parties have found ways to survive, and in some cases to thrive, by taking advantage of higher contribution limits for themselves and their candidates and by tapping many new small donors and their own candidates for contributions.

Has BCRA affected competition in federal elections? One could argue that the 2006 congressional elections featured more competitive races than we have seen in many years. Indeed, the Democrats won enough seats to take control of the House and Senate. Yet it is not clear that BCRA contributed to this increased competitiveness, for other factors surely gave the Democrats a boost—strong opposition to the war in Iraq, extremely low ratings for GOP president George Bush, and various scandals such as the one tying Republicans to corrupt lobbyist Jack Abramoff. There is, however, no evidence that BCRA suppressed competition either. Although some critics called BCRA the "Democratic Party Suicide Bill," the Democrats did better than expected under the new campaign finance rules and actually fared better than the Republicans on some fronts.

One trend in the first two elections since passage of BCRA has been toward new fundraising and spending vehicles that allow big money contributors to continue to spend large sums to influence federal elections. Both big donors and the groups they fund now have a larger variety of choices for raising and spending large sums of money. Donors can make traditional, yet limited and fully reported contributions to candidates, parties, and PACs; or they can give to nonprofits such as 527s and 501(c)s; or they can contribute to for-profit corporations, such as Catalist and the Democracy Alliance. Groups that want to have a political impact can organize under any number of these entities.

While big money has not simply shifted from the parties' soft money accounts to 527s, 501(c)s, and the new for-profit organizations, there certainly has been a good deal of political learning and adaptation in the wake of BCRA as groups and individuals that want to influence federal elections have found new, relatively less regulated ways to do so. BCRA seems to have provided an incentive for large amounts of special interest money to find its way to campaign finance vehicles that allow unlimited fundraising and spending and are subject to little or no public disclosure. These developments may lead to calls for closer scrutiny and more disclosure of these new activities that are clearly intended to influence federal elections. Some critics will see these new campaign finance vehicles as loopholes that need to be brought into the regulatory sphere. Yet others will point to these adaptations by big donors and interest groups as evidence that attempts to restrict campaign contributions and expenditures are futile and should be loosened. [51] One thing is clear: candidates, parties, interest groups, unions, corporations, and wealthy individuals that want to influence federal elections will find ways to do so. These political actors have been quite inventive and effective in finding ways to pursue their electoral goals in a changing legal and regulatory environment, and we should expect them to continue to be.

Overall, BCRA has succeeded in severing the soft money link between big moneyed interests and lawmakers through their parties. It has encouraged parties to engage in more grassroots and voter mobilization efforts and to bring more small donors into their ranks. Yet it has also pushed some political actors to find new, less public ways to spend big sums to influence federal elections. Indeed, interest groups, corporations, and wealthy individuals are generally more difficult to hold accountable for their electoral activities than parties, for the parties' behavior during campaigns will be directly linked to and attributed to their candidates. If a party's activities are questionable, the voters will hold them and their candidates accountable for it on election day. Interest groups, corporations, unions, and individuals can operate less publicly with little public scrutiny and under euphemistic names that reveal little about their political leanings or goals. Future elections are sure to feature new and different ways of raising and spending money as political actors search for more effective and efficient means to influence elections; for example, the potential for *quasi-issue advocacy/quasi-express advocacy* ads in the wake of the *Wisconsin Right to Life* decision. If the amount of unlimited, unregulated, and undisclosed campaign money continues to grow, then these elections are likely to be followed by more efforts to further reform the nation's campaign finance laws and regulations.

NOTES

1. Mark Hosenball, Michael Isikoff, and Holly Bailey, "The Secret Money War," *Newsweek,* September 20, 2004, 22.
2. John McCain and Russell Feingold, "A Campaign Finance Law that Works," *Washington Post,* October 23, 2004.
3. See Raymond J. La Raja, "Expert Witness Declaration Filed for the Plaintiffs in *McConnell v. Federal Election Commission,* Washington, D.C. District Court for the District of Columbia, September 23, 2003; Raymond J. La Raja, "State Political Parties after BCRA," in *Life after Reform: When the Bipartisan Campaign Reform Act Meets Politics,* edited by Michael J. Malbin, (Lanham, MD: Rowman & Littlefield, 2003); Raymond J. La Raja, "Why Soft Money Has Strengthened Parties," in *Inside the Campaign Finance Battle,* edited by Anthony Corrado, Thomas E. Mann, and Trevor Potter, (Washington, D.C.: Brookings Institution Press, 2003); and Sidney Milkis, "Parties versus Interest Groups," in *Inside the Campaign Finance Battle.*
4. Donald Green, "The Need for Federal Regulation for State Party Activity," in *Inside the Campaign Finance Battle;* and Jonathan S. Krasno and Frank Sorauf, "Why Soft Money Has Not Strengthened Parties," in *Inside the Campaign Finance Battle.*
5. Seth Gitell, "The Democratic Party Suicide Bill," *Atlantic Monthly* 292 (1): 106–113.
6. See Robin Kolodny, *Pursuing Majorities: Congressional Campaign Committees in American Politics* (Norman: University of Oklahoma Press, 1998).
7. Federal Election Commission, "Party Finance Activity Summarized for the 2006 Election Cycle," News release, March 7, 2007.
8. Diana Dwyre and Robin Kolodny, "The Parties' Congressional Campaign Committees in 2004," in *The Election after Reform,* ed. Michael J. Malbin, (Lanham, MD: Rowman & Littlefield, 2006), see Figure 3-1, p. 41.
9. Ibid.
10. Ibid.
11. Ibid.
12. Federal Election Commission, "Campaign Guide—Congressional Candidates and Committees," May 2004.
13. Dwyre and Kolodny, "The Parties' Congressional Campaign Committees in 2004," 48–49.
14. Robin Kolodny and Diana Dwyre, "Party-Orchestrated Activities for Legislative Party Goals: Campaigns for Majorities in the U.S. House of Representatives in the 1990s," *Party Politics* 4 (July 1998), 275–295.
15. Raymond J. La Raja, "State and Local Political Parties," in *The Election after Reform,* 60.

16. Ibid.
17. Ibid., 71.
18. Steve Weissman and Ruth Hassan, "BCRA and the 527 Groups," in *The Election after Reform*.
19. Internal Revenue Service, "Exemption Requirement—Political Organizations," www.irs.gov/charities/political/article/0,,id=96350,00.html, June 21, 2007. This section on 527 political committees draws significantly from Diana Dwyre, "527s: The New Bad Guys of Campaign Finance," *Interest Group Politics*, 7th ed., ed. Allan J. Cigler and Burdett A. Loomis, (Washington, D.C.: CQ Press, 2007).
20. Just days before the 2000 Super Tuesday primary, a 527 with no past or track record, Republicans for Clean Air, ran $2.5 million in television ads critical of the environmental record of Sen. John McCain and supportive of Texas governor George W. Bush, both candidates for the GOP presidential nomination. Since 527s do not have to report their contributors' expenditures, it was not clear who was behind the ads until the day before Super Tuesday when news sources revealed that Dallas businessman and Bush family friend Sam Wyly had paid for the ads through the 527 group.
21. Allan J. Cigler, "Interest Groups and the Financing of the 2004 Elections," *Financing the 2004 Election*, Ed. David Magleby (Washington, D.C.: Brookings Institution Press, 2006).
22. Amy Keller, "McCain Takes Aim at 'Shadow' Groups." *Roll Call*, November 18, 2002, available through Westlaw at 2002 WL 8127314.
23. Campaign Finance Institute, "527 Group Fundraising Grew More Slowly in First Quarter of 2006 than 2004," news release, May 19, 2006, http://www.cfinst.org
24. Weissman and Hassan, "BCRA and the 527 Groups," 81.
25. Campaign Finance Institute, "527 Group Fundraising," Table 2.
26. Dwyre, "527s: The New Bad Guys," 224–225.
27. Weissman and Hassan, "BCRA and the 527 Groups," 96–97. Italics in original.
28. Ibid., Table 5.2, 94–96.
29. bid., 93.
30. Anthony Corrado, "The Future of Campaign Finance: Congress, the FEC, and the Courts," Brookings Institution presentation on October 20, 2005, Washington, D.C., quotation from transcript at www.brookings.edu/comm/events/20051020campaign.htm, 7.
31. Weissman and Hassan, "BCRA and the 527 Groups," 90–91.
32. Diana Dwyre and Robin Kolodny, "National Political Parties after BCRA," in *Life After Reform*, 98.
33. Jeanne Cummings, "Companies Pare Political Donations," *Wall Street Journal*, June 7, 2004; Thomas B. Edsall, "Republican Soft Money Groups Find Business Reluctant to Give," *Washington Post*, June 7, 2004; and The Institute of Politics, John F. Kennedy School of Government, Harvard University, *Campaign for Pres-*

ident: The Managers Look at 2004 (Lanham, MD: Rowman and Littlefield, 2006), 211.

34. Weissman and Hassan, "BCRA and the 527 Groups," 90.
35. Stephen R. Weissman and Kara D. Ryan, "Soft Money in the 2006 Election and the Outlook for 2008: The Changing Nonprofits Landscape," A CFI Report, (Washington, D.C.: The Campaign Finance Institute, 2007), 1. Available online at http://www.cfinst.org.
36. Ibid., 2.
37. Lindsay Renick Mayer, "527 Activity Surges in the States." Capital Eye, September 13, 2006 at www.captitaleye.org/inside.asp?ID=231.
38. Center for Responsive Politics, "527 Committee Activity: State-Focused Committees Only" at www.opensecrets.org/527s/527cands.asp?cycle=2006. Data based on records released by the IRS on Monday, May 14, 2007.
39. Cited in Weissman and Ryan, "Soft Money in the 2006 Election," 10.
40. Weissman and Ryan, "Soft Money in the 2006 Election," 14.
41. Lloyd Hitoshi Mayer, "The Much Maligned 527 and Institutional Choice." *Notre Dame Law School Legal Studies Research Paper No. 06-15,* August 14, 2006, 52.
42. Weissman and Ryan, "Soft Money in the 2006 Election," 13.
43. *Catalist: About Us,* www.catalist.us.aboutus.html, June 22, 2007.
44. Ben Smith, "Hillary's Hammer Returns," *The Politico,* April 18, 2007, www.politico.com/news/stories/0407/3595.html, June 22, 2007.
45. Jim VandeHei and Chris Cillizza, "A New Alliance of Democrats Spreads Funding," *Washington Post,* July 17, 2006.
46. Thomas B. Edsall, "Rich Liberals Vow to Fund Think Tanks," *Washington Post,* August 7, 2005.
47. VandeHei and Cillizza, "A New Alliance of Democrats."
48. Ibid.
49. Robert Boatright, Michael J. Malbin, Mark J. Rozell, and Clyde Wilcox, "Interest Group Advocacy Organizations after BCRA," in *The Election after Reform,* 113.
50. Ibid., 137.
51. Weissman and Ryan, "Soft Money in the 2006 Election," 16.

7

The Policy Labyrinth

The debate over campaign finance regulations is often marked by key legislative enactments, such as the Federal Election Campaign Act (FECA) and its amendments in the 1970s and, more recently, the Bipartisan Campaign Reform Act of 2002 (BCRA). These significant pieces of legislation have established the primary rules regarding the raising and spending of money in connection with federal elections. As important as FECA and BCRA are, though, the enactment of such laws represents just one of the four stages of the policy labyrinth that issues such as campaign finance reform follow: (1) policy formation, (2) interpretation and implementation, (3) impact, and (4) assessment. The actions of a wide array of political actors have had a dramatic impact on the development of the nation's campaign finance policies: the legislative activities of members of Congress; the judicial interpretations by justices and judges in the courts; the regulatory implementation of the Federal Election Commission (FEC); and the efforts of candidates, parties, other organizations, and individuals seeking to find ways to influence federal elections.

The congressional debates over the most recent campaign finance legislation—starting in the 105th Congress in 1997 and culminating in BCRA's passage in 2002—offer many valuable lessons for understanding the modern legislative process (particularly for highly contentious bills like BCRA) and highlight the difficulties in trying to balance competing funda-

165

mental values. Chapters 2 and 3 explored the legislative labyrinth through which BCRA traveled, illustrating the unorthodox nature of contemporary congressional policymaking. That winding pathway to passage included pursuing discharge petitions that openly sought to wrestle control of the bill from the Republican majority, strategically compromising to broaden BCRA's support, building upon momentum from outside events such as the Enron scandal, and artfully (and sometimes not-so-artfully) using each chamber's rules to one side's advantage. Further, the legislative journey showed how institutional structures, rules, and processes can affect the substantive outcome of a piece of legislation, such as how the need for sixty votes to end a Senate filibuster can sometimes prevent the passage of a certain piece of legislation even if a majority of senators support it.

Another insight from BCRA's pathway through Congress is recognizing the importance of leadership in the policy labyrinth. One can safely assume that if Senators John McCain and Russell Feingold and Representatives Christopher Shays and Martin Meehan had not fought so diligently for revisions to the nation's campaign finance laws, the issue would have easily fallen off the agenda; particularly in light of the opposition of the majority leadership in the House and Senate through much of the bill's journey. More than issue leaders, these four rose to the level of being policy entrepreneurs who built active and effective networks both within and outside of Congress, and helped bring the issue of campaign finance into the political mainstream. Moreover, even after BCRA became law, the four leaders continued to work to ensure that the intent of the legislation they crafted was not undermined as the Act was interpreted by the courts and implemented by the FEC and others.

In the American system of government, the legislative process is at the heart of policymaking, and rightfully so. The framers saw Congress as the first branch and enumerated the legislative powers in Article 1 of the Constitution. The members of the House and Senate are the only federal government officials elected directly by the people.[1] As Chapters 4, 5, and 6 of this book show, however, the policymaking process is much broader than just the legislative actions within Congress. The laws that Congress enacts must be interpreted and implemented, and from these processes the nuances, implications, and unintended consequences of our nation's laws are fully revealed.

The Supreme Court, in its role as final arbiter of whether a law (or portion of a law) is constitutional, has shaped the way in which campaign finance regulation must be framed if it is to pass constitutional muster. Indeed, lawmakers in Congress, when crafting legislation, often try to predict how the

Court may rule on an issue, and in the case of BCRA much of the debate revolved around how the Court would evaluate BCRA's constitutionality in light of First Amendment free speech concerns. After a bill's passage, the Supreme Court may have many opportunities to review and interpret a law as those affected by it challenge its constitutional underpinnings. BCRA has already been before the Supreme Court more than once, and the Court quite likely will have additional opportunities to consider the constitutionality of the Act's various provisions.

The FEC's regulations have filled in the details that broad-based legislation like BCRA cannot address. These interpretations too can be challenged, and BCRA's sponsors and supporters have taken the FEC to court more than once in an effort to ensure that BCRA is implemented as they intended it to be. The laws and regulations are then put into action during each election cycle as candidates, parties, and others strive to pursue electoral advantages within the regulatory parameters that have been established for them.

Just as important as the affirmative rules that stem from interpretation and implementation, though, are the areas that are left open. Consider, for example, the impact that the Supreme Court's decision in *Buckley v. Valeo* striking down expenditure limitations has had on the nation's campaign finance policies. A cap on the amounts that candidates and others could spend in an election cycle would dramatically alter the landscape in which electioneering activities are conducted. If such a cap were permitted, Congress conceivably could pass a comprehensive law to address electioneering expenditures of all groups (assuming a coalition could in fact be built in support of such a bill).

Instead, as a result of the *Buckley* framework, Congress's only real ability to address issues related to campaign expenditures lies in restricting how certain contributions can be spent, but even then Congress's ability to do so is limited due to First Amendment concerns, such as those seen in *Federal Election Commission v. Wisconsin Right to Life.* BCRA's regulations prohibited certain kinds of contributions (such as those from a corporation's or union's general treasury funds) from being used for certain types of expenditures (for example, electioneering ads containing express advocacy or its functional equivalent during certain defined blackout periods). In *Wisconsin Right to Life,* though, the Supreme Court reined in these regulations as they may be applied to expenditures on *quasi-issue advocacy/quasi-express advocacy* ads in order to protect certain First Amendment rights.

Much like the courts, the actions or inactions of the FEC shape the nation's campaign finance policies as well. As noted in Chapter 5, for example, the regulations promulgated by the FEC in 2002 following BCRA's passage combined with the Commission's decision not to further regulate 527 organizations left the door open for the extensive 527 activity in the 2004 presidential election. Further, as FEC Commissioner Toner noted (as quoted in Chapter 5), the FEC's inaction on 527s, even in the wake of such groups' activity during the 2004 election, may lead to these organizations playing a significant role in determining electoral outcomes in 2008 and beyond.

Once the various rules and regulations in a policy area have been established, the next phase of the policy labyrinth is to determine its impact. As seen in Chapter 6, the impact that BCRA (including its subsequent interpretations and implementation) has had on electioneering depends in part on what one believes BCRA's purpose was. In some ways, BCRA was a success. The flow of funds into national political party organizations has continued at levels generally comparable to amounts prior to BCRA, with the added benefit of all such funds being subject to federal regulation. Thus, contrary to the concerns that BCRA's soft money ban would cripple the parties, they appear to have adapted well to the new campaign finance environment. Further, BCRA brought electioneering communications within sixty days prior to an election within the scope of federal regulation in 2004 and 2006 without curtailing the overall *level* of political speech taking place during such periods, although which groups or individuals ran the ads may have changed as compared to prior years.

On the other hand, however, BCRA's limited scope—that is, its focus on the *twin evils* of soft money and issue ads (particularly sham issue ads)—and the subsequent interpretation by the courts and implementation by the FEC have left open a wide array of electioneering activity that is not subject to extensive regulation. As a result, at the same time political actors operate within the rules regarding the use of regulated funds, they also are seeking out the most effective ways to funnel money to lightly regulated (and entirely legal) activities. Future elections are sure to feature more new campaign finance methods that reveal how political actors adapt as they continue to innovate in a changing regulatory environment.

For some observers, the use of relatively unregulated means of funding electioneering activities, such as through 527s, 501(c)s, or even taxable entities, constitutes nothing more than innovative ways to promote one's ideas in the political marketplace. For other critics, though, these methods represent a continued exploitation of loopholes in the campaign finance system that perpetuates the potential for the corruptive force of big money in politics. Evaluating the impact of these activities is one example of policy assessment.

As the intended and, more importantly, the unintended consequences of new laws and regulations are played out, policymakers will often evaluate whether the new rules sufficiently accomplish their goals or if they create new problems that need to be addressed in future rounds of legislation. In other words, what constitutes the end phase of one level of the policy labyrinth—policy assessment—becomes the beginning phase of the next level as lawmakers utilize the lessons learned through the implementation of the policies to formulate the discussions for the next round of policy formation.

The State of Campaign Finance Policy

The regulations governing the financing of federal elections are premised on the core value of wanting to limit corruption or the appearance of corruption that stems from the presence of large amounts of money surrounding campaigns. This value stems in part from the historical emphasis on the desire to limit the undue influence of people and groups in privileged positions. More directly, though, the Supreme Court's decision in *Buckley* provided that preventing corruption or the appearance of such was the only legitimate governmental interest that would warrant restricting or regulating campaign-related political speech.

The concept of *corruption* or *the appearance of corruption* is malleable and can be shaped to fit many contexts. Given this, what is meant by corruption in the context of campaign finance regulation? In Chapter 1 and Chapter 4, we discussed James Madison's distinction between equality of political rights and inequality in peoples' ability to influence outcomes stemming from the unequal distribution of property; the former being a hallmark of the political system Madison helped create, and the latter a necessary result of a system dependent on individual liberty. Certainly the large sums of money spent on federal campaigns give those with greater resources more opportunity to make an impact on the outcome of elections. Since the resulting outcomes must be tolerated in our political system because of the need to preserve liberty, the idea of corruption in the context of campaign finance regulation does not go to the relationship between campaign funding and who wins the election.

Instead, for money in electoral politics to be corruptive—to the point of justifying restrictions on political speech—it must have a negative impact on the equality of political rights. As noted in Chapter 1, one way this inequality may happen is by distorting the representational relationship between the electorate and elected officials by, for example, giving a greater voice to a minority faction with greater financial resources than a majority view that might not be able to compete financially in the electoral arena. Another way the equality of political rights could be negatively affected is if the constitutionally protected right of *one person, one vote* is undermined. Victoria A. Farrar-Myers has noted,

> The Supreme Court enunciated this premise—one person, one vote—in *Gray v. Sanders,* [372 U.S. 368] (1963), with its roots in the seminal case of *Baker v. Carr,* [369 U.S. 186] (1962). It stands for the proposition that each person's vote should and must be counted equally; that the dilution of one person's vote, with the resulting implication being the increased value of another person's vote, is impermissible in the American political system. [2]

The amount of money flowing through the electoral system can potentially dilute the impact of any individual's vote in a number of ways. The ability of a candidate and/or the candidate's supporters to raise and spend money may determine which candidates even seek office before the average individual ever has the opportunity to vote for or against the candidate. The money spent by candidates, parties, and other groups before an election can sway voters in such a way that the election may be all but decided by election day. Further, once legislators are elected, they can appear to act more favorably to those moneyed interests who helped them get elected, which has the added detrimental effect of contributing to "pervasive public cynicism." [3]

Campaign finance regulations have long sought to limit the dilution of individuals' political rights. But the difficulty that campaign finance regulation proponents have faced in safeguarding these rights is the need to balance the protection of the fundamental right of *one person, one vote* and the representational relationship at the foundation of our political system with another constitutionally protected individual right, namely that of freedom of speech (particularly political speech). As seen throughout this book, the need to maintain this balance has significantly limited the types of regulations that could in fact be enacted. Additionally, regulation proponents in the post–*Buckley* era have often faced a political environment in which key policymakers—whether the president or congressional leaders—have not supported efforts to broaden the system of regulations.

One effect of the constitutional limitations on permissible campaign finance regulations and the political realities of the policymaking environment is that regulation proponents have had to make choices as to what they perceive to be the most significant problems in the current campaign-financing system. The need to make these choices has led to an interesting interplay between the campaign finance regulations and the political parties. On the one hand, political parties play an important and positive role in the electoral process, such as through voter mobilization programs and grass-roots efforts to build the party base. In fact, the desire to strengthen the parties and their ability to undertake party-building activities (particularly in the wake of the weakening of the parties during the 1970s and the emergence of candidate-centered campaigns) led to the FEC regulations that permitted soft money in the first place.

But political parties are leading fundraisers and spenders in the electoral arena. If one is concerned about big money in electoral politics, the role of political parties needs to be addressed. One way that parties, however, are distinguishable from other fundraisers and spenders is that many of the parties' activities are subject to permissible regulation. So long as parties' activities fall within the gambit of federal regulation, the threat of corruption lessens. Thus, for example, the extensive amounts of unregulated soft money that parties were receiving posed a threat to the integrity of the political system (in reform proponents' eyes), but the parties receiving the same level of hard money post–BCRA is not seen as problematic. Similarly, exceptions to the regulatory scheme, such as the amendment to BCRA permitting Levin funds, acknowledge the beneficial role that parties can play in our political system.

This distinction—that money in the electoral process is less of a corruptive force if it is subject to regulation—has come to shape more recent efforts since the mid-1990s, particularly when compared to the 1980s and early 1990s. During that earlier period, for example, PACs caused a great amount of concern among regulation proponents because they represented specialized interests that unduly influenced the political process due to their ability to raise and spend extraordinary amounts of money for elections. As noted in Chapter 1, another concern during this period was the increasing costs of campaigns generally, and several legislative attempts to restrict PAC activity and rein in campaign spending failed during this era. Much of PACs' activities, like those of political parties, were already subject to federal regulation. Similarly, although large amounts of money in the electoral process may be disconcerting, the primary dangers of money's potentially corruptive forces lie in money that flows outside the scope of federal regulation.

Thus, the focus on unregulated money and electioneering activities led to the focus on soft money and issue ads within the context of BCRA. It also has led to the emphasis on 527s and similar groups that are able to legally raise and spend significant amounts of money without being subject to BCRA's limitations and restrictions. Such a focus, however, also implicitly recognizes that (a) the current parameters that campaign finance regulations must meet (i.e., the framework that *Buckley* established) limit the extent of activity that federal law can, in fact, regulate, and (b) whether good or bad for the electoral system, campaign fundraising and spending likely will continue to be excessive.

The system of campaign finance regulation that has emerged following the *Buckley* decision, however, is not without its critics. Certainly, these critics would prefer to strip back the system of regulation in place to allow for a greater flow of political speech—and correspondingly campaign funds—in the system. The natural regulation that would take place through competition in the political marketplace, such critics contend, would sufficiently protect political rights, thus eliminating the need for a governmental regulatory system. Given the system that has developed in the wake of *Buckley*, however, supporters of this free-market approach to campaign finance likely would be able to advance such a system only if the Supreme Court were to overturn *Buckley*, for that decision permits certain restrictions on political speech if the restrictions are narrowly tied to the government's interest in stopping corruption or the appearance of corruption in federal elections. If that were to happen, though, all viewpoints—even those favoring more extensive governmental regulation—would be fighting to gain support for their preferred system.

Campaign Finance, Popular Sovereignty, and the Dynamics of the American Political System

Analyzing the issue of campaign finance seems often to result in a series of contradictions. It is an issue on which, in the words of Sen. Mitch McConnell, R-Ky, "[n]o one in the history of American politics has ever won or lost a campaign," but also one that has the potential to affect electoral outcomes.[4] Campaign finance invokes many fundamental values long underlying the American political system, yet it is often addressed in a partisan environment in which the deciding factor is based on short-term political interests. The regulatory environment that has developed is based on judicial reasoning that has been widely criticized by both regulation proponents and opponents, yet the Supreme Court has decided not to strike it down, in part because legislators, candidates, parties, and other groups all have learned to work within the framework that *Buckley* established.

In 1997, then-House Minority Leader Richard Gephardt, D-Mo., summarized the heart of the campaign finance debate discussed in this book very succinctly: "What we have is two important values in direct conflict: freedom of speech and our desire for healthy campaigns in a healthy democracy."[5] At first blush, one can easily blame the lack of any resolution with respect to these conflicting values on the contradictory and often confusing nature of the matter. Indeed, Gephardt concluded that "[y]ou can't have both" freedom of speech and healthy campaigns in a healthy democracy.[6] Although Gephardt's statement may oversimplify the issue, it does point out that campaign finance would be easier to resolve if one of these values—freedom of speech or fair and open elections—were given primacy over the other. The question remains, though, which should be granted the more privileged position?

Within each round of debate over campaign finance regulations—whether in Congress, in the judicial chambers of the Supreme Court, or within the FEC—proponents of both values have presented strong and valid arguments in support of their position. Even the most recent judicial decision (as of the time this book went to press) featured justices promoting one view or the other. Justice Antonin Scalia, for example, picked up on the quotation from Representative Gephardt above, arguing in *Wisconsin Right to Life,* "If [Gephardt] was wrong, however, and the two values can coexist, it is pretty clear which side of the equation this institution is primarily responsible for. It is perhaps *our most important constitutional task to assure freedom of political speech."*[7] Justice David Souter countered for the other side of the debate stating, "Devoting concentrations of money in self-interested hands to the support of political campaigning therefore threatens the capacity of this democracy to represent its constituents and the confidence of its citizens in their capacity to govern themselves. These are the elements summed up in the notion of political integrity, giving it *a value second to none in a free society."*[8]

An alternative perspective on the issue of campaign finance regulation, however, is to see these apparent contradictions and lack of resolution as beneficial. With so much at stake—from the core values involved to the composition of our government by affecting who is elected to federal office—we may not want the issue of campaign finance resolved in favor of one value or one group at the expense of the others. We would not want a political system that promotes free speech, yet unduly dilutes the *one person, one vote* premise or distorts the representational relationship to benefit a privileged group. Conversely, we would not want to fully sacrifice the right to an open and robust dialogue of political issues of the day in order to keep campaign expenditures in check. Nor would we want a campaign finance system that systematically benefits one group or party—one faction, if you will—leaving others perpetually on the outside of the governing institutions looking in.

Much like the arguments made by James Madison in *Federalist* No. 10, the values and interests invoked by the issue of campaign finance need to be balanced to protect against any interest from gaining too much power within the political system. The mechanism for balancing those interests and the exact nature of that balance are matters open to constant analysis and adjustment. As noted in Chapter 1, though, political participation is vital in determining which values guide the debate. The issue goes to the heart of *popular sovereignty*—that is, the idea that the legitimate exercise of governmental power is premised on the consent of the governed—for it is the electorate that will ultimately be able to decide how the values underlying the campaign finance debate will be allocated and the citizenry who will ultimately decide how they wish to govern themselves.

NOTES

1. The Constitution, as originally written, provided that only the members of the House were directly elected by the people. Senators were initially elected by state legislatures, although the 17th Amendment provided for direct election of senators by the voters. Presidents are technically elected by the electors of the Electoral College based upon the popular vote that occurs within each state.

2. Victoria A. Farrar-Myers. "Campaign Finance: Reform, Representation, and the First Amendment," in *Law and Election Politics: The Rules of the Game,* edited by Matthew J. Streb, Boulder, CO: Lynne Rienner, 2004 (#47).

3. *Federal Election Commission v. Wisconsin Right to Life, Inc.,* Slip Opinion (Dissent), J. Souter, 4. Justice Souter cited the results of a 2002 public opinion poll to support his concern about the relationship among money in elections, governance, and public cynicism: "A 2002 poll found that 71 percent of Americans think Members of Congress cast votes based on the views of their big contributors, even when those views differ from the Member's own beliefs about what is best for the country. ... The same percentage believes that the will of contributors tempts Members to vote against the majority view of their constituents. Almost half of Americans believe that Members often decide how to vote based on what big contributors to their party want, while only a quarter think Members often base their votes on perceptions of what is best for the country or their constituents." Ibid. (internal citations omitted).

4. Alison Mitchell, "Bill Lacks 9 Votes: Supporters Vow to Keep Issue Alive and to Use It in Next Elections," *New York Times,* February, 27, 1998.

5. Nancy Gibbs and James Carney, "The Wake-Up Call," *Time,* February 3, 1997. Justice Scalia quoted this article in his concurring opinion in the *Wisconsin Right to Life* case.
6. Gibbs and Carney, "The Wake-Up Call."
7. *Federal Election Commission v. Wisconsin Right to Life, Inc.,* Slip Opinion (Concurring in part and concurring in the judgment), J. Scalia, 22 (emphasis in the original omitted and additional emphasis added).
8. *Federal Election Commission v. Wisconsin Right to Life, Inc.,* Slip Opinion (Dissent), J. Souter, 5 (emphasis added).

INDEX

Note: Boxes, figures, notes, and photos are indicated by b, f, n, and p following the page number.

Abramoff, Jack, 159
ACLU. *See* American Civil Liberties Union
ACORN, 156
ACT. *See* America Coming Together
Administrative Procedures Act of 1946, 127
AFL-CIO, 156
Air America Radio, 156
Alaska Right to Life Committee v. Miles (2006), 113
Aldrich, John H., 138n4
Alito, Samuel, 112, 113–114
Allen, Tom (D-Maine), 38
Alvarez, Lizette, 62n37
Amendments. *See* Bipartisan Campaign Reform Act; Legislation and legislative process
America Coming Together (ACT), 148, 150, 151, 156
American Civil Liberties Union (ACLU), 35, 54–55
American Civil Liberties Union of Nevada v. Heller (2004), 113
American Financial Groups, 155
Anti-Federalists, 3
Armey, Dick (R-Tex.), 61

Baesler, Scotty (D-Ky.), 38, 61n27
Bailey, Holly, 161n1

Baker v. Carr (1962), 170
Barcia, James (D-Mich.), 95
Barr, Bob (R-Ga.), 63n59
BCRA. *See* Bipartisan Campaign Reform Act
Bickel, Alexander M., 119n4
Bipartisan Campaign Reform Act (BCRA; McCain-Feingold Bill; Shays-Meehan bill). *See also* Federal Election Commission—Bipartisan Campaign Reform Act; *McConnell v. Federal Election Commission*
  amendments and, 47–54, 55–57, 63n56, 63n59, 70, 72, 73, 77, 78–80, 81–82, 84–85, 95n9, 96n19, 97n30
  Blue Dog bill, 38, 61n27, 68
  Clinton, William and, 46
  Commission bill, 48, 53, 63n53
  effects of, 168
  elections of 2000 and, 73–75
  Enron scandal and, 82–84
  Feingold, Russell and, 30, 52, 70–71, 73, 126, 142, 166
  Freshmen bill, 38–39, 41, 45, 48, 50, 52, 57, 64n60
  historical background of, 8–19, 30–35

House actions (Shays-Meehan) on, 35–57, 66, 66–70, 80–86
interpretation and implementation of, 8, 92, 123–124, 126–130, 137, 167
issue leaders for, 52, 91
judicial review and appeal under, 23, 108–109, 110–111
McCain, John and, 29, 52, 70–72, 73, 75, 90, 91, 126, 128, 142, 166
McConnell, Mitch and, 71–72, 86, 92, 97n30, 99, 108, 158
Meehan, Martin and, 35, 41, 45, 46, 47, 50, 51, 52–53, 56, 66–67, 84, 91, 126, 127, 166
political issues of, 33–35, 41–42, 50–51, 55–56, 68, 70, 71–73, 75–76, 77, 79, 81–84, 99–100, 125, 142–149
provisions of, 30–33, 39, 41, 86–90, 91–92, 157, 167
rulemaking process for, 123–124
Senate actions (McCain-Feingold) on, 28–35, 47, 49, 57, 59n10, 66, 70–73, 75, 76–80, 84–85
Shays, Christopher and, 35, 41, 45, 46, 47, 50, 51, 52–53, 56, 57, 61n27, 66–67, 68–69, 77, 80–81, 84, 86, 90, 91, 126, 127, 166
Supreme Court and, 108–116
twin evils (soft money/issue ads) of, 39, 86, 92, 109, 111, 168, 171
voting and passage of, 53–57, 64n60, 65–66, 70, 75–86, 93, 124, 126
Bipartisan Campaign Reform Act— constitutional and legal issues
Buckley v. Valeo and, 109, 115, 118
Bush, George W. and, 65
corporate electioneering, 113–115
corruption and, 111
federal regulation of campaign finance and, 109, 111–112
free speech and First Amendment issues, 35, 49–51, 56, 71, 72, 92, 97–30
majority judicial support for, 109

McConnell v. Federal Election Commission and, 99–100, 108–109, 110, 111–112, 114, 115, 117, 158
questions about constitutionality, 99–100, 108–109, 117, 120n28, 167
severability and judicial review, 51, 53–54, 70, 108, 109
soft money and issue advocacy and, 109, 110–111, 113, 114–115, 157–159
views of individual justices, 109, 113–114
Wisconsin Right to Life and, 113–115
Blogs, 24
Blue Dog Coalition, 37, 38, 44, 61n27, 68
Blunt, Roy (R-Mo.), 62n46
Boatright, Robert, 158, 163n49
Bonior, David (D-Mich.), 41, 51
Bradley, Bill, 74
Breaux, John (D-La.), 77, 78
Breyer, Stephen, 109, 112, 114
Broder, David, 59n11
Brownback, Sam (D-Kans.), 71, 96n19
Bruni, Frank, 95n4
Buckley, James (Conservative-N.Y.), 12
Buckley v. Valeo (1976), 1, 7–8, 12–13, 14, 16–17, 20, 23, 25n6, 102–105, 107, 108, 110–111, 113, 115, 116, 117–118, 167, 172
Buffett, Warren, 54
Bundling. *See* Political action committees
Bureaucracy, 123–124, 129, 135
Bush, George H. W., 15, 76p
Bush, George W.
527 groups and, 151
campaign finance reform and, 65, 66, 75–77, 80, 131–132, 153
elections and, 74, 157
nominees of, 126, 131–132
recess appointments of, 131, 132
Bush (George W.) administration, 132

Business issues. *See* Corporate and
business issues

California, 53
Campaign finance. *See also* Bipartisan
Campaign Reform Act;
Constitution and constitutional
issues; Corruption; Federal
Election Campaign Act
American political system and,
172–174
amounts raised, 74
costs of campaigns, 13
expenditures, 167
Federalist No. 10 and, 6
historical context of, 8–19, 103
hydraulic theory of, 149–150, 152
income tax checkoff and, 10
issues of, 2
legislative issues and, 2, 165
"mischiefs of faction" and, 3–8
state of campaign finance policy,
169–172
twin evils of, 19, 20, 39, 86, 92, 109,
111, 168, 171
Campaign finance—loopholes
BCRA and, 126–127, 128, 160
candidate conduct and, 21
contribution limits and, 15–16
disclosure of contributions, 8–9
issue ads, 17, 157–158
reforms and, 17–19, 128, 168
Campaign finance—reforms. *See also*
Bipartisan Campaign Reform Act;
Federal Election Campaign Act
clash of values and, 99–100
contributions versus expenditures,
105
criticisms and concerns, 13–14,
15–16, 34–35, 58–49, 71
debates surrounding, 2, 9, 21–23
historical context of, 8–19
independent expenditures, 18, 25n3
issue ads and, 17, 18, 62n35, 71, 88
limits and limitations, 8, 9, 11–14,
15–16, 17, 22, 54–55, 62n35, 79,

89–90, 102, 104–106, 112, 116,
149
multiple layers of, 19–22
political aspects of, 125
scandals and, 11–12, 23, 82–84, 166
Campaign finance—soft money. *See
also* Political parties; 527 groups
501(c) committees, 155
amounts raised, 17–18, 19, 28, 74
BCRA and, 126–127, 133, 160
campaign finance reforms and,
86–88
corruption and, 71–72, 109
definition of, 17
elections of 1996 and, 17
FEC proposed regulations for,
126–128, 171
issue ads and, 17, 18, 19, 71
origins of, 16
political parties and, 142–143
Supreme Court and, 109
Campaign Reform and Election
Integrity Act of 1998, 43
Campaign Reform Project's Business
Advisory Committee, 54
Campaign Reporting and Disclosure
Act (1998), 43
Campaigns. *See* Elections and
campaigns
Campbell, Tom (R-Calif.), 50, 57,
62n40, 63n55
Candidates. *See also* Campaign finance;
Elections and campaigns
campaign money and, 147
challengers, 14, 147
contributions by, 145–147
incumbents, 14, 146, 147
issue ads and, 17, 34
money raising by, 10, 146
spending by, 13, 14f
selection of, 9–10
soft money and, 75
Cantor, Joseph E., 26n12, 61n29
Carney, Eliza Newlin, 140n48
Carney, James, 175nn5–6
Caruso, Lisa, 62n39

Casper, Jonathan D., 121n55
Castle, Michael N. (R-Del.), 95n5
CAT. *See* Conservative Action Team
Catalist, 156–157
CED. *See* Committee for Economic Development
Center for Responsive Politics, 157
Chafee, Lincoln (R-R.I.), 96n19
Christian Coalition, 56
Cigler, Allan J., 97n34, 139n35, 162n19, 162n21
Cillizza, Chris, 163n45, 163n47
Citizens Club for Growth, 155
Clean Air Act amendments (1970), 124
Clinton, William J. "Bill"
    allegations, 25n11
    campaign finance reform and, 15, 32, 46, 54, 66, 72, 73, 75
    elections of 1996 and, 74
    judicial nominees of, 126
    scandals and impeachment, 46–47, 52, 62n42, 95n2
Club for Growth, 155
Cochran, John, 97nn30–33, 97n40, 139nn23–24
Cochran, Thad (R-Miss.), 75, 78
Colorado Republican Federal Campaign Committee v. Federal Election Commission (1996), 105–106
Commission bill, 48, 53, 63n53
Committee for Economic Development (CED), 69
Common Cause, 41, 44, 46
Common Sense Ohio, 155
Conference committees, 84
Congress. *See also* House of Representatives; Senate; individual members
    BCRA and, 124–125
    bureaucracy and, 124
    Buckley v. Valeo and, 117–118
    campaign finance reform and, 15
    Congressional Review Act and, 129
    control of, 147
    "Dear Colleague" letters, 63n47
    delegation of powers by, 135

electoral connection of, 125
leadership of, 90
staff members, 46, 52, 54
Congress—specific
    102 (1991–1993), 15, 64n64
    103 (1993–1995), 15
    104 (1995–1997), 40
    105 (1997–1999), 19, 22, 28–59, 65, 67, 68, 70, 73, 77, 94, 95n9
    106 (1999–2001), 66–73, 77, 94
    107 (2001–2003), 75–86, 91, 94
Congressional Accountability Act (1995), 36
Congressional Black Caucus, 51, 81, 135
Congressional Hispanic Caucus, 81
Congressional Review Act (1996), 129
Conservative Action Team (CAT), 50–51
Constitution and Constitutional issues. *See also* Supreme Court
    anonymous speech, 111
    Article 1, 166
    checks and balances, 20–21, 101
    elections, 106, 174n1
    equality of opportunity, 103
    flag burning, 28
    judiciary, 100–101
    minority versus majority interests, 93
    one person, one vote, 170
    ratification, 3
    separation and sharing of powers, 20–21, 123, 127
    Tenth Amendment, 39
Constitution and Constitutional issues—campaign finance
    campaign finance and reforms, 12–13, 21–22, 28, 35, 54–55, 57, 71, 93, 99–100, 102, 104–105, 107–108, 110–112
    First Amendment and freedom of speech, 1, 7, 13, 21–22, 28, 35, 71, 93, 104–108, 110–116, 117, 157–159, 169, 173
    "magic words" test, 18, 19, 110, 113, 115
    political speech, 21, 25n8, 111, 112, 114, 169, 170, 172, 173

Contract with America (1994), 36, 37
Core values
  balance and, 6
  campaign finance and, 8, 21, 102, 107, 172–173
  clashes of, 24
  judiciary and, 100
Cornfield, Michael, 96n24
Corporate and business issues
  527 groups, 152
  campaign finance, 8, 10–11, 54, 69, 82–83, 113
  issue ads, 157–158
  power of corporations, 9
  vehicles for influencing elections, 156–157
Corrado, Anthony, 25n4, 26n14, 140n40, 161n3, 162n30
Corruption. *See also* Constitution and constitutional issues—campaign finance
  Buckley v. Valeo and, 116
  campaign finance
    regulations/legislation and, 9, 12, 13, 25n6, 102–106, 109, 111–112, 168, 169
  contribution limits and, 112
  definitions and concepts of, 106, 110, 111, 169
  Madison, James and, 7
  McConnell, Mitch and, 71–72, 103–104
  McConnell v. Federal Election Commission and, 109, 110, 111
  money and, 7, 12, 71–72, 83, 103–104, 109–110, 116, 159, 168, 169–170, 171
  PACs and, 18, 171
  protection against, 21
  regulation and, 171
  Supreme Court and, 106, 110, 116
Courts, appellate. *See also* Judiciary; Supreme Court
  Court of Appeals for the District of Columbia Circuit, 104

District Court for the District of Columbia, 99, 108, 128, 129, 136
Courts, appellate—cases and rulings. *See also* Supreme Court—cases and rulings
  Alaska Right to Life Committee v. Miles, 113
  American Civil Liberties Union of Nevada v. Heller, 113
  Majors v. Abell, 113
Cummings, Jeanne, 163n33
"Curse of American Politics" (Dworkin), 1

Dahl, Robert, 121n54
Daschle, Tom (D-S.D.), 33, 34, 80, 84, 131, 132
Data Warehouse, 156
Davidson, Roger H., 61nn25–26, 61n34, 138nn4–5
Davis, Tom (R-Va.), 44
DCCC. *See* Democratic Congressional Campaign Committee
Dean of the House. *See* Dingell, John
Delay, Tom (R-Tex.), 49, 50, 51, 52, 55–56, 62n46, 63n59
Democracy. *See also* Factions
  campaign finance and, 173
  elections and, 7, 14
  fundamental characteristics of, 1, 110
  individual rights and liberties in, 6, 103, 170
  political participation and, 2
  republican form of government and, 5
Democracy Alliance, 156–157
Democratic Caucus, 41, 42, 51, 61n31
Democratic Caucus Campaign Finance Reform Task Force, 51
Democratic Congressional Campaign Committee (DCCC), 51, 54, 63n50, 143, 145, 146
Democratic Governors Association, 153
Democratic National Committee (DNC), 19, 143, 145, 156

Democratic Party. *See also* Bipartisan
  Campaign Reform Act; Political
  parties; individual Democrats
  527 groups and, 134, 135, 151, 153,
    154*b*
  allegations, 25*n*11
  Blue Dog Coalition, 37, 38, 38, 44,
    61*n*27, 68
  campaign finance reform and, 15,
    41–42, 51, 76, 143, 145, 148
  elections and, 145, 153, 159
  financial situation of, 28, 42, 51, 77,
    135, 143, 145
  labor unions and, 32–33
  scandals of, 52
  selection of candidates by, 10
"Democratic Party Suicide Bill," 143,
  159
Democratic Senatorial Campaign
  Committee (DSCC), 143, 145
Dewar, Helen, 64*n*61, 95*nn*8–9
DeWine, Mike (R-Ohio), 91
Dingell, John (D-Mich.), 48, 53
Dionne, E. J., Jr., 64*n*62
Discharge petitions. *See* Legislation and
  legislative process
DNC. *See* Democratic National
  Committee
Dole, Bob, 74
Doolittle, John (R-Calif.), 55–56,
  61*n*27, 62*n*46, 84
Dorgan, Byron (D-N.Dak.), 60*n*14
Drinkard, Jim, 96*n*20
Drucker, David, 138*n*18
DSCC. *See* Democratic Senatorial
  Campaign Committee
Dworkin, Ronald, 1
Dwyre, Diana, 59*n*3, 139*n*35, 146,
  161*nn*8–11, 161*nn*13–14, 162*n*19,
  162*n*26, 162*n*32

Edsall, Thomas B., 163*n*33, 163*n*46
Electioneering communications, 33
Elections and campaigns. *See also*
  Campaign finance; Candidates
  BCRA and, 159–160

Buckley v. Valeo and, 118
  campaign communication, 16–17
  campaign finance regulations and,
    110–111
  candidate orientation of, 10
  congressional, 10, 14–15, 153
  costs of, 171
  corruption and, 111
  Kennedy, Anthony and, 106
  money raised and spent, 7, 10,
    143–148, 149, 151–153, 169–170
  one person, one vote, 169–170
  party orientation of, 9–10
  political factors of reelection, 125
  political speech and, 111, 116
  presidential elections, 10, 12, 153
  primary elections, 10, 9
  role of, 7
Elections and campaigns—specific
  1904, 9
  1992, 30
  1994, 19, 148
  1996, 17, 19, 32, 52, 59, 74, 156
  1998, 28, 30, 68, 70, 74, 95*n*2
  2000, 23, 66, 73–75, 80, 91, 143, 145,
    149, 150, 152, 156, 158, 162*n*20
  2002, 23, 143, 145, 148, 151, 152, 153
  2004, 24, 100, 133, 135, 136, 141,
    143, 145, 147, 148, 149, 151, 152,
    153, 155, 157, 158, 168
  2006, 24, 133–134, 143, 145, 153,
    154*b*, 155, 157, 159, 168
  2008, 133, 137, 168
EMILY's List, 156
Enron scandal, 23, 82–84, 166
Environmental Protection Agency
  (EPA), 124
EPA. *See* Environmental Protection Agency
Executive branch, 100, 101, 123

501(c) committees, 155–156, 168
527 organizations
  advertising by, 150–151
  BCRA and, 133, 149, 151–154
  campaign finance and, 132, 133, 135,
    141, 155–156, 168, 171–172

corporations and, 152
definitions and rules of, 150, 151
electioneering ads and, 158
elections and, 149, 151–153, 157,
　158, 168
FEC and, 133–137, 155
individual contributions to, 151–152,
　153, 159
McCain, John and, 74, 136
as political groups, 24, 73, 132–134,
　136, 148
political parties and, 151
spending of, 153, 154*b*
state activity of, 153
527 Reform Acts, 135–136
Factions, 3–8, 20, 21
Fall, Edward, 8
Farhi, Paul, 59*n*11
Farrar-Myers, Victoria A., 25*n*1, 59*n*3,
　96*n*24, 170, 174*n*2
Farr, Sam (D-Calif.), 57, 61
Fazio, Vic (D-Calif.), 41, 51
FEC. *See* Federal Election Commission
FECA. *See* Federal Election Campaign Act
Federal Corrupt Practices Act (1925), 8–9
Federal Election Campaign Act (FECA;
　1971, 1974). *See also Buckley v.*
　Valeo
　BCRA and, 32
　campaign contributions and
　　expenditures, 10, 102, 103, 104
　Supreme Court and, 12–13, 102–108,
　　116
　Watergate scandal and, 11–12
Federal Election Commission (FEC)
　commissioners, 126, 128–129,
　　130–131, 137
　FECA and, 12
　Feingold, Russell, 129–130, 136
　fines of, 136
　McCain, John and, 129, 135, 136
　Meehan, Martin and, 135
　opposition to, 127–130
　political aspects of, 23, 125, 126, 127,
　　130, 137
　reform of, 23

　role of, 21, 137, 167
　Shays, Christopher and, 130, 135
　soft money and, 16
Federal Election Commission—
　　Bipartisan Campaign Reform Act
　527 groups and, 133–137, 150, 151,
　　154–155, 167–168
　court rulings on, 128–129
　criticisms and opposition to, 23, 123,
　　126, 127–130, 167
　first proposed regulations for, 126–128
　legislative approach to, 129–130
　revised regulations for, 128, 129
　rulemaking process and, 125–126,
　　130, 131, 137, 167
Federal Election Commission v.
　Massachusetts Citizens for Life, Inc.
　(1986), 107
Federal Election Commission v. National
　Conservative Political Action
　Committee (1985), 107
Federal Election Commission v. Wisconsin
　Right to Life (2007), 113–115,
　158–159, 167, 173, 174*n*3
Federalist Papers (Hamilton, Jay,
　Madison, 1787–1788)
　Constitution and, 3
　No. 10 (Madison), 1–2, 3–8, 20, 21,
　　174
　No. 51 (Madison), 20–21
　No. 78 (Hamilton), 100–101
Federalists, 3
Federal Register, 127
Feingold, Russell (D-Wis.), 17, 19, 20*p*,
　23, 29–30, 31*p*, 59*n*9, 161*n*2. *See*
　also Bipartisan Campaign Reform
　Act
Filibusters. *See* Senate
"Filling the amendment tree," 32,
　60*n*13
Flag burning, 28
Fleischer, Ari, 80
Foerstel, Karen, 25*n*2, 97*n*29,
　97*nn*33–38, 138*n*1, 138*n*8,
　138*n*10, 138–139*nn*19–22,
　139*nn*25–31

Forbes, Michael P. (R/D-N.Y.), 63, 95n5
Freedom of speech. *See* Constitution
    and Constitutional issues—
    campaign finance
Free Speech Coalition, 49–50, 62n46
Freshman Democratic Task Force, 45
"Freshmen bill". *See* Bipartisan
    Campaign Reform Act
Frost, Martin (D-Tex.), 51, 54, 143

Ganske, Greg (R-Iowa), 95n5
Gejdenson, Sam (D-Conn.), 41, 51
Gephardt, Richard (D-Mo.), 41, 51,
    61n27, 172–173
Germond, Jack W., 63n57
Gibbs, Nancy, 175nn5–6
Gillespie, Ed, 135
Gill, Tim, 157
Gingrich, Newt (R-Ga.), 22–23, 35,
    36, 37, 38, 40–41, 54, 62n38, 68,
    95n2
Ginsburg, Ruth, 109, 114
Giroux, Gregory L., 140n42, 140n44
Gitell, Seth, 161n4
Gluckstern, Steven, 157
Goodling, William (R-Pa.), 41
GOP (Grand Old Party). *See*
    Republican Party
Gore, Al, 25n11, 46, 74, 80
Goss, Porter (R-Fla.), 41
Government, 26n16, 100–101
Government, federal, 9, 10, 39,
    100–101
"Granny D." *See* Haddock, Doris
Grassroots efforts, 148–149
Gray v. Sanders (1963), 170
Green, Donald, 161n5
Greenwood, Jim (R-Pa.), 63n55
Grunwald, Michael, 95n7

Haddock, Doris ("Granny D"), 69
Hagel, Chuck (R-Neb.), 77, 79
Hamilton, Alexander, 3, 100–101
Hard money. *See* Political parties
Hassan, Ruth, 140n39, 151–152, 162n18,
    162n24, 162n27, 162n31, 163n34

Hastert, Dennis (R-Ill.), 23, 67–68, 81,
    82, 84, 95n2
Hatch Act (1939, 1940), 9
Henneberger, Melinda, 60n21, 62n35
Henry, Ed, 59n4, 60n13
Hollings, Ernest (D-S.Dak.), 85
Holmes, Steven A., 61n32
Hosenball, Mark, 161n1
Houghton, Amo (R-N.Y.), 63n55
House of Representatives. *See also*
    Bipartisan Campaign Reform Act;
    Congress; Gingrich, Newt;
    Hastert, Dennis; Legislation and
    legislative process; individual
    members
Blue Dog bill, 38, 61n27
campaign contributions and
    expenditures by, 13, 14f, 16f, 147
campaign finance reform in, 35–57
debate in, 42, 43, 54, 61n27
Freshmen bill, 38–39, 41, 45
incumbent candidates of, 14
investigations of, 32
lawsuits and, 127
legislative process in, 27–28, 42, 45
open process in, 45, 47–48
rules in, 30, 37, 38, 42–43, 44, 48,
    54, 61n27, 81
Speaker of the House, 40p, 67–68,
    95n2
staffers of, 54
suspension of the rules, 42–44, 45,
    61n34
unanimous consent in, 55
House of Representatives—committees
Committee of the Whole, 54, 63n54
conference, 84
Rules, 38, 47, 81
House resolutions
    H.R. 34 (1998), 43
    H.R. 259 (1997), 38, 61n27
    H.R. 2183 (1998), 50
    H.R. 2608 (1998), 43
    H.R. 3485 (1998), 43
    H.R. 3526 (1998), 47, 50
    H.R. 3582 (1998), 43

Hutchinson, Asa (R-Ark.), 38, 41, 61*n*27, 96*n*19

Ickes, Harold, 156
Illegal Foreign Contributions Act (1998), 43
Independents, 74
Individual donors, 153, 156, 159. *See also* Corporations; 501(c) committees; 527 groups
Interest groups. *See also* 527 groups; individual groups
  BCRA and, 160
  campaign finance reform and, 38, 41, 51, 52, 55, 69–70, 85
  citizen advocacy groups, 55
  FEC and, 23
  good-government groups, 41
  pro-life groups, 69–70
  public interest groups, 52, 77
  public policy and research groups, 69
Internal Revenue Code, Section 527. *See* 501(c) committees; 527 groups
Internal Revenue Service (IRS), 150
Internet, 24, 74
IRS. *See* Internal Revenue Service
Isikoff, Michael, 161*n*1
Issue advocacy ads. *See also Federal Election Commission v. Wisconsin Right to Life*
  527 groups and, 150–151
  BCRA and, 111, 113, 157–159, 168
  campaigns and, 17, 29, 34
  corporate and union ads, 113–115, 157–159
  definitions and concepts of, 18, 33, 114–115
  electioneering communications, 33, 88, 109, 110, 111, 128, 150–151, 157, 168
  express advocacy and, 33, 114–115, 147, 158–159
  First Amendment issues of, 71, 110–111
  independent expenditure communications, 147

  quasi-advocacy ads, 158, 160, 167
  reforms and, 19, 29, 88
  sham issue ads, 113, 115, 157–158
  soft money and, 62*n*35, 148
Issue leaders, 52, 90, 91
Issue networks, 50, 52, 70, 91, 166

Jay, John, 3
Jeffords, James (R/I-Vt.), 33, 60*n*16, 84, 85*p*, 93
Johnson, Nancy L. (R-Conn.), 63*n*55, 95*n*5
Judiciary. *See also* Courts; Supreme Court; individual cases and rulings
  campaign finance and, 102–117
  founders' view of, 100–101
  judicial activism and restraint, 121*n*54
  judicial review and interpretation, 23, 116–118, 123
  precedent (*stare decisis*) and, 107–108
  role of, 21, 100, 101
Justice, Department of, 37, 54

Kangas, Edward, 95*n*6
Keating Five scandal, 59*n*8
Keller, Amy, 59*n*4, 59*n*12, 60*nn*13–14, 60*n*17, 60*n*19, 62*n*41, 62*n*44, 62*n*46, 63*n*48, 138*n*15, 139*n*37, 162*n*21
Kelly, Sue (R-N.Y.), 63*n*55
Kindleberger, Richard, 61*n*24
Kingdon, John W., 58, 64*n*65
Kennedy, Anthony M., 99, 106, 109, 110, 111, 114, 117
Kerry, John, 132–133, 139*n*36, 157, 158
Knutson, Lawrence L., 96*n*22
Kohlberg, Jerry, 54
Kollar-Kotelly, Colleen, 128
Kolodny, Robin, 146, 161*n*6, 161*nn*8–11, 161*nn*13–14, 162*nn*32
Krasno, Jonathan S., 161*n*5
Kurmholz, Sheila, 157

Labor unions, 9, 10, 32–33, 71, 151, 158

La Raja, Raymond, 148, 161*n*3, 162*n*15
Lay, Kenneth, 83*p*. *See also* Enron
    scandal
Leach, Jim (R-Iowa), 63*n*55
Leadership meetings, 51
League of Conservation Voters, 155
League of Women Voters, 41
Legislation and legislative process. *See*
    also Bipartisan Campaign Reform
    Act; House of Representatives;
    Federal Election Campaign Act;
    Policymaking; Senate
    amendments, 32–33, 45, 47–49,
    60*n*13, 70
    briefing books and strategic
    materials, 51–52, 63*n*51
    campaign finance and, 2, 8–19, 20,
    24, 109
    carry-over of, 67
    checks and balances and, 20–21
    collective action problems and, 125
    Congressional Review Act and, 129
    congressional staffers and, 54
    debate, 40, 54
    discharge petitions, 37–38, 41, 44,
    44–45, 61*n*27, 62*n*38, 68, 70,
    83–84, 166
    divide-and-conquer strategies, 45
    executive branch rules and
    regulations, 123
    flowchart model of, 27
    free votes, 45, 64*n*64, 68, 77
    implementation of, 123–126, 137
    incremental nature of, 91–92
    issue networks and, 50
    judiciary and judicial review, 23, 100,
    101, 116–118, 123, 137
    leadership and, 52, 90–91, 166
    legislative delay, 82
    Madison's "principal task" of, 6
    modern strategies of, 27, 32, 33, 41,
    44, 48, 53, 55, 57–59, 64*n*64,
    93–94, 97*n*30, 165–166
    poison pill amendments, 33, 47, 48,
    50–53, 54, 55, 56, 57, 67, 70,
    78–79

    political factors of, 58, 94, 124–125
    presidential support, 46
    problems of, 31, 38, 39–40
    Queen-of-the-Hill rule, 48,
    64*n*60
    reconciliation of House and Senate
    versions, 71, 84
    rules and, 48, 93–94, 166
    scheduling and timing of, 40, 42,
    67–68, 70, 81
    soft money and, 109
    "strike the last word" amendment,
    54
    Supreme Court and, 166–167
    thrown votes, 72
    whips and whipping, 42, 51
Legislative branch, 101. *See also*
    Congress; House of
    Representatives; Senate
Lenhard, Robert, 136
Levin, Carl (D-Mich.), 61, 78, 142, 149
Levin funds and money, 78, 127, 142,
    149, 171
Levin, Sander M. (D-Mich.), 51
Lewinsky, Monica, 62*n*42, 95*n*2
Lewis, Peter, 151, 157
Lightman, David, 60*n*23
Limits and limitations. *See* Bipartisan
    Campaign Reform Act; Campaign
    finance—reforms; Federal Election
    Campaign Act
Lindner, Carl, Jr., 155
Livingston, Bob (R-La.), 95*n*2
Loomis, Burdett A., 139*n*35, 162*n*19
Los Angeles Times, 23
Lott, Trent (R-Miss.), 32, 33, 34, 72,
    131, 132

Madison, James, 1–2, 3–8, 26*n*16, 93,
    103, 169. *See also Federalist Papers*
Magleby, David, 162*n*21
Majors v. Abell (2004), 113
Malbin, Michael J., 140*n*39, 158,
    161*n*3, 161*n*8, 162*n*18, 162*n*32,
    163*n*49
Maloney, Carolyn (D-N.Y.), 53

Mann, Thomas E., 25n4, 97n39, 161n3

Marbury v. Madison (1803), 101, 119n5

Mason, David, 126, 130

Mayer, Lindsay Renick, 163n37

Mayer, Lloyd Hitoshi, 156, 163n41

Mayhew, David, 125, 138n6

McCain-Feingold Bill. *See* Bipartisan Campaign Reform Act

McCain, John (R-Ariz.), 17, 19, 20p, 23, 29, 31p, 36, 59n8, 66, 73–74, 96n11, 123, 161n2. *See also* Bipartisan Campaign Reform Act

McCarthy, Eugene (Democratic-Farmer-Labor-Minn.), 12

McConnell, Mitch (R-Ky.), 28–29, 30p, 34, 35, 52, 58, 71–72, 104, 131–132, 172. *See also* Bipartisan Campaign Reform Act

McConnell v. Federal Election Commission (2003), 99–100, 108–109, 110, 111–112, 114, 115, 128

McGovern-Fraser Commission (1968), 10

Media, 11, 38, 42, 44, 52

Media Fund, 156

Meehan, Martin T. (D-Mass.), 17, 20p, 21, 23, 35, 36p, 37, 39, 46p, 51, 79p, 83, 136. *See also* Bipartisan Campaign Reform Act

Metcalf, Jack (R-Wash.), 63n55

Michigan, 74

Milkis, Sidney, 161n3

Miller, Dan (R-Fla.), 63n59

Mintrom, Michael, 63n52

Mitchell, Alison, 95n1, 95n3, 96nn15–16, 96n18, 174n4

Money. *See* Campaign finance; Corruption

Morella, Constance A. (R-Md.), 45, 95n5

Motor-voter law, 49, 62n45. *See also* Voter guides and mobilization

Murray, Matthew, 140n47

National party committees. *See* Political party committees; individual committees

National Republican Congressional Committee (NRCC), 63n50, 143, 145, 146

National Republican Senatorial Committee (NRSC), 28, 71, 143, 145

National Right to Life Committee (NRLC), 69–70, 95n7

Nelson, Suzanne, 138n14, 138n16

Neustadt, Richard, 138n2

New Hampshire, 74

New York, 3

New York Times, 23, 42, 44, 136–137

Ney, Bob (R-Ohio), 81–82

Nixon, Richard M., 11

Nixon (Richard M.) administration, 11

Nixon v. Shrink Missouri Government PAC (2000), 105, 106, 107, 111, 117

Nonprofit organizations, 154–156. *See also* 501(c) committees; 527 groups

Northup, Anne M. (R-Ky.), 62n46

NRCC. *See* National Republican Congressional Committee

NRLC. *See* National Right to Life Committee

NRSC. *See* National Republican Senatorial Committee

Obey, David (R-Wis.), 57

O'Connor, Sandra Day, 109, 110–111, 117

Oleszek, Walter J., 61nn25–26, 61n34, 138nn4–5

Ortiz, Daniel R., 25n4

PACs. *See* Political action committees

Parker, Mike (R-Miss.), 63n55

Paxon, Bill (R-N.Y.), 62n46

Paycheck Equity Act (paycheck protection measure), 32–33, 34, 48–49

Paycheck Protection Act, 43

Pelosi, Nancy (D-Calif.), 135

Pence, Mike (R-Ind.), 135–136

Perry, Bob, 151, 142, 153
Peters, B. Guy, 138n3
Phillips, Kate, 140n43, 140nn50–52
Pierce, Emily, 139nn32–33
Podesta, John, 46
Policy circles, 52
Policy entrepreneurs, 52–53, 90–91,
    166
Policymaking
  incremental nature of, 91–93
  judiciary and, 100, 101, 116–118,
    123
  legislative process and, 166
  policy assessment, 168–169
  policy labyrinth, 165–169
  political factors of, 170–171
Political action committees (PACs)
  527 groups and, 136, 150
  bundling by, 15, 17, 25n10
  FECA and, 10–11
  influence of, 171
  issue ads and, 158
  regulation of, 171
  reliance on, 13, 18–19
  total contributions, 16f
Political issues. *See also* Political parties
  BCRA, 124
  checks and balances, 20–21
  electoral connections, 125
  politics by other means, 116–117, 137
  political rights, 7
  regulations, 170
Political parties. *See also* Democratic
    Party; Republican Party
  BCRA and, 24, 142–149, 153, 168, 171
  campaign finance and, 10, 135–136,
    146–149, 159, 170–171
  candidates and, 9–10, 147
  control of Congress and, 147, 159
  farm teams of, 147, 148
  grassroots efforts of, 148–149
  hard money and, 19, 24, 143, 145,
    147, 148, 171
  interparty competition and, 143, 147,
    148
  regulation of, 171

soft money and, 16, 17–18, 19, 23,
    24, 142–143, 148, 149, 151–152,
    153, 171
  state and local parties, 148–149
  special rules and, 48
  whipping and, 42
Political party committees, 142–148,
    152. *See also* individual committees
Pomper, Gerald, 26n14
Popular sovereignty, 174
Porter, John Edward (R-Ill.), 63n55
Posner, Richard, 113
Potter, Trevor, 25n4, 161n3
Progress for America, 150
Progress for America Voter Fund, 136
Public Citizen, 41
Public Interest Research Group, 41
Publicity Act (1910), 8

Ramstad, Jim (R-Minn.), 63n55
Randall v. Sorrell (2006), 99, 112, 117
Recess appointments, 131
Regulations and regulatory processes, 2,
    7–19, 20, 103–104, 137, 170–172,
    173
Rehnquist, William, 109, 111
Reiner, Rob, 157
Republican Conference, 40
Republican forms of government,
    5f, 6
Republican Governors Association, 153
Republican National Committee
    (RNC), 143, 145
Republican Party (GOP). *See also*
    Bipartisan Campaign Reform Act;
    Contract with America; Political
    parties; individual Republicans
  527 groups and, 134, 135, 151, 153,
    154b
  allegations, 25n11
  broken promises of, 40–44
  campaign finance reform and, 15, 28,
    34, 37, 40–44, 48, 50, 51, 54, 56,
    57, 63n55, 68, 76, 93, 143, 145,
    148–149
  elections and, 17, 19, 28

financial situation of, 28, 42, 51, 71, 77, 135, 143, 145
GOP farm team of, 147
political situation of, 68, 147–148
Republicans for Clean Air, 162n20
Revenue Act of 1971, 10
RNC. *See* Republican National Committee
Roberts, John, 112, 113–114, 115
Roll Call, 49, 129
Roosevelt, Theodore, 8
Roth, Bill (R-Del.), 96n19
Roukema, Marge (R-N.J.), 57
Rozell, Mark J., 158, 163n49
Rulemaking, 126–127
Ryan, Kara D., 153, 163n35, 163nn39–40, 163n42, 163n51

S. *See* Senate resolutions
Sandstrom, Karl, 131
Sanford, Mark (R-S.C.), 41
Scalia, Antonin, 109, 111, 114, 115, 173
Schaffer, Bob (R-Colo.), 63n59
Schiff, Steven H. (R-N.M.), 42
Schwartz, Bernard, 157
Seiger, Jonah, 96n24
Senate. *See also* Bipartisan Campaign Reform Act; Congress; Legislation and legislative process; individual members
    amendments in, 60nn13–14
    campaign contributions and expenditures by, 13, 15f, 16f, 147
    campaign finance reform in, 28–35
    cloture in, 33, 34, 35, 71, 96n17
    conference committee of, 84
    elections of 2000 and, 75
    filibusters in, 33, 34, 35, 45, 57, 66, 68, 71, 72, 75, 76, 77, 85, 96n17, 166
    investigations of, 32
    lawsuits and, 127
    legislative process in, 27–28, 32–33
    political issues in, 70
    recess appointments and, 131
    rules in, 30, 34, 60n13, 96n17, 127

unanimous consent agreements in, 34
Senate resolutions
    S. 25 (1997), 30
    S. 1593 (1999), 71
Sierra Club, 156–157
Simpson, Alan K. (R-Wyo.), 125
Sinclair, Barbara, 27, 58, 59n1, 64n63
Shays, Christopher (R-Conn.), 17, 20p, 21, 23, 35–37, 39, 41, 45, 46p, 63, 79p, 83, 95n5. *See also* Bipartisan Campaign Reform Act
Shays-Meehan bill. *See* Bipartisan Campaign Reform Act
Shrink Missouri case. *See Nixon v. Shrink Missouri Government PAC*
Smith, Ben, 163n44
Smith, Bradley, 126, 128, 130, 131, 135
Smith, Linda (R-Wash.), 56–57
Snowe, Olympia (R-Maine), 33
Soft money. *See* Campaign finance—soft money; Political parties
Solomon, Gerald (R-N.Y.), 62n43
Sorauf, Frank, 161n5
Soros, George, 151, 152, 153, 157
Soros, Jonathan, 157
Souter, David H., 109, 114, 115, 121n47, 173, 174n3
Specter, Arlen (R-Pa.), 96n19
State of the Union address (1998), 46
Stein, Rob, 156
Stevens, John Paul, 107, 109, 110–111, 114, 117
Stone, Peter H., 63n49
Streb, Matthew J., 25n1, 174n2
Sullivan, Emmet G., 136
Supreme Court. *See also* Courts, appellate; Judiciary; individual justices
    Bipartisan Campaign Reform Act and, 108–116
    campaign finance and, 99–100, 116–118, 166
    Federal Election Campaign Act and, 102–108
    opinions and decisions of, 120n26

strict scrutiny test of, 119*n*15
views of individual justices, 102–116,
    117, 173
Supreme Court—cases and rulings
    Baker v. Carr, 170
    Buckley v. Valeo, 1, 7–8, 12–13, 14,
        16–17, 20, 23, 25*n*6, 25*n*9,
        102–105, 107, 108, 110–111, 112,
        113, 115, 116, 117–118
    *Colorado Republican Federal Campaign
        Committee v. Federal Election
        Commission,* 105–106
    *Federal Election Commission v.
        Massachusetts Citizens for Life,
        Inc.,* 107
    *Federal Election Commission v.
        National Conservative Political
        Action Committee,* 107
    *Federal Election Commission v.
        Wisconsin Right to Life,* 113
    Gray v. Sanders, 170
    Marbury v. Madison, 101
    *McConnell v. Federal Election
        Commission,* 99–100, 108–109,
        110, 111–112, 114
    *Nixon v. Shrink Missouri Government
        PAC,* 105, 106, 107, 111
    Randall v. Sorrell, 99, 112
Swift Boat Veterans for Truth, 132–133,
    139*n*36, 158

Taft-Hartley Act (1947), 9
Tanner, John (D-Tenn.), 61*n*27
Task Force on Campaign Finance
    Reform (Democratic), 41
Taylor, Andrew, 97*n*26, 97*nn*30–31,
    97*n*40
Teapot Dome scandal (1922), 8, 9, 11
Thomas, Bill (R-Calif.), 43, 53–54, 55,
    63*n*58
Thomas, Clarence, 105–106, 109, 110,
    111, 114, 117
Thompson, Fred (R-Tenn.), 79
Tiefer, Charles, 60*n*13, 60*n*18

Tierney, John (D-Mass.), 57
Tillman Act (1907), 8, 9
Tobacco issues, 29, 37
Toner, Michael, 129, 131, 133–134, 168
Tone, Robin, 96*n*10, 96*n*12
Tully, Matthew, 96*n*25

Unanimous consent agreements
    (UCAs). *See* Senate
Upton, Fred (R-Mich.), 63*n*55, 63*n*59

VandeHei, Jim, 62*n*41, 62*n*44, 62*n*46,
    63*n*48, 163*n*45, 163*n*47
Vermont, 112
Vietnam and Vietnam War, 29,
    132–133, 139*n*36, 158
Voter guides and mobilization, 56–57,
    148, 149, 150, 171. *See also* Motor-
    voter law

Wamp, Zach (R-Tenn.), 41, 44, 50,
    62*n*40, 63*n*55
Washington Post, 44
Watergate scandal (1972), 11
Weintraub, Ellen, 131, 132
Weissman, Stephen, 140*n*39, 151–152,
    153, 162*n*18, 162*n*24, 162*n*27,
    162*n*31, 163*nn*34–35,
    163*nn*39–40, 163*n*42, 163*n*51
Wellstone, Paul (D-Minn.), 97*n*30
White, Byron, 104–105, 107
White, Rick (R-Wash.), 47, 53, 61*n*27
Whitfield, Edward (R-Ky.), 62*n*46
Wicker, Roger (R-Miss.), 62*n*46
Wilcox, Clyde, 158, 163*n*49
Willis, Derek, 96*n*25, 97*n*26,
    97*nn*30–31, 97*n*40, 138*n*12
*Wisconsin Right to Life. See Federal
    Election Commission v. Wisconsin
    Right to Life*
Witcover, Jules, 63*n*57
Wolf, Frank (R-Va.), 44
"Worker gag rule," 32–33
Wynn, Albert (D-Md.), 135–136